Technology, E-learning and Distance Education

Second edition

Technology, E-Learning and Distance Education is the essential guide for anyone wanting advice on how to choose the right technology at the right cost for a course or flexible learning programme.

The underlying principle of this new second edition is unchanged from the first – technology is not inherently good or bad for teaching – it's the way that teachers and administrators use it that matters.

Fully updated to include all the latest technologies in this fast-moving field, this second edition presents a user-friendly model to help you to make your decisions, and explores the spectrum of media available, including print, radio, video, online learning and synchronous conferencing. Exploring the strengths and weaknesses of each medium, the book considers issues such as cost, pedagogy and usability.

Technology, E-Learning and Distance Education will be a valued tool for any teacher, educator, trainer manager or administrator wanting to ensure that they provide a learning programme that is tailored to the needs of their learners.

Dr Tony Bates is an international education consultant and has the Cisco Chair in E-learning at the Southern Alberta Institute of Technology. He was formerly Director of Distance Education and Technology, Continuing Studies, at the University of British Columbia, Canada, where he was responsible for managing the development and delivery of 100 distance education courses. **Janice Picard** is an expert on synchronous communications technologies. She is currently pursuing a PhD in Management Learning at Lancaster University in the UK. Her research focuses on problems in collaborative team work in networked learning.

RoutledgeFalmer Studies in Distance Education
Series Editors: Desmond Keegan and Alan Tait

Technology, E-learning and Distance Education

Second edition

A. W. (Tony) Bates

Routledge
Taylor & Francis Group

LONDON AND NEW YORK

Second edition published 2005
by Routledge
2 Park Square, Milton Park, Abingdon, Oxon OX14 4RN

Simultaneously published in the USA and Canada
by Routledge
270 Madison Ave, New York, NY 10016

Originally published 1995 as *Technology, Open Learning and Distance Education*

Reprinted 2006, 2007, 2008

Routledge is an imprint of the Taylor & Francis Group, an informa business

© 1995, 2005 A. W. (Tony) Bates

Typeset in Sabon by
HWA Text and Data Management, Tunbridge Wells
Printed and bound in Great Britain by
MPG Books Ltd, Bodmin

British Library Cataloguing in Publication Data
A catalogue record for this book is available from the British Library

Library of Congress Cataloging in Publication Data
A catalog record for this book has been requested

ISBN 10: 0–415–28436–8 (hbk)
ISBN 10: 0–415–28437–6 (pbk)
ISBN 13: 978–0–415–28436–3 (hbk)
ISBN 13: 978–0–415–28437–0 (pbk)

Contents

Figures

Tables

Preface to the second edition

Harold Wilson once said: 'A week is a long time in politics.' Ten years is an eternity in educational technology. For example, the first edition of *Technology, Open Learning and Distance Education*, published in 1995, makes no reference to the World Wide Web. It is hard to believe that there were no educational programmes using the Web before 1996. What is more remarkable about the first edition though is that it has continued to sell steadily over all this period. There lies an important lesson.

Technology is constantly changing and new technological developments can have profound effects on education, as in the case of the Web. Nevertheless, there are underlying constants in educational technology that do not change, and which, if understood, can help decision makers in their choice and use of technology for teaching. This book re-examines and applies the fundamentals discussed in the first edition in the light of new technology developments since that book was first published.

All books are hard to write and this one is no exception. The main challenge has been deciding what to keep from the old edition and what to add, without making the book so long that it would be unreadable. Should we forget about television, radio, audio-cassettes and print, now that the Internet and the World Wide Web are seen as the future of distance education? The examples and data used in the first edition are sometimes over 20 years old. Does it make any sense to include them now?

Certainly, much of this book is completely new. Five chapters, one an overview of developments in distance education and e-learning in the last ten years, two on Web-based learning, and two on synchronous conferencing technologies, are completely new. Four chapters, on print, television, and radio and audio cassettes, and the final chapter (previously the executive summary), have been revised. Two chapters, the introduction, and the chapter on selecting technologies, have been edited and slightly revised, but are basically unchanged.

I have resisted the post-modernist tendency to believe that everything new is good and that there are no lessons to be learned from the past. Indeed, I believe quite the opposite. There are many useful lessons from the past that apply with as much force to new educational technology developments, and we ignore those lessons at our peril. Chapter 2 illustrates that point in particular. Furthermore, this book is really about a methodology for decision making. If the method stands the test of time, and works just as well for new technologies as for old, then it has strong validity.

Then there is the choice of title. I have substituted 'e-Learning' for 'Open Learning' with some regret, because over the last ten years, distance education has become more closely identified with the commercialization of e-learning than with open access. E-learning has had a dramatic effect on both campus-based teaching and distance education. However, I wanted to address in particular the confusion between e-learning and distance education in many people's minds. Neither distance education nor e-learning is dead. Despite what critics say, both are thriving, but although there is considerable synergy between them, they are different concepts.

The acknowledgements in the first edition still apply, but I want to add my thanks to others. I will always be indebted to Lord Perry of Walton, the first Vice-Chancellor of the Open University, and Glenn Farrell, former President of the Open Learning Agency. I would also like to acknowledge the contributions of my former colleagues in the A/V Media Research Group at the Open University, and later colleagues at the Distance Education and Technology unit at the University of British Columbia. Special thanks go to Janice Picard, without whose substantial contribution I could not have written the chapters on synchronous conferencing technologies. Also, I must give thanks to a series of editors at Routledge who have shown amazing patience with my continual procrastination in getting this revised edition finished. Lastly, my wife, Pat Porter, has had to suffer continuously from my frustration and bad temper when I have been stuck or unable to do the writing for this edition. Thank you, Pat, for sticking with me!

1 Emerging trends: convergence and specialization in distance education

THE DIVERSITY OF DISTANCE EDUCATION

Sunni is a 12 year old Kutchi nomad, with her family travelling an ancient dirt road between Bamian and Mazar-i-Sharif in Afghanistan. She is walking beside one of the family's mules. She is listening to a recording of Ali Dhost, one of Afghanistan's most popular singers, on her brother's portable CD player. Between two of the songs, she hears a short, humorous 'message' from Ali about the need to boil well or river water for at least five minutes for drinking. The message is part of a UNICEF health campaign.

Frank McGuinness is sitting in a ballroom on a Saturday morning in the Hotel Vancouver in Vancouver, Canada, with six other fellow students, watching a video-conference of a business professor lecturing and demonstrating marketing techniques from Queen's University in Kingston, Ontario, 3,000 kilometres away. Frank is paying C$44,000 to take an executive MBA from Queen's, while he works as an electrical transmission engineer for the local power company.

Gloria Gonzales Roca is a 24 year old wife and mother, with two young children, living in Tonala, a small town just outside Guadalajara, Mexico. She has taken two years off teaching, but is planning to return next year. She is working on her computer, studying a master's program in educational technology jointly offered by Tec de Monterrey in Mexico and the University of British Columbia in Canada. She is working online with two other students, one in Canada and one in Slovakia, Europe, on a group assignment.

Chandra Arasaratnam is a student in the city of Ratnapura, Sri Lanka. He is studying a Bachelor of Technology (Civil) run by the Open University of Sri Lanka. He studies mainly at home through a combination of print materials, audio-cassettes, and a four-week practical course taken on site in Colombo. He has access to computing facilities in his local study centre. He hopes to get a job as a road engineer with the city once he has completed his studies.

Sharon Geibert is a first year sociology student at Indiana University-Purdue University at Indianapolis, United States of America. She is one of over 2,000 students taking Introductory Sociology. Although technically a full-time, on-campus student, she studies a good deal of this course from home, as most of her study is done online, combining textbook reading, Web searches, and online small group discussion forums. She drives to the campus about twice a week for her face-to-face Introductory Sociology class, to meet fellow students, to use the library and to take face-to-face classes in other subjects.

All these are students learning wholly or partly at a distance. All are using technology. All are enjoying their studies and expect to succeed. At the same time, the organizations providing their education are facing many challenges. What technologies should we invest in? What are the educational benefits or limitations? What will it cost to teach with technology? Is it sustainable? How will students and professors react? Is there any real difference between technology-enhanced classroom teaching and technology-based distance education? Can teachers do this without help? How do we organize and manage teaching with technology?

These are some of the issues I try to address in this book. In particular, I want to look at how the world of distance education and learning is changing, and the implications of this both for conventional institutions and for well-established distance teaching universities.

TECHNOLOGY AND DECISION MAKING

This book is primarily about decision making: making choices and implementing them. I will show that technology is neither good nor bad in itself but it is the way that it is used that matters. To make good decisions then about technology in education, we need to understand the relative educational strengths and weaknesses of different technologies, and what needs to be done to use technologies effectively.

Good decision making is particularly important given the rapid development in technology, and especially communications technologies. Hardly a conference on education goes by without a major part being devoted to technological change. Those who invested heavily in technology for teaching even five years ago are seeing cheaper, more powerful and more functional technology arriving every day. Technology indeed provides educators and governments with the capacity to transform radically our whole education system and nowhere is this truer than in the area of flexible and distance learning. Furthermore, the technology continues to change.

However, the focus in discussions of educational technology tends to be more on the actual technology itself, the information highway, the hardware, new software, and the potential for change. It is certainly important to understand the technology, but even more important to understand its strengths and weaknesses in terms of its actual applications. Also important is an understanding of managerial, administrative and operational requirements for the successful use of technology in distance education and training.

Although this book should appeal to experienced distance education practitioners, its main targets are key decision makers in education and training. For instance, a school superintendent, wondering how best to provide science courses to upper grade students in small rural high schools. Or a Dean of Humanities in a university, wondering how to take back the administration of Arts undergraduate distance education programmes from the Division of Continuing Education, now that student tuition fees are increasing. Or a World Bank team, wondering how to deliver quality education into remote rural regions of poor, developing countries. Or a university Vice-Chancellor, wondering how to increase enrolments without losing quality, but with no extra funding from government. Or a college head of department, wondering how to respond to demands from faculty and students for more online courses. Or a State Commissioner for Higher Education, who has received a request from the state university for $20 million to enhance and update its state-wide campus video-conferencing infrastructure, but who feels in his bones that this is not the right investment at this time. Or a politician and her civil servants seeking ways to meet the growing demand for access to higher education, but faced with pressure from the Minister of Finance to reduce expenditure.

All these key people are being faced with choice and decisions about distance education technologies and systems. Technology is the infrastructure, the bones, of distance education. The book then is not so much about technology-based curriculum design (see Bates and Poole, 2003 for this), as about decision making regarding technology *systems* for distance teaching and learning, including human, economic and organizational factors.

After reading this book, you will know what distance education is, how it differs from e-learning, and why it will remain relevant in the twenty-first century. You will be able to select and use different technologies in relation to your educational goals and local circumstances. You will have a set of questions or criteria to protect yourself and your organization from the temptations of vendors selling the latest breakthrough in learning technology. You will understand some of the barriers to the adoption of technologies for distance teaching and learning, and what needs to be done to remove those barriers. Perhaps even more importantly, when you have read this book, you should be able to deal with rapid technological change and have a clear vision of how to deliver quality education and training to learners, wherever they may be.

One of the basic premises of this book is that newer technologies such as the World Wide Web are not necessarily better (or worse) for teaching or learning than older technologies such as print or video-conferencing. New technologies are just different, and we need to understand the differences and the appropriate circumstances for applying various technologies for effective distance teaching and learning. The choice of technology should be driven not by its novelty but by the needs of the learners and the context in which we are working.

Another premise is that lessons learned in the past from research into some of the older technologies are often still relevant for the newer technologies. Whenever a new technology emerges in education people in general ignore what has been learned in previous contexts. In most cases, though, many of the lessons learned from previous applications of technology are just as relevant for the new technology application, yet the same mistakes are made. For instance, the need to reorganize and redesign teaching to exploit fully a new technology is often ignored. We shall see that the failure to learn from prior experience in distance education has led to many costly disasters in online learning in the last few years.

A third major premise is that there is a direct link between the use of technology and different ideologies of teaching and learning. The effectiveness of a technology cannot be judged without making some basic assumptions about what constitutes effective teaching and learning, and the goals and purposes of education and training. Therefore some space is taken in the early part of the book to discuss some of the basic differences in approach to education and training, and how these relate to the use of different technologies.

Lastly, it is easy to be seduced by the excitement of the latest technology, but technologies do not roll out evenly and all at once. Even in more advanced industrial countries, there will still be some target groups who will have access only to print, television and possibly the telephone. In developing countries, many of the newer technologies, for instance, the Internet, will be beyond the reach of most of the target group for distance education for many years to come.

Distance education is one of the few areas of education where for over 30 years technology has been central to the teaching task. A feature of distance education institutions is that they are deliberately designed and structured to exploit the cost and educational benefits of technology. Distance education has therefore provided a valuable test bed for understanding the potential and limitations of a wide range of technologies in education. At the same time, one of the main conclusions reached in this book is that while distance education has historically been at the leading edge in applying technology to education, recent technological advances are making the distinction between conventional and distance education more and more blurred. Technology is dramatically affecting *all* educational institutions.

First though we need to address the issue of distance education itself, and whether this remains a useful concept in the twenty-first century.

DEFINING OPEN LEARNING, FLEXIBLE LEARNING AND DISTANCE EDUCATION

Although these three terms are often used to mean the same thing, there are significant differences.

Open learning

Open learning is primarily a *goal*, or an *educational policy*. An essential characteristic of open learning is the removal of barriers to learning. This means no prior qualifications to study, and for students with disabilities, a determined effort to provide education in a suitable form that overcomes the disability (for example, audio tapes for students who are visually impaired). Ideally, no-one should be denied access to an open learning programme. Thus open learning must be scalable as well as flexible. Openness has particular implications for the use of technology. If no one is to be denied access, then technologies that are available to everyone need to be used.

Distance education

Distance education, on the other hand, is less a philosophy and more a *method* of education. Students can study in their own time, at the place of their choice (home, work or learning centre), and without face-to-face contact with a teacher. Technology is a critical element of distance education.

Flexible learning

Flexible learning is the provision of learning in a flexible manner, built around the geographical, social and time constraints of individual learners, rather than those of an educational institution. Flexible learning may include distance education, but it also may include delivering face-to-face training in the workplace or opening the campus longer hours or organizing weekend or summer schools. Like distance education, it is more of a method than a philosophy, although like distance education, it is often associated with increased access and hence more openness.

Differences and similarities

Open learning may include distance education, or it may depend on other flexible forms of learning, including admission to open-access face-to-face programmes. However, distance education programmes may not be open. That is certainly the case at the University of British Columbia (UBC). Students who wish to take distance courses and receive a UBC degree must meet UBC's admission requirements (which are set very high), and take the necessary course pre-requisites. For undergraduate education, at least half the programme must be done 'in residence', that is, by taking face-to-face classes on campus. Thus in practice students who live out of province or in foreign countries cannot obtain a UBC undergraduate degree wholly at a distance.

At the same time, the same distance courses at UBC may also be partly open to students in other institutions. Approximately 20 per cent of UBC's distance students – over 1,000 course enrolments – are registered with other institutions (mainly the Open Learning Agency). Students pay the course tuition fee (which more than covers the marginal cost of an extra student) to UBC, even if registered with another institution. Such students can take any UBC distance education course without meeting UBC admission standards (so long as sufficient instructors can be found). However, to obtain a degree, students taking these courses who do not meet UBC admission standards must transfer the credits from the UBC course into another institution's programme and receive qualifications from that institution (that institution also has to agree to this). Thus it is more accurate to say that UBC distance courses are partly open to non-UBC students, so long as they can find an institution willing to accept the UBC course credits.

If an institution is deliberately selective in its students, it has more flexibility with regard to choice of technology for distance education. It can for instance require all students who wish to take a distance education programme to have their own computer. It cannot do that if its mandate is to be open to all students.

Both openness and distance are rarely found in their 'purest' forms. No teaching system is completely open (minimum levels of literacy are required, for instance), and few students ever study in complete isolation. Thus there are degrees of openness and 'distance'.

Indeed, distance is more likely to be psychological or social, rather than geographical, in most cases. For instance, the vast majority of UBC undergraduate distance education students are not truly distant. The majority (83 per cent) live in the Greater Vancouver Region, and almost half within the City of Vancouver. Only 6 per cent of the undergraduate enrolments in 1999–2000 were from outside the province (because of the residential requirement). On the other hand, two thirds of UBC's distance students (67 per cent) were working. The main reason for most UBC students taking distance courses is the flexibility they provide, given the work and family commitments of students and the difficulty caused by timetable conflicts for face-to-face classes. Only 17 per cent gave reasons to do with distance or travel (Distance Education and Technology, 2001).

Although open learning and distance education can mean different things, the one thing they both have in common is an attempt to provide alternative means of high quality education or training for those who either cannot take conventional, campus-based programmes, or choose not to.

Three generations of distance education

It has been argued (Kaufman, 1989; Nipper, 1989) that there are three generations of distance education. The *first generation* is characterized by the predominant use of a single technology, and lack of direct student interaction with the institution providing the teaching or awarding accreditation. Although educational television and radio would also fit this description, the main form of first generation distance education was print-based correspondence education.

Typically a private company would provide reading lists of books and articles to students who would study independently. The company would hire tutors or instructors mainly to mark assignments and possibly to give feedback to students, before the students took a competitive examination from a recognized or accredited institution.

Second generation distance education is characterized by a deliberately integrated multiple-media 'print + broadcasting' approach, with learning materials specifically designed for study at a distance, but with communication with students mediated by a third person (a tutor, rather than the originator of the teaching material). Second generation distance education is sometimes described as industrial in nature (see Peters, 1983). Second generation distance education institutions can serve very large numbers of students. Daniel (1996) describes those with over 100,000 students as mega-universities.

Quality design of materials, highly centralized production and delivery, one way transmission of information modified by independent learner activities aimed at student cognitive development, large bureaucratic systems, and very cost-effective results are typical characteristics of second generation distance education. They are considered industrial in nature because they use methods of mass production and delivery of standardized products. Autonomous distance teaching universities such as the British Open University, the Anadolu Open University in Turkey, and the Universidad National de Educaciòn à Distancia in Spain are examples of second generation distance education.

Third generation distance education is based on two-way communications media such as the Internet or video-conferencing that enable interaction between the teacher who originates the instruction and the remote student. Perhaps even more importantly, communication is facilitated *among* students, either individually or as groups, but at a distance. Third generation technologies result in a much more equal distribution of communication between student and teacher (and also among students).

Third generation systems are sometimes described as knowledge-based or post-industrial (see Campion and Renner, 1992, and Farnes, 1993). Small, relatively autonomous teams manage course design, development and delivery. Often but not exclusively more constructivist approaches to teaching and learning, dependent on student dialogue and discussion, and relatively flexible Web-based administrative services, are found in third generation distance education. Third generation distance education is characterized by economies of scope – customized courses, quickly produced, for relatively low initial investment (although operating costs can be substantial). Examples of third generation distance education are often found in conventional universities with a distance education operation (dual mode institutions), and in some of the smaller training organizations.

Kaufman (1989) characterizes the three generations as a progressive increase in learner control, opportunities for dialogue and emphasis on thinking skills rather than on mere comprehension. More significantly, third generation distance learning is leading to new types of organization, discussed in more detail in Chapter 2.

Online learning and e-learning

The main reason for the growth of third generation distance education is the rapid expansion of the Internet and in particular the World Wide Web. However, this is influencing not only distance but also conventional education. The World Wide Web is a particular component of the Internet, allowing digital materials to be created, stored, accessed and interacted with over the Internet. The Internet also includes e-mail, bulletin boards and digital video-conferencing, either separate from or combined with the World Wide Web. The terms e-learning and online learning are often used interchangeably, although e-learning can encompass any form of telecommunications and computer-based learning, while online learning means using specifically the Internet and the Web.

E-learning, distributed learning, mixed mode, blended and hybrid courses

Distributed learning is a term that usually encompasses both on-campus and distance courses delivered online (from the computer term, 'distributed intelligence' (Twigg, 2001)). Mixed mode, hybrid and blended are all terms used to designate a combination of face-to-face and online teaching. However, I prefer to use the term 'mixed mode' in the specific context of a reduction in class time to accommodate more time spent studying online, whereas hybrid or blended could mean just adding online teaching to regular class time (or to print-based correspondence courses). However, there is no consistency yet in terminology.

At the same time as classroom teachers were moving to online components of their teaching, so too were many print-based distance education operations. Many institutions started adding e-mail, online Web articles and online discussion forums to their already existing print-based courses. Often these additional online activities are optional, so as not to reduce access to students without Internet facilities.

It can be seen then that defining an online course is not straightforward. Institutions often claim they are offering online courses when all they have done is merely added an online component to what is basically a face-to-face, print-based or broadcast-based course. However, even courses designed from scratch as 'online' courses will often contain printed readings, either in the form of required textbooks or as collections of printed articles distributed to students by mail. Some mainly online courses require attendance at a summer institute or weekend classes.

These are not just issues of terminology. Governments and institutions are increasingly requiring institutions to report on how many online or e-learning courses have been produced or delivered, without any clear definition of what constitutes an online course. I don't believe that there is any particular virtue in being fully online. Choice of technology should be driven by the needs of the subject matter and of the students. However, there is a tendency by many institutions to over-inflate their claims to being an online learning institution, so we need to define our terms.

Therefore, for the sake of clarity I use the term *'fully online'* if the students must have access to a computer and the Internet to do the course, and can take the course without having to attend any face-to-face classes. In other words, fully online courses are distance courses. In this definition, students may also need to read printed books and articles, and may attend face-to-face classes on an optional basis. I use the term *'e-learning'* where courses may have anything from a relatively small Web-based component of a course or program to a fully online offering.

Bates and Poole (2003) have described these developments graphically in Figure 1.1.

Thus new developments require new terminology. However, the use of terminology by those who believe they are inventing something new is not always helpful. 'Virtual' has been used to describe so many different forms of online provision that it is now virtually meaningless. Distributed learning is useful only as long as it is not seen as being the same as distance education. Blended, hybrid and mixed mode are useful descriptors for campus-based e-learning, but again we need to be clear whether this is merely adding to regular classroom teaching or actually replacing or transforming it.

It can be seen then that distance education can operate with or without online learning. E-learning encompasses a wider range of activities than distance education. Distance education students tend to have quite different characteristics, such as being older, more independent learners and requiring specialist learning support. We shall see that there are significant pedagogical differences between distance education and classroom teaching or even mixed mode instruction. Thus even though there is convergence in the use of technology between classroom-based teaching and distance education, distance education remains a dynamic and distinct form of education.

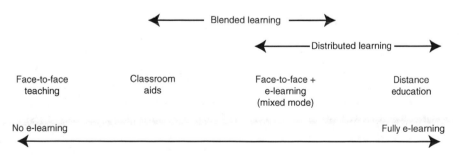

Figure 1.1 The continuum of technology-based learning (from Bates and Poole, 2003, p.127)

WHY E-LEARNING, OPEN AND DISTANCE LEARNING?

There are several quite different reasons why governments, the private sector and individual students have given strong support to open and distance learning, and to e-learning:

Economic competitiveness

Governments in economically advanced countries in particular have recognized the importance of knowledge-based economies. Unable to compete with low labour costs in developing countries, more advanced economies are trying to create highly productive (and high wage) knowledge-based industries, such as computing, telecommunications, financial systems, and education itself. Such industries depend on a highly educated work force, thus leveraging an advantage over less economically advanced countries.

Governments see two quite distinct roles for e-learning. They see e-learning as a new knowledge-based industry, able to lever the advantage of advanced educational systems to create educational products and services that can be marketed internationally. The second role is to use e-learning to improve the quality of education and to produce technology-savvy graduates, able to use new technologies in the new economy.

Business also sees a value in e-learning as a way of increasing competitiveness through ensuring that the work-force is continually learning and improving, without the high costs of travel and time away from work. In particular, e-learning is seen as an essential component of knowledge management, allowing companies to become 'learning organizations' (see Senge, 1990, and Rosenberg, 2001).

Lifelong learning

Vocational training is undergoing radical change. For the last 50 years, there have been three main methods of vocational training: on-the-job 'apprenticeship' (essentially learning at work with a master craftsman); public sector classroom teaching (either as day release or evening classes); and company-organized, in-house training (seminars/ courses). These three methods are all primarily based on personal contact between teacher and taught, and are hence time and place dependent. They are all also costly to employers, if there are travel and accommodation costs or employees are away from regular work while training. Such methods are also inflexible, from a learner's perspective.

In the last few years, though, e-learning in particular has been applied on a large scale in vocational training. There are several reasons for this. First is the changing nature of work. Because of rapid developments in technology, the idea of being trained as a youth for the same job for life – as, for example, through the apprenticeship system – is becoming less and less tenable. Most people are likely to change careers at least two or three times. Within a particular job, the need for continuing training is rapidly increasing.

Job mobility is increasing, especially across national frontiers. An employee of a large company in Europe can increasingly expect to move around Europe, or at least within his or her own country. This makes the provision of continuing education difficult through traditional means, if at one time you are in Frankfurt, a year later in Toulouse, and the next back in the United Kingdom.

Lastly, because training is costly, efforts are being made to find more cost-effective ways to train. Open learning centres, where employees can 'drop-in' for training during breaks, after work, or during slack periods at work, or e-learning, where employees can learn either at home, or at their desk or work-place, both suggest greater flexibility and lower costs. In particular, a wide range of companies and institutions has been created to provide e-learning for the workforce.

Open and distance learning provide the flexibility needed for adults to continue their education or training while still working or with family responsibilities. Some governments and employers have stressed the importance of lifelong learning and distance education for increased economic productivity. Companies in particular see the value of employees learning in their own time. Individuals see the value of having flexibility and access to learning, without sacrificing time away from home. In particular, in a volatile job market (especially in the knowledge-based industries), individuals feel the pressure to continue their education. Lastly, the rapid growth of knowledge in areas such as health, technology, and management require people working in these areas to continue to study and learn, just to keep up with the knowledge base of the job. E-learning and distance education are ideal methods of lifelong learning.

Social equity and access

Many adults are unable to enter or complete higher education on leaving the school system for academic, personal or economic reasons. Open learning gives a second chance to such people by removing the barriers of access to higher education. The more selective, restricted or expensive the conventional education system, the greater the need for open educational provision. Distance education fits well the needs of those wanting open access but are working or who have family responsibilities.

Better education

The arrival of the Web as an educational tool in the mid 1990s coincided with pressure from some influential educational theorists in North America to move away from an emphasis on the transmission of knowledge to the social construction of knowledge. Online discussion forums enable discussion, reflection and dialogue over time and in different places, all functions supporting the social construction of knowledge. The link between different theories of learning and the use of technology will be discussed in more detail throughout the book, but one argument often put forward by proponents of e-learning is that it facilitates better than traditional classroom teaching the kind of learning outcomes needed in a knowledge-based society.

Cost effectiveness

In many countries, demand for places in the conventional education system far exceeds the supply. Under the right circumstances, open and distance learning systems have proved that they can provide quality education and training to large numbers at lower unit costs than conventional education systems. The jury is still out on the cost-effectiveness of e-learning. However, there is often a belief by key policy makers that in the long term, e-learning must be more cost-effective, because it will replace high labour costs with low-cost technology.

Geography

In geographically remote or sparsely populated areas, it is not economically possible to provide a full range of educational and training opportunities through conventional institutions. Distance education enables learning and training to be delivered more effectively and economically in such communities.

Commercialization of education

There has been a very strong movement in the United States to develop e-learning as a commercial activity. Wall Street analysts (particularly Michael Moe and Henry Blodgett of Merrill Lynch) projected a vast untapped new dot.com business in e-learning. As a result, not only private companies but also several major universities invested very heavily in online education businesses. We shall see in the next chapter that this was a grossly over-optimistic scenario, which came crashing down in the dot.com bust of 2000–1. Nevertheless, the pressure on public institutions to diversify their sources of funding, and the drive by some major American companies to offer private educational services, has resulted in e-learning still being considered a potential moneymaker.

Are these arguments true?

The validity and evidence for such arguments will be assessed as we go through the book. In a sense though it does not matter whether they are true; it is what policy makers believe that drives action. In reality, it is not so much any single argument as the combination and range of arguments that have led to the rapid and ongoing development of e-learning and distance education.

It should be noted though how varied and contradictory are some of these arguments. From a decision-making perspective, it is essential to be clear as to the main motives for using technology for teaching in education, and in particular to be clear whether it is e-learning, open access or distance education that is the most appropriate solution for the problem under question.

THE GROWTH OF DISTANCE EDUCATION

In the last 30 years, 'second generation' open and distance learning has spread to many countries, and become an important part of most modern educational systems. Since 1996, 'third generation' distance education has spread rapidly in economically advanced countries, and even to niche markets in developing countries. Open learning and distance education projects now exist at school and career, technical and vocational, and college and university levels, as well as in the private sector, in the form of work-based training. There are now examples of thriving open and distance education initiatives operating across all subject areas, at all academic levels, and in every continent. The same is increasingly true for e-learning.

It might be thought that the demand for distance access would start to decline in countries such as the United States and Canada, where over half the high school graduates now go on to post-secondary education. Also, the Open University in Britain has felt the pressure as the proportion of the high school graduates going to conventional universities increased from around 10 per cent in the 1970s to 35 per cent by the year 2000. At the same time, conventional universities, especially the former polytechnics, have moved aggressively into online learning in the United Kingdom. Nevertheless, despite increasing competition from other universities, the British Open University's enrolments figures have remained remarkably stable at around 150,000 to 180,000 students a year.

We shall see in the next chapter that the commercial market for e-learning was badly overestimated at the end of the 1990s. Nevertheless, several institutions in different countries have been tracking their distance education enrolments over a number of years. Their data suggest that in the United States, Canada and some countries in Western Europe, demand for degree programmes, continuing professional education, and workplace training delivered by distance methods has been steadily increasing by an average of around 10 per cent per year since 1996. This compares with enrolment increases in traditional education of around 2 to 5 per cent per year. These trends have been quite consistent since the advent of Web-based online learning in 1996.

Most of the growth in distance education in these countries has been in online learning. Thus increasing access to conventional education is being more than offset by increased demand for flexibility and for lifelong learning, and especially for online learning. It seems that third generation distance education will continue to grow in these economically advanced countries, although it will be interesting to see how increased use of e-learning on the campus will affect fully online distance education enrolments in dual-mode institutions.

In countries such as Pakistan, Turkey, Venezuela, the Philippines or Indonesia, where only a small proportion of high school graduates can access public post-secondary education or even high schools, the demand for distance education will continue to increase, mainly through their large public national autonomous universities. Online learning though will still be mainly a marginal or niche market for some time to come.

In rapidly developing countries such as Malaysia, Mexico, India, Thailand, Singapore, South Korea, Taiwan, Brazil and the new European Union entrants from Eastern Europe, online and distance learning will grow even more quickly over the next ten years. This is because their prosperous middle classes are developing faster than their conventional education systems. It is in these countries particularly that we are likely to see new models of education emerging based on e-learning and distance education, with private and for-profit education playing a much larger role than in the most economically advanced countries. We will also see more failures and disappointments in these countries. It will also be interesting to see the impact of these e-learning developments on the enrolments in the large autonomous open universities in some of these countries.

CONCLUSIONS

Distance education illustrates well the relationship between the use of technology and the need to reorganize to maximize its benefits. Distance education, when properly organized and structured, also illustrates the capacity to reach new target groups and to expand the range of educational provision through the use of technology. Distance education is also being revolutionized by the development of the Internet.

Open and distance learning – or at least the provision of education and training in more flexible ways than regular, full-time attendance at a single campus-based institution – are growing rapidly. Technology is an essential component of most (but not all) open learning initiatives. The quite parallel online developments in distance and classroom teaching, leading to convergence of at least some activities common to both classroom and distance teaching, therefore raise a number of questions.

Is distance education any longer a different or separate activity from classroom teaching? Is distance education an obsolete concept, now incorporated into distributed learning? This argument is often put forward by strong advocates of e-learning, who see e-learning as an educational paradigm shift, making obsolete all forms of distance education that preceded it (see for instance Harasim *et al.*, 1995, and Garrison and Anderson, 1999).

This though is a fundamental mistake. Although e-learning or online learning can be a component of both classroom and distance learning, e-learning is not synonymous with distance education. Distance learning can exist without online learning, and online learning is not necessarily distance learning. Students who cannot or will not access a campus have very different needs from those that do, whether or not they are studying primarily by e-learning. To merely replace the term distance learning with distributed learning then confuses rather than clarifies.

Second, distance education traditionally has been strongly associated with the educational philosophy of openness, of making it easier for students to access learning. We shall see in the next chapter that e-learning has become strongly associated with the privatization of education. Increased access and equal opportunity have not been the driving forces behind many e-learning initiatives; commercialization and profit have been the drivers. Thus e-learning comes from a very different ideological background. Nevertheless, as in the example of UBC, distance education is not necessarily synonymous with open learning, nor is e-learning synonymous with the privatization of education. These are decisions people have made as a result of changing ideologies, not because of new technologies.

Another development resulting from the increased move towards e-learning is the challenge to institutions in how to manage and organize these new developments. Especially in dual-mode institutions, distance education has been seen as a separate activity, on the periphery of mainstream classroom teaching, and somewhat esoteric in its organizational needs. Therefore separate departments or institutions of distance education were established. The growing convergence though between e-learning in the classroom and e-learning at a distance has raised questions about how best to organize and support e-learning. Should academic departments be responsible for the design, production and management of all forms of teaching, or should teaching be organized around different target groups or methods? What kind of help do instructors need to use e-learning effectively, and what working methods will be needed to ensure quality?

Once instructors are trained in the use of technology, do they need specialist support at all for online courses? Should separate distance education units be disbanded, and their specialists (instructional designers, Web programmers) fired or reallocated to regular teaching departments or faculties? Is there any longer a need for separate distance education institutions? Do we need new types of institution to exploit better these developments? Who should make such decisions, and on what basis?

These questions will recur throughout the book. However, I will argue that the needs of students who study entirely at a distance are quite different from those who are taught on campus or in classes. Distance students require different approaches to course design, development and learner support. Classroom teachers incorporating online teaching can benefit from some of the approaches developed for distance learners, but these need to be adapted to a classroom context. Similarly, distance educators can benefit from some of the e-learning applications in classrooms. Nevertheless, whether students are fully distant or not, the main issues in e-learning are quality standards, teacher and student workload and costs.

The value of distance education is its ability to reach learners not well served by conventional educational institutions. The value of technology in teaching is its ability to meet better the newly emerging educational needs of an information society, and to improve the quality of learning. The intelligent application of technology and distance education is critical to economic well-being, particularly in Europe, North America and other more economically advanced countries. Although there are important exceptions, the value of distance education is generally greater when applied to more mature students, with jobs and families, compared to younger people in full-time education.

In summary, neither e-learning nor distance education is a panacea for education, not does e-learning replace distance education as a concept. Nevertheless, e-learning and distance education are both evolving very quickly. Indeed, we will see in the next chapter how these developments are leading to 'disruptive' behaviour in existing organizations. Senior managers of established institutions ignore at their peril emerging technologies. New technologies require new organizational responses. This applies just as much to distance education operations as to classroom-based institutions. Therefore in the next chapter I will look at how educational institutions have responded over the last ten years to the challenge of change with respect to e-learning and distance education.

2 The impact of technology on the organization of distance education

Distance education has resulted in major changes to the organization of educational provision. The obvious difference is that students are no longer required to attend a campus at regular periods. As a result, distance education has required quite different organizational structures from those of conventional educational institutions. Furthermore, as technology changes, so does the need to reorganize institutions to lever the benefits of new technology. Institutional reorganization due to technology change applies as much to distance teaching organizations as to conventional institutions.

In this chapter, I will analyse the different approaches to the organization of distance education, and in particular, will look at how the Internet has resulted in the emergence of new forms of distance education. (I draw heavily on Dirr, 2001 and on Ryan and Steadman, 2002 for this analysis.)

AUTONOMOUS DISTANCE EDUCATION INSTITUTIONS

Autonomous distance education institutions are institutions that are totally dedicated to distance education.

Print and broadcast based open universities

The establishment in 1969 of the British Open University (UKOU) marked a turning point in the development of distance education, in two ways. Not only was the UKOU designed solely and specifically for open access to distance education at degree level but it was also designed as a multiple media teaching institution, combining print, broadcasting, and face-to-face tuition in an integrated manner. Since it opened in 1971, the Open University has served over two million students. In 2002–3 it had over 180,000 undergraduate and postgraduate students, of which over 70 per cent were in regular employment. It is ranked regularly in the top ten universities in the United Kingdom based on formal independent assessments of its teaching and research.

The Open University's provision of higher adult education at a distance, through the use of technology, has led to an organizational structure quite different from that of conventional universities. Although it hires tenured research faculty, has a large administrative campus, and uses facilities in other colleges and universities for local study centres and summer schools, it has no students on campus (except some postgraduates doing research). It does though have major media design and production facilities, huge warehousing, and an army of administrators and part-time local face-to-face tutors, counsellors and regional administrative staff and centres. It is thus an excellent example of the structural changes in organization that can result from the systematic large-scale application of technology to education.

Since the creation of the Open University, over 25 similar autonomous university institutions dedicated solely to distance education have been established in different countries throughout the world. These are institutions that operate across whole countries, states or provinces. They are enabled by government to award their own accreditation, in the form of degrees, diplomas or certificates (hence they are autonomous). They use a variety of media, and usually have large numbers of students. Daniel (1996) lists eleven 'mega-universities' in this category, each with over 100,000 students. The largest are the Radio and Television University of China (RTVU) and the Anadolu Open University of Turkey, both of which have over 500,000 students enrolled each year.

The large autonomous open universities have had some difficulties in embracing fully online courses. Such institutions are primarily open in philosophy, and there has been a concern that many students will not have convenient and ready access to a computer and the Internet. Thus even though in 2003 it describes itself as Britain's leading e-university, the UKOU designates its programmes as primarily 'information technology enhanced' (Open University, 2003). Although most of its courses are supplemented by e-mail, discussion forums and Web sites, and although it has a number of innovative educational technology projects, only 14 of the British Open University's courses were delivered entirely over the Internet in 2002–3. The original media of print, television and audio still provide the core learning materials for most of their programmes, although information technology plays an increasingly important part in many courses.

The dominance of the more traditional media at the Open University is unlikely to change, even if most homes in Britain eventually get Internet and computer access, because the Open University's core organization is built around the production of 'second generation' distance education programmes based on print and broadcasting. Although most students on most courses are exposed to information technology-based learning in some way, the Open University cannot change from an institution of mass education to one based on low-cost, customized Web-based programming, without completely reinventing itself.

At the same time, the UKOU continues to provide a highly valued service to large numbers of students. It is very cost-effective, providing quality degrees at approximately half the full cost of traditional universities in Britain. Most importantly, it is still a truly open university. These characteristics are even more relevant for the other large open universities in less economically advanced countries, where computer access is far less widespread and where cost is a critical factor. However, we shall see later in the book that it is more difficult to provide the type of learning essential in a knowledge-based society through the mass education approach of large autonomous open universities.

Online autonomous distance universities

In 2002–3 there were almost no public, accredited universities that were fully online, in the sense that students were required to have a computer and Internet access for all courses, with no or minimal face-to-face classroom attendance, and all programmes were delivered online.

The nearest to a fully online public university is probably the *Open University of Catalonia* (Universitat Oberta de Catalunya (UOC)). It opened in 1996, and in 2003–4 it had 25,000 students, mainly from Catalonia, the region around Barcelona in Spain. Enrolments are increasing by about 10 per cent per year, while enrolments in conventional Spanish universities are declining. UOC's courses are developed primarily in the Catalan language, but some programmes are also available in Spanish. Most of its courses are now fully online. It offers 19 bachelors degrees, 9 masters programmes and a unique online Ph.D. programme on the information society.

UOC is funded directly by the regional government of Catalonia. Other public universities in Spain, including Spain's national open university, Universidad Nacional de Educación a Distancia (UNED), are funded by the central Spanish government. UOC has a core of full-time academic staff who manage programmes, hiring professors on contract from other universities to develop and teach courses. Courses are developed using a project team of contract professors, instructional designers, project managers, and Web and multimedia designers. UOC has developed its own technology infrastructure, called Virtual Campus, for student administration and teaching. UOC does have regional study centres with computer and Internet access, but attendance is optional if students have a computer and Internet access at home (as most do).

Although publicly funded, UOC has an interesting and unique 'business model'. Government funds go to a 'holding company' or Foundation. The holding company allocates funds to the Open University of Catalonia, but some funds are also allocated as stock to companies that are wholly or partly owned by the Foundation. For instance, one company, which is a 50:50 partnership between the Foundation and a private publisher, is responsible for the publication, marketing and distribution of UOC's courses in Spanish. Any profits from the operation of the companies flow back to the Foundation (and partners).

Athabasca University (AU), based in Alberta, Canada, is another autonomous distance teaching university that is moving rapidly towards being a mainly online university, although it still has a substantial inventory of primarily print-based courses, enhanced with e-mail and online discussion forums and student services. AU describes itself as Canada's Open University (which might be disputed by Télé-université in Québec). AU has about 30,000 students in over 600 courses leading to undergraduate and master's degrees. Enrolments increased by about 10 per cent per year between 1998 and 2003.

Thus despite the great deal of attention given to online learning between the first educational applications of the Web in 1996 to the dot.com bust at the turn of the century, there are still very few public educational institutions that are fully online.

Virtual institutes

A number of institutions run 'virtual' or online components within otherwise traditional distance education or campus-based operations. These are usually limited to a specific number of courses or programmes, often in the form of pilots or deliberately innovative and leading-edge technology applications. Some are more research and development projects than sustainable teaching programmes (for example, the Knowledge Media Institute at the UKOU). Others are specific programmes in an organization still dependent on older forms of distance education.

Thus the *Indira Ghandi National Open University* in India, which otherwise depends heavily on print and broadcasting for its programmes, offers an Advanced Diploma and a Bachelor degree in Information Technology, using a combination of CD-ROM and Internet technologies. NIIT in India also offers online programmes to computer engineers and scientists. The Virtual University of Pakistan offers a federally recognized Bachelor of Computer Science, using a combination of television broadcast, Internet and private sector computer institutes.

Instituto Tecnológico y de Estudios Superiores de Monterrey *(Tec de Monterrey)*, a large private not-for-profit university in Mexico, has a distance education system very much in transition. Although its undergraduate programmes are delivered mainly by face-to-face teaching in 33 campuses throughout Mexico, its graduate and continuing education programmes are delivered by Tec de Monterrey's Virtual University (Universidad Virtual) throughout Mexico and also to 13 other Latin American countries by satellite television.

All of the Tec de Monterrey campuses have both wired and wireless networks, thus moving the on-campus teaching increasingly into a mixed mode (i.e. face-to-face plus online learning). The university provides financial plans to help the students buy a laptop computer.

The Virtual University offers full graduate degrees at a distance. In the second semester of 2002 the VU had 5,772 graduate students. One-third of these students are fully online. The VU also includes 55,000 students participating in continuing education programmes in 2002, delivered in online, satellite or mixed mode for in-company training and for non-governmental organizations, teachers and workers in the public sector. The VU will increase the number of online students as most of its satellite television programs were changed to online delivery for the August semester of 2003.

These examples of online programmes that are part of a wider range of modes of delivery within public post-secondary institutions indicate the complex and diverse ways in which distance education is developing.

DUAL-MODE INSTITUTIONS

These are conventional teaching institutions with on-campus students which also offer full programmes at a distance. Usually, the distance students sit the same examinations as the on-campus students.

Typical dual-mode institutions are Pennsylvania State University, the University of Wisconsin, the University of Maryland, and the University of Maine, in the United States, the University of British Columbia, the University of Guelph and the University of Saskatchewan in Canada, the University of Southern Queensland, Deakin University and Charles Sturt University in Australia, and the University of Derby in Britain. Dual-mode institutions are particularly prevalent in federal systems of government, where states or provinces are responsible for higher education. Their existence also explains why national autonomous open universities have not taken root in the United States.

In the past, distance courses in dual-mode institutions were of two main kinds: primarily print-based, usually with some additional media support, such as audio cassettes or telephone tutoring, and delivered to students at home; or primarily 'remote classroom' lectures delivered to satellite campuses by video-conference or satellite TV transmission. Often the numbers of distance students in dual mode institutions are relatively small (between 1,000 to 10,000 course enrolments, equivalent to 100 to 1,000 full time student equivalents). Hence their operations administratively have to be much more streamlined or integrated with campus-based systems, compared with the autonomous institutions dedicated to open and distance learning.

Since 1996, when the Web first became established in online learning, many dual mode institutions have increasingly been moving into Internet-based delivery. A few online distance education operations are very large in terms of the total number of enrolments. For instance, the *University of Maryland University College* offers more than 500 courses and 80 undergraduate and graduate certificate and degree programmes completely online to more than 87,000 student enrolments (equivalent to about 10,000 full-time students). US military personnel account for approximately 23,000 of these student enrolments.

The *University of British Columbia's* distance education programme was a typical mid-size operation. In 2002–3 its Distance Education and Technology unit (DE&T) administered 107 distance courses and 5,700 course enrolments, equivalent to 720 full time students. There were 53 fully online courses with just over 2,000 student enrolments. Student enrolments in DE&T increased by about 10 per cent per year over the previous seven years. All new course production since 1996 was fully online, but there still remained approximately 50 print-based courses that had not yet been redesigned or replaced by 2004. These were mainly the larger courses, with over 200 enrolments per term or semester. Although these print-based courses did not allow for the regular student and instructor interaction found in the online courses, it was difficult to find professors willing to convert the remaining old print-based courses to online courses. To maintain teacher–student ratios of around 1:30, essential for online teaching in many subjects, more contract instructors would need to have been hired. Thus moving these large courses from print-based to online teaching not only would have increased costs, but also would have made it difficult to find enough well-qualified contract instructors.

Many distance education units will continue to run print- and broadcast-based courses in parallel with online courses for some time, because of their large inventory of 'second generation' courses, and because print-based courses for large course enrolments have relative cost advantages. Some institutions have opted to add new information technologies to existing courses, but as a consequence have lagged behind in developing fully online courses from scratch. Yet others have started online operations separate from the print-based distance education programmes. Therefore it is difficult if not impossible for distance education programmes to move quickly from second to third generation distance education without a large infusion of capital for new course development. In summary, dual-mode institutions are major suppliers of post-secondary distance education programmes. Many are moving quite quickly to fully online distance delivery, while others are moving more slowly.

FOR-PROFIT DISTANCE EDUCATION INSTITUTIONS

Revenue generation, globalization, economies of scale, internationalization of the curriculum, competitive advantage, and local adaptation are all reasons that have led public and private universities to develop for-profit spin-off companies in recent years.

Private and corporate institutions were most affected by the dot.com boom and bust of the late 1990s, although commercial developments in online learning have also had a profound effect on public universities and colleges in many countries. There is still considerable confusion about exactly what is happening in the United States, because of the size, diversity and naked entrepreneurial spirit of that country. Thus new public, private and corporate online learning organizations are created and collapse on an almost daily basis. It is also difficult to categorize the for-profit sector, as new organizational forms and new types of institution are being created, modified, and reconstituted. However, certain patterns are now beginning to emerge, and in particular, some hard lessons have been learned about commercial IT-based distance education.

Private e-learning universities

In this complex field, the simplest organizations to describe are the private, for-profit companies. For-profit educational companies in the United States account for a small but growing share of the education market. According to the *Chronicle of Higher Education* (July 19, 2001) for-profit companies grew from 3 per cent to 8 per cent of the education market between 1989 and 1999, mainly in certificate and associate degree programmes. The three most successful private companies that are operating fully online post-secondary programmes on a sustainable basis are Jones International University, the University of Phoenix Online, and Capella University.

Jones International University (JIU), founded in 1993 and headquartered in Engelwood, Colorado, was established as a fully online university in 1995. JIU was the first private online university to be fully accredited in the United States by the Higher Learning Commission, a member of the North Central Association. All JIU programmes are delivered entirely via the Internet, including an electronic library, academic advising, and technology support. In 2003 it offered two bachelor's degrees, three master's degrees, and six certificates, mainly in business and information technology. In the same year there were 86 students who graduated.

The University of Phoenix (owned by the Apollo Group) provides standardized face-to-face programmes designed at their headquarters but delivered to over 100,000 students by contract faculty (usually working professionals) through local centres in most major cities in the United States. *The University of Phoenix Online* (UoPOnline), now a wholly Internet-based operation, started in the early 1990s as part of the University of Phoenix, and was spun off as a separate company within the Apollo Group in 1999. Like Jones International University, UoPOnline has survived the dot.com boom and bust. In 2001 it was trading profitably (Ryan and Steadman, 2002).

In 2003, UoPOnline had 26,000 students enrolled. In 2004 it offered one associate degree, 14 undergraduate degrees, 26 Master's degrees, and four Ph.D. programmes, all completely online. Its programmes focus on business, technology, health care, education, and social sciences. It also offers a number of customized certificates for corporate clients. A UoPOnline master's degree will cost approximately US$25,000 in fees. It should be noted that UoPOnline in 2003 was not accredited by NCA as a university or college as recognized by Chapter IV of the United States Department of Commerce, but as a vocational/adult education organization.

Capella University is a fully online university with headquarters in Minneapolis. Capella, like Jones International and the University of Phoenix, is also accredited by the North Central Association. Capella offers courses, certificates and degree programmes in business, technology, education, human services and psychology. In 2003 it had 6,500 enrolled students and more than 500 online courses.

There are many other private distance education companies in the United States, but these will nearly all be unaccredited. These private online universities are working in a large but narrowly focused niche market of business and information technology programmes for adult learners – what Daniel (quoted in Ryan and Steadman, 2002, p. 52) describes as 'low-hanging fruit'. It is a market where there is high demand and where learners have the means to pay the full cost of instruction.

Not-for-profit university spin-offs

One interesting development has been the creation of arms-length spin-off companies from prestigious accredited not-for-profit universities. The university retains at least majority ownership, but the spin-off company operates outside the normal internal university academic approval procedures and on a strictly commercial basis.

In 1998 New York University, a prestigious not-for-profit private university, set up NYUOnline, with an investment of $21.5 million (*Chronicle of Higher Education,* November 28, 2001). Temple University, a large public university in Pennsylvania, set up an online programme as a for-profit business as 'Virtual Temple'. In 2000, the British Open University made its third foray into the United States since its establishment in 1969, investing US$20 million in a US subsidiary, the United States Open University.

In 2000, Cornell University, a public university in New York State, created eCornell, an e-learning company established and wholly owned by Cornell University and which incorporated many of the resources of the former Office of Distance Learning. In 2003, eCornell was working with four schools of Cornell University, offering 23 Web-based non-credit or certificate courses in the areas of human resources, hotel administration, food and beverage management and medical education.

Although the University of Phoenix Online, Jones International University and eCornell have managed to survive, other for-profit online universities have crashed and burned. NYUOnline and Virtual Temple closed as separate divisions, NYU rolling back NYUOnline into its School of Continuing and Professional Studies, which in 2003 offered five Master's programmes and a number of certificates through online study. Harcourt, a major publisher, invested US$10 million in 2000 in Harcourt Virtual College but closed the college within 12 months after being bought out by another publisher, Thomson. The United States Open University lasted little more than 18 months, closing at the end of 2001, although it did get 600 enrolments, and two partners, the University of Maryland–Baltimore and Indiana State

University. We shall see that these were not the only for-profit online learning initiatives to fail in 2001.

PARTNERSHIPS AND CONSORTIA

Partnership and collaboration between universities, and between universities and colleges, in distance education is increasing. Collaboration avoids duplication of courses within a state system, allows development costs to be shared, and provides local support and cultural adaptation.

Collaboration takes a number of forms. I define a partnership as a formal, ongoing working relationship between two separate organizations. Each partner will have roughly equal status and investment in the partnership. I define a consortium as a formal arrangement between several institutions to collaborate or share resources.

University joint degree programme partnerships

The simplest form of collaboration is a joint degree offered by two universities, or by colleges in partnership with a university. Cleveland State University and the University of Akron offer a joint Master's programme in Social Work exclusively taught through distance learning via two-way interactive television. Edmonds and Bellevue Community Colleges have combined with Washington State University to offer joint BA/Associate degrees. Students take on-campus courses at the colleges, and complete their degree by distance courses from Washington State University.

UBC has partnered with Tec de Monterrey in Mexico to offer a joint Master in Educational Technology delivered entirely online, in both English and Spanish. The programme started in 2002–3, with over 200 students taking the Spanish version, and 80 taking the English version. The programme is expected to grow to over 400 students studying in English, and 1,000 in Spanish.

Public–private partnerships

Partnerships between universities and colleges and private sector organizations are becoming more common. *eCollege*, based in Denver, Colorado, is one of the largest providers of 'integrated technology and service solutions that support the success and growth of online educational programs'. Basically, eCollege enables a department or institution to get and maintain its programmes online. In 2003 eCollege had over 200 clients, including public and private universities, career colleges, community colleges, school districts, and state departments of education.

OnlineLearning.net, part of the Online Higher Education division of Sylvan Learning Systems, Inc. in the United States, had more than 20,000 enrolments in 1,700 online courses between 1996 and 2003. It had an agreement with the National Education Association for in-service teacher training courses. As part of this initiative, OnlineLearning.net had the exclusive worldwide electronic distribution rights to graduate-level extension and graduate-credit courses in teacher education developed by the University of California–Los Angeles Extension (a public university) and the University of San Diego Department of Continuing Education (a private university).

Such service companies have helped many institutions without prior distance learning or e-learning experience to enter the field, and as such have speeded up the development of e-learning.

State or national consortia

In some educational jurisdictions, distance education is centrally co-ordinated to avoid duplication among institutions. From 1979 until 2003, British Columbia in Canada offered a collaborative open and distance-learning programme, primarily at university undergraduate level. The Open University of British Columbia was administered by the Open Learning Agency (OLA). *The Open University of British Columbia* was essentially a collaboration among the OLA and three universities (UBC, Simon Fraser University and the University of Victoria), each of which offered distance education programmes. The Open University of B.C. allowed open access, the OLA provided primarily first and second year courses and general degrees in Science and Arts, and the three universities made available their third and fourth year more specialist undergraduate distance courses to students registered with OLA. Thus students could obtain a degree of the Open University of British Columbia (accredited nationally) by taking approved courses from a variety of providers.

A new provincial government was elected in 2002, and with the rapid growth of online courses from colleges and new universities created since 1979 in the province, the new government decided to close OLA and transfer its services to other institutions within the province. The 16,000 students enrolled in the Open University of B.C. programme were transferred to the newly restructured University of the Caribou, based in Kamloops, a town in the interior of British Columbia.

Virtual universities or colleges are often in reality consortia that have agreed to share collections of online courses from different institutions. Michigan Virtual University (MVU) is a not-for-profit corporation established in 1998 to deliver online education and training opportunities to the Michigan workforce. MVU contracts for the delivery of its programmes and services through the colleges and universities in Michigan and private training providers. MVU does not independently grant degrees; instead, credentials are granted by the organization providing the programme. The primary motivation for creating MVU was to provide high-quality, convenient, and cost-effective education and training to Michigan's workforce.

The Kentucky Virtual University serves as a clearing-house for courses and programmes offered online by 27 accredited Kentucky colleges and universities and accredited professional development providers. Like MVU,

Kentucky Virtual University does not grant degrees. These are awarded by the institution where the student is enrolled and to whom the students pay tuition fees. The Kentucky Virtual University offers a 24 × 7 virtual library, research help from reference librarians, call centre specialists, 24 × 7 technical support and an online bookstore.

The *Canadian Virtual University* is a consortium of 13 Canadian universities offering over 250 programmes available through the Internet or by distance education. Students can select from any of the 2,000 courses offered by any of the participating universities. Most full Bachelor degree programmes however come from two members, Athabasca University and the Open University of British Columbia, and most Master's degrees are offered by Royal Roads University, British Columbia.

One of the largest consortia is the Southern Educational Regional Board's *Electronic Campus*. This covers over 200 colleges and universities across 16 states in the south-east United States, often allowing students to take out of state programmes from partner institutions at in-state tuition rates.

The *Western Governors' University* in the United States is another form of consortium. It opened officially in June 1998 and has governors from 19 western and mid-western states as Board members. WGU received accreditation in 2003 from the Interregional Accrediting Committee (a committee of four regional accrediting commissions) to offer associate, Bachelor's and Master's degrees. It has 25 leading business partners, including AT&T, Cisco, Dell, Google, Hewlett Packard, Microsoft, Oracle, Sun Microsystems and Thomson Learning. In 2004, it had 2,600 students and 46 students who graduated that year.

WGU was created because of the founding governors' frustration that universities and colleges were not responding to the needs of business and industry, and were not preparing students properly for the new world of work. As a result, WGU is based on the concept of *competency-based learning*. The business partners are important because they help to determine the competencies required.

Students can achieve their qualifications in two ways. The most innovative is by demonstrating set standards of competency through successful completion of tests and assessment, irrespective of prior courses taken. Alternatively, students can take courses from WGU-recognized providers that produce the requisite competencies. WGU 'brokers' and validates these courses. (Go to http://www.wgu.edu for more information.) Its three degree areas are information technology, business, and education.

The National Technological University in the United States is another degree-awarding consortium, with 26 leading universities offering nation-wide post-graduate distance courses in engineering and management, via satellite television and the Internet. Founded in 1984, and headquartered in Fort Collins, Colorado, NTU offers 19 Master's programmes, over 1,400 individual courses and hundreds of professional development programmes. Often these courses are delivered into the workplace, providing company staff with the latest developments in research in engineering, computing and management. NTU purchased the PBS Business Channel in 1999 then was acquired itself by Sylvan Ventures in 2002.

Consortia may range widely in their mandate and functions. Some, such as the SERB's Electronic Campus and the Clyde Virtual University, Scotland, are primarily just a common Web site listing all the online courses or materials available from partner institutions. Others, such as the California Virtual Campus provide system-wide listing of online courses and licensing of software and joint professional development in e-learning for the state's community colleges. The e-University was an organization that funded, co-ordinated and marketed courses from the conventional universities in Britain. Consortia may also develop quality standards for distance learning and act as a lobbying group for funding and support within the system (for example, the Western Interstate Commission for Higher Education).

In an ideal consortium (from a learner's point of view), universities or colleges, together with a separate central or co-ordinating institution or council, offer an integrated programme of studies through distance learning leading to full qualifications (degrees, etc.). Students are able to take courses from any of the participating institutions, with full credit transfer between institutions. As well as course integration and collaboration, institutions may also share common production and/or distribution facilities, including electronic highways.

International consortia

Distance learning is not limited by geographical boundaries. Very small states find it difficult to offer a full range of educational opportunities within national boundaries. Open and distance learning allow small or isolated states to share teaching and facilities, and to use technology to communicate across large distances. Two examples of where a number of different countries have co-operated in this way are the University of the West Indies and the University of the South Pacific.

For-profit consortia

There are several international consortia of universities offering programmes by distance, where commercial partners play a leading role. *NextEd* (www.nexted.com) is a private company that provides services to approximately 13 universities and colleges from Australia, New Zealand, the United Kingdom, and the United States. Several of these universities are members of the Global University Alliance. NextEd enables students in countries such as China and Malaysia to take programmes from the partner universities. NextEd provides the local administrative and technological support structures needed to ensure success in marketing distance education programs in a foreign country. In 2000 over 2,600 students from 21 countries were enrolled in 200 courses hosted by NextEd.

In the United Kingdom, the *e-University* was essentially constructed as a collaborative organization, with central funding for e-learning programmes contracted from different conventional institutions that would be integrated into coherent programmes. The UK government contributed £62 million (approximately US$100 million) towards its development between 2001 and 2004. The main purpose of the e-University was to market British online programmes internationally, but it was closed early in 2004 due to spiralling costs and lack of income from sales.

Universitas 21 is a network of 17 public research universities from the United Kingdom, Australia, Canada, China, Singapore, Sweden, Germany, New Zealand and the United States. In September 2000, Thomson Learning, a division of Thomson Corporation, and Universitas 21 announced a partnership to found an 'e-university' called *U21global*. The member universities have a somewhat curious role in this partnership, mainly providing $25 million of the total US$90 million of the start-up financing, and supervising quality control of the U21global programmes through a jointly owned spin-off company called U21pedagogica.

Thomson Learning is responsible for new course development and delivery, since initial programming and staff for U21global come from Thomson's textbook division, plus contracting of temporary instructors, who do not have to be hired from the U21global participating institutions. Furthermore, for students who take U21global courses, there is no transferability of credits or guaranteed admission to the universities that are members of U21global. Nevertheless, students who graduate from U21global will be issued with a diploma containing the seals of all the member universities. As Ryan and Steadman (2002) state (p.25):

> ... the issues raised by the U21global venture are potentially of serious concern to publicly-supported higher education systems. It is unclear how U21pedagogica, the accrediting body of the U21 universities, can call on sufficiently wide expertise to validate proposed programmes without the deep expertise that a comprehensive university uses in its usual accrediting procedures, which proceed from departmental level, where the expertise resides, through the various academic bodies of the university.

Put another way, how can a publicly accredited and funded research university allow its seal to be used for a degree program that may have had no input from its own professors?

Cardean University is a for-profit private university owned by UNext Inc., who invested $120 million in the project (Ryan and Steadman, 2002). Cardean University is accredited by the Accrediting Commission of the Distance Education and Training Council and authorized to grant degrees by the Illinois Board of Higher Education. Cardean is in fact an academic consortium of five elite institutions: Carnegie Mellon, the University of Chicago, Columbia

Business School, London School of Economics and Stanford University. According to the Cardean Web site, educators from these universities collaborate with Cardean course designers and technology experts to offer online courses leading to a Cardean M.B.A. However, Ryan and Steadman (2002) claimed that UNext was to provide the teaching staff. In 2002 Cardean offered approximately 150 short business courses that articulate into the M.B.A., but had only just over 200 students enrolled. Cardean has also developed agreements to provide professional business training to General Motors and a number of other major American companies in a partnership with Thomson Learning.

Fathom was an educational consortium set up to market the talent and knowledge of some of the world's leading higher education institutions. Members included the American Film Institute, British Library, British Museum, Cambridge University Press, Columbia University, London School of Economics, Natural History Museum, New York Public Library, RAND Corporation, Science Museum, University of Chicago, University of Michigan, Victoria & Albert Museum, and the Woods Hole Oceanographic Institution. Three main types of content were offered on the Fathom website: features, seminars, and non-credit e-courses. Features and seminars were free, while e-courses charged a fee for enrolment. In other words, this was primarily a non-credit continuing education operation. Despite the stellar names contributing to the consortium, Fathom folded in 2002, but not before the members had invested many millions of dollars in the operation. Columbia University, which took the lead position in the consortium, invested over US$20 million in the project. As Ryan and Steadman (2002, p.13) concluded:

> Fathom's experience would indicate that the strategy of attracting individual consumers to an online liberal education product is not a successful business model, presumably because so much material of a generalist nature is available on the internet, and because an unknown name (Fathom) will struggle to attract sufficient numbers for viability.

WORKPLACE TRAINING AND CORPORATE UNIVERSITIES

Perhaps the most interesting development in recent years has been the increased interest shown by commerce and industry in distance teaching and especially in e-learning.

Private e-learning companies

E-learning companies fall into three main categories:

- Content providers offering online courses or 'just-in-time' modules to corporate clients. Content providers may develop the courses themselves then sell them, or collect together courses from other providers through an e-learning portal and licensing agreements, or may develop or customize specific e-learning programmes for a corporate client.

- Technology providers develop and sell learning platforms and other e-learning technologies such as synchronous learning software, video-conferencing equipment, or course and student management systems.
- Service providers act as consultants and provide 'turn-key' e-learning solutions to corporate clients, that is, needs analysis, design and implementation of e-learning solutions. This may include providing content and technology as part of the package.

Following its merger with Smart Force in 2002, SkillSoft Inc. is one of the largest private e-learning companies in the world, with annual revenues of approximately US$250 million in 2003. With world corporate headquarters in Dublin, Ireland, SkillSoft claims more than 2,800 clients and 4.5 million registered online users, and an inventory of over 300,000 learning objects. To put its size in perspective, its annual revenues are roughly equivalent to the annual provincial government grant to the University of British Columbia, a university with 36,000 full-time students.

Corporate universities

While e-learning companies sell to corporate clients, corporate universities develop or manage their own in-house e-learning programmes. Cunningham *et al.* (2000) provide a good description and analysis of typical corporate universities. Certainly in terms of British usage, most are not universities in the sense of independent, research-oriented institutions, but glorified training operations focused on company business objectives. In the American usage, there is sometimes a 'tongue-in-cheek' humour about such enterprises, such as Macdonald's Bachelor of Hamburgerology. There is nevertheless an underlying seriousness about trying to ensure that organizations maximize what in business jargon is called their human resource capital – their employees – by providing a culture of continuous learning and improvement.

Many corporate universities use classroom-based teaching, but some have moved into distance learning in a big way. The Ford Motor Company invested $100 million in FORDSTAR, a video-based programme for training repair and service staff, now widened to include marketing and new product information for dealers, and Internet-based training. FORDSTAR makes use of spare capacity on Ford's dedicated satellite system. In 2004 it was delivering 270 hours of weekly programming over 15 satellite channels to 400,000 participants. General Motors, Motorola and Arthur Anderson Professional Learning are other corporate universities that have moved some of their training online.

Another interesting development is the Volkswagen AutoUniversity, which plans to combine campus-based education with online learning. With manufacturing plants on several continents, and marketing, sales and distribution worldwide, the AutoUniversity aims to provide postgraduate degree pro-grammes focused initially on sustainable mobility and international business leadership. At its inception, its programmes are directed solely at its own employees. However, the aim is to open its programmes to suppliers and other business associates, then to the general public, as the AutoUniversity eventually aims to receive recognition as a public university from the state government (Land).

In addition to the approximately 2,000 corporate universities operating in 2002, and the 700 or so large e-learning companies, there are thousands of small- to medium-sized companies that specialize in online training for corporate clients. For instance, eLearningBC is an alliance of more than 70 public and private businesses, corporations, consulting firms, and government service providers in British Columbia, offering a variety of e-learning services to corporate clients. (BC has a population of just under four million people.)

Professional associations

Lastly, professional associations are beginning to get into e-learning. For instance, the Chartered General Accountants of Canada provides Internet and CD-ROM based professional development programmes for its 55,000 members, and has partnered with Laurentian University, a public university in Ontario, to deliver a fully online MBA aimed at its members.

VIRTUAL SCHOOLS

Online and distance learning can be found in a growing number of secondary school systems (see Dirr, 2001, for a fuller account). The main reason for virtual high schools is to enable students in small or specialist schools to have access to specialist subject teachers from outside their community. Thus virtual schools tend to operate mainly in rural areas, although recently there have been some projects in North America aimed at students in urban schools as well, providing an alternative mode of study to face-to-face classes.

In 2003 the US Department of Education Star Schools program listed 100 virtual schools, defined as those entities which offer courses designed for k-12 learners and which offer at least some Web-based courses. At the same time, the Ontario Institute of Educational Studies at the University of Toronto listed 24 public providers of distance education programmes for the school sector in Canada.

HOW BIG ARE DISTANCE EDUCATION AND E-LEARNING?

Table 2.1 attempts to summarize the increasing diversification of distance education provision on a global basis.

Table 2.1 Types of distance education institutions

Type of distance institution	Status	Media	Student numbers (estimates)[4]
1. *Public distance education institutions* National open universities, e.g. UKOU, CRTVU, Anadolu, UNED	Public	Print + broadcasting + ICT[1]	4,000,000
Public online universities, e.g. Open University of Catalonia	Public	Fully online	50,000–100,000
Virtual institutes, e.g. Virtual University of Tec de Monterrey, IGNOU, NIIT, VUP	Private	Satellite TV and fully online	100,000–150,000
2. *Dual-mode institutions*[2] e.g. UBC, Deakin, USQ, Charles Sturt, U of Wisconsin	Public	Print + correspondence + ICT	650,000
Extension, U of Maryland UC, Penn		fully online	250,000
State, U of Derby, U of Saskatchewan		satellite TV; video-conferencing	100,000
3. *For-profit distance education institutions* Private universities, e.g. UoPOnline, Capella, JIU	Private	Fully online	50,000–100,000
University for-profits, e.g. e-Cornell	Private	Fully online	5,000
4. *Partnerships and consortia*[5] University and college joint degrees, e.g. UBC/Tec de Monterrey	Public + private	Fully online	1,000
Public–private partnerships, e.g. eCollege	Public + private	Fully online	50,0000

(continued ...)

Table 2.1 Types of distance education institutions (continued)

Type of distance institution	Status	Media	Student numbers (estimates)[4]
State/national consortia, e.g. WGU, KVU, OUBC, SERB, e-university NTU	Public + private	Print + correspondence	20,000
		Fully online	50,000–100,000
		Satellite TV + ICT	20,000
International consortia, e.g. UWI, USP	Public	Satellite TV, audio-conferencing	10,000
For profit consortia, e.g. NextED, Universitas 21, Cardean, Fathom	Public + private	Fully online	3,000
5. *Workplace training*[3] e.g. FORDSTAR	Private	Satellite TV	500,000
e.g. IBM, HP		Video-conferencing	250,000
e.g. GM, SkillSoft, KnowledgeNet		Fully online	2,500,000– 5,000,000
6. *Virtual schools*	Public (mainly)	Fully online	150,000
	Totals[4]		
	Distance learners		9 million
	Public distance		5 million
	Private distance		4 million
	Print + broadcasting		5 million
	Fully online		4 million
	Public fully online		0.6 million
	Private fully online		3.4 million
	E-learners on campus[6]		3–4 million

Note: superscript numbers relate to main text.

Methodology

It should be stated that Table 2.1 is not based on a proper survey of all distance education institutions worldwide (such a study by the International Council for Distance Education, OECD, UNESCO or similar body would be extremely timely). Particularly with regard to student numbers, the numbers in Table 2.1 are no more than intelligent guesses. The main aim with student numbers is not to give precise data, but to provide ballpark figures so that the magnitude of differences between the various sectors of distance education can be assessed, and some of the hype and criticism that has been generated around e-learning can be more realistically evaluated.

The data are drawn from multiple sources, but in particular Daniel (1998), Cunningham *et al.* (2000), Dirr (2001), Ryan and Steadman (2002), Li Chen *et al.* (2003) and many articles from the *Chronicle of Higher Education*. I have used Peterson's *Guide to Distance Learning Programs 2003* to identify distance teaching organizations and the size of their operations in the United States, and the CREAD directory for programmes in Latin America. I also used the International Centre for Distance Learning database at the British Open University.

I have used other directories from distance education organizations such as the Canadian Association of Distance Education, the Open and Distance Learning Association of Australia, and the Brazilian Association of Distance Education. And above all I have used Google and the Web to go to institutional and corporate web sites to ensure data for 2003–4 were accurate. I hope that Table 2.1 and the subsequent analysis will provoke further studies to ensure more precise figures. The numbers in the following list relate to Table 2.1.

1 Many autonomous distance education institutions have what the UK Open University calls Internet-enhanced courses, but most are primarily print and broadcast based.

2 The public dual-mode category is difficult to analyse in terms of student numbers and mode of delivery. It is by far the most numerous in terms of institutions (I counted just over 1,000 institutions with at least some distance programmes as well as campus-based operations), and the great majority of these are in transition from print-based to online teaching. Because of the backlog of print-based inventory, it appears that at least two-thirds of courses being offered are still primarily print-based. However, this figure is changing rapidly, at roughly 15 per cent a year being moved to fully online delivery. In addition there are some institutions that have no print-based inventory going straight to online distance delivery. NOT included in this category are blended or mixed-mode courses, that is, courses requiring regular campus attendance. An estimate for this sector is given at the end of the 'total' section in Table 2.1.

3 The number of students in workplace and distant corporate training is the most difficult figure to estimate. Meister (1998) stated that there

were approximately 200 genuine corporate universities, in the sense of offering in-house training. Some of these have several hundred thousand employees taking programmes. However, many corporate university programmes are primarily classroom-based. In addition, there are thousands of small training companies who offer online programmes. For corporate training, a module may be as short as two minutes, so counting 'learner sessions' can be very misleading. The figure of four million is an estimate of the number of individuals who would have used e-learning as part of their employment in one year, and this is probably a bad under-estimate (OneTouch Solutions – http://www.onetouch.com/aboutus.html – alone claims 3.4 million clients a year). Much more focused and detailed research is needed on this sector.

4   I have used student numbers, in the sense of individuals taking at least one distance education course or module in 2003. However, many institutions report only course enrolments. Students though can take several courses or modules in one year. For university distance programmes, in general I have assumed an average of one and a half semester courses per student per year when student numbers were not given. This is based on average figures for many dual-mode institutions.

5   I have tried to avoid double-counting. Many of the categories overlap in student numbers. For instance, most students counted in consortia will also be counted by the institution in which they are registered (approximately 20 per cent of UBC's 5,500 registrations are from consortium institutions). At the same time, there were students in consortia who are registered with organizations such as the Western Governors University and the Open Learning Agency, and not with other institutions.

6   In terms of e-learning on campus, estimating accurately is again difficult. However, figures from the major learning resource management system (LRMS) companies give some guidance. The two major LRMS companies for higher education are WebCT and Blackboard Inc. WebCT and Blackboard cover about 80 per cent of the market, with the rest made up of a number of different proprietary LRMS. WebCT had approximately 2.5 million student licences and Blackboard about 1.5 million. WebCT estimates that approximately 80 per cent of the applications of WebCT are to support on-campus courses. If we make the same assumption for other LRMS providers, we get an estimate of approximately four million on-campus e-learners in higher education.

This is a snapshot taken in 2003. I have tried to be conservative in estimating numbers, and will have missed many small distance education operations, so the actual numbers are probably higher. What I am concerned with though are the trends, and the relative size of the different categories of distance education providers. This is discussed in more detail below

Patterns

Overall size of distance education

I have estimated the number of distance learners, that is individuals who experienced some form of distance learning during 2002–3, to be around nine million. Education fully at a distance seems to account for about 5 per cent of a nation's higher education provision in most economically advanced countries. In some fast developing countries, it is much higher (15 per cent in China, according to Li Chen *et al.*, 2003)

Diversity and volatility

The most striking result from the analysis is the diversity and volatility of distance education in 2002–3. In 1995 there were really just three main categories of distance education: public national autonomous distance teaching universities, public dual-mode institutions, and workplace training. We have seen though since then the emergence of fully online universities in both the public and private sectors, university for-profit spin-off companies, public and private partnerships, national and international consortia, extensive penetration of e-learning into the corporate training market, and the development of virtual schools. In addition, there has been a large penetration of e-learning into traditional campus-based teaching.

Failed commercial operations

Although some of these new initiatives have been clearly successful in terms of sustainability and market penetration, others have been nothing short of a disaster. In particular, some very prestigious universities got it badly wrong in their attempts to cash in on the e-learning bonanza. The UK e-University lost £62 million, equivalent to $1 billion dollars. Columbia University, New York University, Temple University, the University of Chicago, the University of Melbourne, the e-University and the UKOU each lost between US$10 million and US20 million in trying to set up for-profit e-learning organizations. While $10 million is relatively small beer for institutions such as the University of Chicago (which has endowment funds of over $3 billion), $10 million would have paid for ten years of distance education programming at UBC.

More fundamentally, most of the institutions that lost money did not really understand the business of e-learning and the underlying cost structures of quality distance education. Nearly all the institutions that lost money were new to distance education. The main misunderstanding was to believe that e-learning was primarily about commodifying content. Although content is important, it constitutes probably less than 50 per cent of the operational costs of a successful high quality online distance education operation. In particular, we shall see that in the education sector interaction between students and teachers is essential. The costs of learner support seem to have been underestimated in many of the business plans.

Furthermore, the business models of the prestigious universities were developed on the basis of keeping their main operation, and in particular their tenured research faculty, isolated from distance education, what one might call the quarantining of distance education. It is hard to feel sympathy for public and not-for-profit universities that looked for a quick profit while holding their noses about the business they were investing in. Compare this with the University of Phoenix Online, which has been in distance education for over ten years, and which has focused on a particular niche market, providing consistent and high quality learner support, even if its content is sneered at by the same prestigious universities. Nor have commercial companies, and publishers in particular, fared much better. Publishers such as Harcourt and Thomson have either lost money or are still waiting to see a return on their investments in the university e-learning sector.

The limited achievements of consortia

In particular, consortia such as Universitas 21global, Cardean and Fathom seem too cumbersome to work. The numbers enrolled in 2002–3 in such consortia (under 5,000 in total) are very disappointing, given the hoopla and level of investment. Even the public sector consortia are struggling. At a maximum, they account for no more than 150,000 students in 2002–3, most of whom are registered with dual-mode institutions. WGU has fewer than 3,000 enrolments. Most consortia provide weak forms of collaboration and little added value for learners other than a common web site that lists courses. One trend that may emerge then is smaller, simpler university-to-university partnerships, such as the one between UBC and Tec de Monterrey, where just two partners work together to provide a joint international degree.

All successful collaborative programmes depend on more or less automatic credit transfer, whereby students can combine courses from different institutions towards one common degree. A flexible administrative system that allows students to access and be tracked across different courses in different institutions is another requirement. Lastly, there also needs to be an accredited body that can award degrees when students accumulate credits from different institutions, and that can ensure coherent programmes built from multiple providers.

Is distance education dead?

In terms of technology, the common assumption among many post-secondary administrators and e-learning pundits that distance education is dead is clearly mistaken. Distance education is certainly changing, with many more players, different forms of organization, improved pedagogy through the use of more interactive technologies, and increasing commercialization. Nevertheless, although e-learning plays an increasingly important role, distance education remains a distinct activity.

In 2002–3, there were still more distance students in print and broadcast-based distance education programmes than in fully online programmes (five million to four million). In the public sector, print and broadcast-based distance education still accounted for almost ten times more distance students than fully online programmes (five million to 600,000). The very large national open universities are likely to continue to operate mainly as print and broadcast-based operations. Although the number of print-based courses in dual-mode institutions is decreasing, they are being replaced relatively slowly. Furthermore, for some of the larger enrolment courses in dual-mode institutions, print-based distance education may remain, because of the costs of replacing them with online learning.

Another reason why distance education remains distinct from e-learning is that the learner support requirements of students who are fully distant are quite different from those students using e-learning as part of their campus education. Distance learners are more likely to be older, working, and have families than on-campus e-learners. Thus while there is convergence between distance learning and e-learning in terms of pedagogy, and to some extent administrative systems as they go web-based for on-campus students, marketing, advising, credit transfer, prior learning assessment, learner support, and credentialling requirements remain distinct for most distance learners.

Trends

Trends are more important than the actual figures. The overall trend is towards more online courses and fewer print-based courses in distance education. Private suppliers of online learning are increasing. Distance education continues to grow in the public sector, but more slowly than has e-learning in general. There has been rapid growth in the use of e-learning for company training and to support classroom teaching on university and college campuses.

It is interesting however that unlike the 1970s and 1980s when governments created large national autonomous open universities, governments have generally been reluctant to create new post-secondary institutions that are fully online (the Open University of Catalonia is an exception). Instead, governments have tended to encourage consortia of existing conventional universities and colleges moving into online learning for the first time. We have seen though that conventional institutions and consortia have not in general been successful in widening access, increasing quality, or becoming financially sustainable through the use of online learning. There certainly seems to be an opportunity for political parties to make their mark by creating new virtual institutions designed from the beginning to exploit fully the potential of the Internet, possibly through a public–private partnership.

The private sector now accounts for almost half of all distance learning globally, mainly through company training. In terms of formal post-secondary education, though, the private sector impact is still quite small, though growing. For instance, private universities such as the University of Phoenix Online, NIIT in India, and Tec de Monterrey in total probably account for no more than 100,000 distance education university or college students in 2002–3, compared with five million in the public sector. The large numbers still come from the national autonomous open universities, which account for approximately four million students.

However, private sector university and college distance education will probably continue to grow rapidly, especially in Mexico, Brazil, Chile, China, Malaysia, Korea, India and other newly emerging economic powerhouses, where influential and impatient middle classes are increasing faster than the provision of good quality public sector education. Much of this private sector expansion of distance education in these countries will be online.

In poorer countries, and for the poor in rapidly developing countries, the large public sector print- and broadcast-based autonomous open universities will continue to be important. However, the rapid development of parallel online private sector distance education institutions will force a much-needed review of the quality of learner support in the public open universities in these countries.

CONCLUSIONS

Distance education has continued to grow and evolve over the last eight years. Although print and broadcasting remain important for many distance education operations, the Web in particular has transformed not only the pedagogy of distance education, but also its organizational structures. There have been major interventions from the corporate and private sector to exploit the commercial potential of online distance education, with mixed results. Although new forms of technology-based learning are developing and there is some convergence in teaching methods between conventional and distance teaching institutions, distance education remains a distinct and dynamic part of the education and training system.

In recent years, the development of e-learning has resulted in less emphasis on openness and access, and more emphasis on commercialization, profit or at least cost-recovery in post-secondary education. Nevertheless, distance education still has a critical role in serving those who have difficulties for personal, social or economic reasons in accessing conventional campus-based education. Especially for the poor and disadvantaged, for lifelong learners, for those having to work to pay their way through university, and for those already in the workforce, distance education, whether based on e-learning or on the older technologies of print and broadcasting, remains a powerful tool for economic development and personal advancement.

3 Selecting and using technologies in distance education

Chapter 2 demonstrated the variety of ways in which distance education and e-learning are evolving. Although e-learning is becoming increasingly important within both distance education and campus-based teaching, it is not the only technology available. Even within e-learning, decisions need to be made about the use of specific media, such as text, audio and video. Decision makers have to decide under what circumstances e-learning will be appropriate and whether the older technologies of print or broadcasting, or newer technologies such as Web-casting and mobile wireless, might have advantages for distance or open learning.

Also, history suggests that new technologies do not necessarily replace older technologies. Despite the Internet, other media such as newspapers, radio and television are still active and thriving. To survive, the older media have had to change and hence they have become more focused and specialized. In fact, the range of technologies available to educators is increasing all the time. In such a context, we need some kind of framework to enable decision making about the choice and use of technology for teaching.

THE TECHNOLOGICAL EXPLOSION

For over 3,000 years, from Moses and Socrates onwards, the teacher, in direct, personal contact with the learner, has been the main means of communicating knowledge. Indeed, this remained the primary form of educational communication until the fourteenth century, when the invention of the printing press allowed for the first time the large-scale dissemination of knowledge through books. Printed books, however, did not replace the teacher. A consequence of the improved availability of printed matter was that many more of those engaged in government, commerce, medicine, law and agriculture had to be literate to cope with the explosion of ideas and knowledge that followed.

So teachers retained their importance in the educational process, since they were required to help large numbers of children develop the skills of reading and writing, to such a scale that it became necessary to found schools and colleges to allow greater numbers to be educated in an economical manner. Thus not only did the invention of books require more teachers, it also led to a radical reorganization of teaching and an opening of access to education.

The Industrial Revolution by and large reinforced these developments, without really changing the basic organization of education. To meet the needs of growing industrial and imperial nations, school and university education expanded rapidly and the curriculum was broadened, but the Industrial Revolution curiously made little impact on the technology of education. The introduction of the postal service did stimulate the start of correspondence education, and the telephone was later to be used to some extent for distance education, but on balance the technology of teaching remained almost the same from the fifteenth century well into the twentieth.

Then came radio. In a remarkably prescient publication in the *Radio Times* of 13 June 1924, the newly appointed first Director of Education at the BBC, J.C. Stobart, speculated about the possibility of a 'broadcasting university'. The first adult education talk, broadcast on October 6th, 1924 by the BBC, was actually about fleas. It was entitled 'Insects in Relation to Man' (Robinson, 1982). The first schools radio programme was broadcast by the BBC in 1926. By 1981, the BBC was broadcasting over 450 radio programmes a year in the continuing education area.

From the 1930s onwards, 16 mm. film became used extensively in schools, to become eventually replaced to a large extent by the development of educational television, which was introduced towards the end of the 1950s. In Britain, the British television organizations were broadcasting well over a thousand schools and a thousand adult education television programmes a year in 1981 (Bates, 1984). Until the late 1970s, then, the rate of change, while accelerating, had nevertheless been reasonably sedate, as can be seen from Table 3.1.

Table 3.2 though shows the rapid expansion of new technologies introduced into education since 1980.

Beneath this pile of rapidly changing technology are the poor teachers, administrators and learners. It is not surprising that there is often confusion,

Table 3.1 The development of new technologies in teaching up to 1980

Development	Years in operation
Teachers	3,000
Printed book	500
Postal service	150
Telephone	90
Radio	60
Film	50
Television	20

Table 3.2 The development of new technologies in teaching since 1980

Audio cassettes	Video cassettes
Audio-conferencing	Computer-based learning
Audio-graphics systems	Cable TV
Viewdata/Teletext/Teledon/Minitel	Satellite TV
Laser video-discs	Video-conferencing
Computer conferencing	Compact discs
Internet	Electronic mail
World Wide Web	LCD projectors
Digital video discs	Search engines (e.g. Google)
Fibre Optics	Mobile phones
Learning objects	Wireless networks
Portals	e-Portfolios
Simulations	Expert systems
Virtual reality	

Note: in approximate order of invention, reading left to right

fear and hostility with regard to the use of technology in education and training. We need then some form of analytical framework to enable skilled decision making about the appropriate use of media and technology in distance education and in e-learning.

THE STRUCTURAL CHARACTERISTICS OF MEDIA AND TECHNOLOGIES

I will begin the analysis by examining the physical or structural characteristics of media and technologies.

Media and technology

First, it is useful to make a distinction between *media* and *technology*. The term *media* is used in this book to describe generic forms of communication associated with particular ways of representing knowledge. Text, audio, face-to-face communication and video are all media. Each medium not only has its own unique way of representing knowledge, but also of organizing it, often reflected in particular preferred formats or styles of presentation.

A single medium such as video may be carried by several different delivery *technologies* (satellite, cable, video-cassette and so on), and incorporate a unique blend of *symbol systems* (voice, moving pictures, graphics, captions) and *formats* (news, documentaries, drama and so on).

In education, the five most important media are:

- Direct human contact (face-to-face).
- Text (including still graphics).
- Audio.
- Video.
- Digital multi-media (incorporating text, audio and video).

While certain technologies are closely associated with each medium, a variety of different technologies may be used to *deliver* these media, as Table 3.3 indicates.

Broadcast (one-way) and communications (two-way) technologies

A major structural distinction lies between technologies that are primarily *one-way* or 'broadcast', and those that are primarily *two-way,* or 'communicative'. Television and print, for example, are broadcast or one-way technologies, as the end user cannot change the 'message'. One advantage of broadcast technologies is that they ensure a common standard of learning materials for all students. This is particularly important in countries where teachers are poorly qualified or of variable quality. One disadvantage is that additional resources are needed to provide interaction with teachers or other learners.

The telephone and video-conferencing are examples of two-way technologies, in that users at both ends can communicate with each other. The significance of two-way technologies is that they allow for interaction between learners and teachers, and perhaps even more significantly, between a learner and other learners.

Synchronous and asynchronous technology

Another distinction is between synchronous and asynchronous technologies. *Synchronous* technologies operate in real time. Synchronous teaching has the benefit of spontaneity and immediacy, provided that it is offered at times and places that are convenient for students. Video-conferencing is a good example of a synchronous technology. Although the learner may be distant from the teacher, both teacher and learner must be present at the same time in video-conferencing. Similarly, broadcasting is a synchronous technology, in that learners have to present at the time of broadcast.

However, video cassettes are an *asynchronous* technology, because they can be accessed at any time. A synchronous broadcast television programme can be shifted to an asynchronous form by recording it onto a video cassette. An online, text-based discussion forum is also an asynchronous technology. Learners can log on at times of their own choosing to access the contributions

Table 3.3 The relationship between media, technology and educational applications of technology

Media	Technologies	Educational applications
face-to-face	classrooms, labs	lectures, seminars, experiments
text (including graphics)	print	course units, supplementary materials, correspondence tutoring
audio	cassettes, radio, telephone	radio programmes, telephone tutoring, audio-conferences
video	broadcasting, video-cassettes, video-discs; cable, satellite, fibre-optics, microwave; video-conferencing	television programmes, video-conferences
digital multi-media	computers, World Wide Web, telephone, cable, satellite, fibre-optics, CD-ROM, DVD, wireless	PowerPoint, computer-aided learning (CAI, CBT), e-mail, discussion forums, learning objects/databases, Webcasts, WebQuests, online courses, Web conferencing

to the discussions. The significance of asynchronous technologies is that they allow more control and flexibility for the learner.

For instance, research at the UK Open University (Bates, 1981; Grundin, 1981) found that students much preferred to study from audio cassettes than from radio broadcasts (although in these studies the content was identical). The extra control gives learners more time to study the materials, as they can stop, go back, and go over materials as many times as they wish. The same control characteristics apply equally to books, video cassettes, compact discs, and Web sites.

A classification of educational technologies by structural characteristics

Table 3.4 summarizes different media and technologies by their structural characteristics.

Table 3.4 indicates that the World Wide Web is the only technology that combines text, audio and video, and all four structural characteristics of technology: broadcast and two-way communication; and synchronous and asynchronous communication. Thus a major reason why the Web has such potential is that its media and structural characteristics provide more options for teaching and learning.

Table 3.4 A classification of educational technologies by structural characteristics

Media	Broadcast (one-way) applications		Communication (two-way) applications	
	Synchronous	*Asynchronous*	*Synchronous*	*Asynchronous*
Face-to-face	lectures	lecture notes	seminars, tutorials, lab. classes	
Text		books, course units, supplementary materials		mail, fax, correspondence tutoring
Audio	radio	audio-cassettes	telephone-tutoring, audio-conferencing	
Video	broadcast TV cable TV satellite TV	video-cassettes	video-conferencing	
Digital	Web-casting, PowerPoint	web sites, CAL, web streaming, learning objects, multimedia, DVDs, CD-ROM, pdf files, databases	Web-conferencing chat MUDs	e-mail, online discussion forums

The distinctions between media and technologies will become less meaningful as they become integrated into a single technology or transmission system. Nevertheless, there are still significant physical and educational differences between media. One major difference lies in the bandwidth required (uncompressed video requires 1,000 times the bandwidth capacity of an audio telephone call). More importantly, we shall see later that there are different educational applications associated not just with different media, but also with different technologies within a single medium. The educational importance of these structural characteristics will be explored in more detail in later chapters.

RATIONALE FOR A NEW FRAMEWORK FOR DECISION MAKING

Without generally agreed educational criteria for media and technology selection in education and training, technology decisions have tended to be made primarily for commercial, administrative or political reasons. Typical factors that have influenced decision making about educational technologies are as follows:

- The availability of spare broadcasting capacity (an important factor initially influencing the BBC's partnership with the UK Open University – see Perry, 1976);.
- An offer from technology suppliers of free or cheap equipment or services (for instance, IBM Thinkpads for campus-wide computing).
- The comfort level of academics with technologies that replicate traditional teaching formats (for instance, video-conferencing).
- The enthusiasm of a key decision maker for a particular technology (for instance, a college president influenced by a presentation at a conference).

When such factors influence the adoption of a new technology, the technology is more likely to be added to existing teaching methods, rather than replacing more costly or less effective teaching approaches.

Consequently, without strong educational criteria, three decision-making scenarios are common. The first is basically to do nothing. The reasons for using technology are not clear, or there is a well-judged recognition of ignorance, or there are too many choices. Doing nothing is safer. The second is 'sympathetic anarchy': an organization leaves it to individual, enthusiastic teachers or trainers to use whatever technologies they can lay their hands on. Again, though, if there is not institution-wide support behind a particular technology based on educational criteria, the technology eventually ends up in cupboards (or in cyber-cupboards: un-maintained Web sites), as individual enthusiasts run out of either money or support within the system, or move on to other jobs.

The third is 'monomedia mania': a government, company or institution decides to invest heavily in a single technology for all teaching or training throughout its system. This can lead to leap-frogging between competitive institutions, as new technologies develop. Thus one bank may decide to use a Web site for staff training in every branch. A little later, another bank, with similar training requirements, will install desktop video-conferencing in every branch. Not to be outdone, a third bank comes along and develops a system based on 'just-in-time' use of learning objects. 'Monomedia mania' is usually driven by the decision to go for the latest or most sophisticated technology available at the time of the decision. No comparative analysis though is done on the appropriateness of older or more established technologies.

Strategic and tactical decision making

Another limitation has been the confusion between strategic and tactical decision making. There are two quite different levels of decision making involved in selecting and using media and technologies in e-learning and distance education.

The first is the decision to set up a *system* of teaching based on technological delivery. This might be to create a new open or distance teaching institution, or to use technology to extend the reach of an existing campus-based institution. The decision to use the Internet as a main teaching technology, for instance, will require capital investment, and recurrent expenditure in the form of regular, specialist staff. Once servers and desktop computers are purchased, networks installed, and professional and technical staff hired, the monster must be fed, in other words, the facilities need to be used. Establishing a general facility for technological delivery is a *strategic* decision. Once major investment has been made in a particular technology or set of technologies, it is difficult to move quickly into other technologies.

Sometimes strategic decisions are made on the basis of what technology has already been developed for other than teaching purposes. Thus a company may have invested in information technology for business and internal communications reasons, but may then wish to widen the technology application to education and training. One common instance of this has been the development of in-house administrative software, onto which later educational applications are then grafted. There are however often difficulties with such a strategy, as teachers find the in-house software more limiting than course authoring software from commercial providers.

The second level of decision making is concerned with the most appropriate use of the media and technologies already available to an organization. What is the best mix of available media and technology for a particular course? What is the best way to combine text, audio and video for a particular teaching context? Do all courses need the same amount of multimedia or Web-conferencing, or would it be better to concentrate multimedia on some courses rather than others; if so, which? These are *tactical* decisions.

Ideally, strategic decisions should be driven by the teaching needs of the institution, that is, by the kinds of decision taken at the tactical level. It is though an iterative process: if a heavy investment is made in video-conferencing facilities (a strategic decision), a different kind of course is likely to result than if investment has been made in another technology, such as the Web. Thus strategic decision making may result in different learning objectives being achieved, thus influencing tactical decisions.

The continuing reduction in the costs of technologies, and their increasing accessibility, is making it easier for individual teachers to enter directly at the tactical level, by picking and choosing different software 'off-the-shelf' for particular purposes, without waiting for strategic investment by the institution. In other words, the price of entry for teachers is low, particularly for Internet applications, when the institution is already investing in it for other reasons. Thus technology investment for administrative purposes is also resulting in many institutions moving into e-learning and even distance education for the first time. Without a strategic approach, however, short-term tactical decisions can lead to duplication and waste, as different parts of the organization start to build a patchwork quilt of different software and educational applications.

Furthermore, the ubiquity of the Internet and the Web has led many policy-makers and teachers to assume that this technology is automatically better for teaching and learning than previous technologies. We have seen that the Web in particular can combine four of the five media (text, audio, video, digital multimedia) within a single technology, and can also combine both one-way and two-way communication, and synchronous and asynchronous communication. The Web therefore does have very powerful characteristics that lend itself to a wide variety of ways of teaching and learning.

However, it also has some disadvantages, such as lack of access for certain groups of learners, high cost in some contexts, and a possibility of dehumanizing the learning context. Thus there are circumstances where other media (such as face-to-face teaching) may be more appropriate. A good theoretical model will allow such discriminations to be made on a logical and empirical basis. These are all reasons why a more systematic approach to media and technology selection is needed in education.

An alternative framework

Thus a model for technology selection and application is needed which has the following characteristics:

- It will work in a wide variety of contexts.
- It allows decisions to be taken at both a strategic or institution-wide level and at a tactical or instructional level.
- It will identify critical differences between media and technologies, thus enabling an appropriate mix of media and technologies to be chosen for any given context.
- It gives equal attention to instructional and operational issues.
- It will accommodate new developments in technology.

The factors I believe to be important for selecting and using technology in open learning and distance education can be stated as a set of questions (roughly in order of importance) that each institution needs to answer:

A   Access: how accessible is a particular technology for the targeted learners?
C   Costs: what is the cost structure of each technology? What is the unit cost per learner?
T   Teaching and learning: what kinds of learning are needed? What instructional approaches will best meet these needs? What are the best technologies for supporting this teaching and learning?
I   Interactivity and user-friendliness: what kind of interaction does this technology enable? How easy is it to use?

O   Organizational issues: What are the organizational requirements, and the barriers to be removed, before this technology can be used successfully? What changes in organization need to be made?
N   Novelty: how new is this technology?
S   Speed: how quickly can courses be mounted with this technology? How quickly can materials be changed?

The **A C T I O N S** framework then asks questions around a specific set of factors, irrespective of the type of institution or teaching programme. The answers to these questions enable appropriate decisions to be made regarding the choice and application of different technologies. In other words, these *questions* need to be asked in any context; the *answers* though will depend on the context.

ACCESS

No matter what the quality of teaching with technology, learning will not occur if learners cannot access the technology. The first question to ask then is, 'Who are students that we want to reach?' The answers to such a question will depend on the mandate of the institution, and the type of programme to be delivered. Thus a selective research university aiming for the best undergraduates to feed its graduate research programmes will answer very differently from an open university committed to widening access. For a highly selective research university it may be acceptable to mandate that all students must have a laptop computer. However, an open university needs to accommodate learners denied access to conventional institutions, equity groups, the unemployed, the working poor, and workers needing up-grading or more advanced education and training. Thus an open institution needs to use technologies that are already easily available to all its potential students.

The second question to be asked is, 'What is the most appropriate location for study for the intended learners?' There are several possible answers, depending on the characteristics of the target group:

- On campus.
- At home.
- In a local centre dedicated to open learning.
- At a local public education institution, with shared facilities for campus-based and distance students.
- At work – which could be either at an individual workstation or in a company learning center.
- At a commercial centre, such as an Internet café.

If students have to come to *campus* anyway, it may be possible to provide computer labs and Internet access for students on campus. However, there are likely to be high costs for the institution to do this. If an institution's policy is open access to anyone who wants to take its courses, the availability of equipment already in the *home* (usually purchased for entertainment purposes) becomes of paramount importance.

Sometimes it may be possible for a distance education institution to provide equipment or facilities at relatively low cost to students in their homes. For instance, a *home experiment kit*, such as chemical apparatus, may be supplied to a student. The kit is returned after completing the course, then reissued to other students on the following year's course, thus spreading the initial capital cost over several years. However, again this is likely to be an expensive decision for an institution, as there are high costs of design and high administrative costs in tracking materials, in checking and maintaining equipment when it is returned and in establishing penalties for not returning or looking after equipment.

Open access, home-based learning will be limited in many countries to relatively few technologies. Also, studying at home is not always convenient, especially if living conditions are crowded or if there is only one television set or computer for the whole family.

An alternative is to make technology available through *local study centres*. These can be of two kinds: those established specifically and mainly for the use of open and distance learners; and those which may be located in existing colleges or schools, where facilities or at least rooms are shared between distance and open learners and campus-based students. The disadvantage of study centres is that students have to travel to the study centre, thus losing the flexibility of being able to study anywhere at any time, although for some learners study centres may be a better learning environment than watching television programmes at home.

The *workplace* is becoming an increasingly important location for distance learning, and especially for e-learning. Often employers have technology that is not available in the home. For instance, if all personnel in a company have a computer and access to the company's intranet, it may be possible to use it also for training purposes. However, there are difficulties in using workstations for study purposes. Employers may not want study interfering with day-to-day operational requirements, especially if it is not immediately work-task focused. Employees may be just too busy to find time during work hours to study. As a result, some employers have established local site-based training centres, which may be no more than a room with equipment dedicated for training purposes, where employees can 'drop in' for training.

The rapid growth of Internet or cyber-cafés has enabled relatively low cost access to the Internet in many countries throughout the world. However, because of the noise, presence of rowdy teenagers, and lack of space, these may not be ideal locations for studying. (For a good discussion of learning centres, see Naidoo, 2001).

Access to and availability of equipment is likely to be the most powerful discriminator for assessing the appropriateness of a particular technology for distance learners. Home access to technology will often be the most convenient for distance learners and the most economical delivery location for institutions.

COSTS

A cynic once defined an accountant as someone who knows the cost of everything and the value of nothing. Like most jokes, there is a serious point in it. It is very dangerous just to look at costs without also examining benefits. Nevertheless, a proper understanding and analysis of costs is essential for making sensible decisions about the use of technology in education.

The main questions to be asked regarding costs of e-learning or distance education technologies are as follows:

- What are the main costs in developing and delivering programmes? What counts as a cost?
- What are the main drivers of costs? In other words, what causes costs to increase or decrease?
- How do cost structures vary between different media and technologies (including face-to-face teaching)?
- What needs to be included in a business plan, if costs are to be covered or recovered?
- How do you relate costs to benefits?

It is not always clear what constitutes a cost in teaching. For instance, a professor's salary usually remains the same, irrespective of how much or little time she spends on teaching. If she spends more time on teaching online than face-to-face, is this an extra cost? Why should the university administration worry, especially if she chooses to spend her time that way? It should be seen as an extra cost, because if she were not spending more time teaching online, she could be spending more time doing research, for instance. There is a lost opportunity cost then if teaching online takes her more time. Furthermore, other professors may refuse to teach online, if they see this as causing more work. Thus time spent on designing, developing and delivering teaching with technology is perhaps the most important cost factor.

Similarly, it is important to identify not just actual costs, but the drivers of costs. For instance, we have found that the time professors spend teaching online is directly related to their method of working, and in particular to how a course is designed. E-learning will take more time than face-to-face teaching if a professor works alone or with a graduate student, than if he works in a team of professional instructional designers and Web programmers. Student numbers also drive costs, but not necessarily in a linear way. We shall see that some technologies are more cost sensitive to student numbers than other technologies.

Common questions asked are, 'Are online courses cheaper or more expensive than face-to-face courses?' 'Are broadcast television courses more expensive than online courses?' The answers to such questions depend on the *cost structures* of technologies. For instance, broadcast television courses are likely to be cheaper per student than online courses when student numbers exceed 5,000 per course. This is because broadcast television production (development) costs are high, but their transmission (distribution) costs are relatively low (if a transmission network is already in place). Online learning has moderate development costs, but relatively high delivery costs, so online learning becomes more expensive relative to television as student numbers increase. Thus we need to separate development from distribution costs and take account of the impact of student numbers in order to make cost comparisons between different technologies.

Another critical issue is the affordability of a technology-based programme. To determine the affordability of a programme means calculating the costs of the programme against the likely revenues generated. A typical example is a programme that aims to recover its full costs and perhaps even generate a profit from student tuition fees, scholarships or additional grant money. In order to make such a judgement a business plan is necessary. This means analysing the costs of development, delivery and maintenance of a programme and the likely revenues that such a programme will generate.

Lastly, another economic issue is the likely return on investment in a particular technology for teaching. Such a concern is not related just to costs, but also to benefits. For instance, commercial companies usually invest in technology to provide competitive advantage. Reducing costs may provide competitive advantage, but competitive advantage can also be increased by providing benefits to consumers, even at extra cost. In educational terms, e-learning may cost more, but the resulting benefits may be worth the extra cost. This, however, requires benefits as well as costs to be identified and measured. All these cost factors will be examined in detail as we examine the different technologies for e-learning and distance education.

TEACHING AND LEARNING

There are three critical questions that need to be asked about teaching and learning in order to identify appropriate technologies:

- What kinds of learning need to be developed?
- What instructional strategies will be employed to enable the learning needed?
- What are the unique educational characteristics of each technology, and how well do these match the learning and teaching requirements?

I will briefly discuss the first two questions, to illustrate some of the issues involved in answering them. The third question will be discussed through an analysis of each technology in the following chapters.

Different kinds of learning

Embedded within any decision about the use of technology in education and training will be assumptions about the learning process. These assumptions, although often implicit, are nevertheless likely to be reflected in one or other of the major theories of learning. It is worth saying something briefly about these theories of learning, since the choice and use of technology should be driven by a coherent and conscious view of how people learn.

Behaviourism

The design of teaching machines, and subsequently the major part of computer-based training, have been strongly influenced by the theories of behaviourists such as Skinner (1969). The essential feature of behaviourism is that it denies or ignores the role of conscious strategies or self-will in learning. Learning takes place through the impact of the external environment, which rewards or punishes 'trial-and-error' behaviour. Learners seek rewards or avoid punishment, and in this way learn 'appropriate' behaviour. The teacher's job is to manage the learners' environment to create the most appropriate learning outcomes.

Cognitive theories

Although behaviourism has its value for certain kinds of learning (e.g. rote memory, correcting deviant or psychopathic behaviour, learning certain motor skills), most cognitive psychologists (that is, psychologists who study thinking and learning) believe that simple behaviourism is inadequate for explaining a great deal of human behaviour. Some cognitive psychologists follow the behaviourist tradition of looking for explanations of learning and thinking in terms of physical rules that ignore consciousness or self-will. Although much more sophisticated than simple behaviourism, most research into artificial intelligence follows this tradition. This has led to the development of machine-based intelligent tutoring systems, which use computer programs to embody teaching strategies.

On the other hand, there are many cognitive psychologists who emphasize the importance for learning of conscious intellectual strategies. Bruner (1966) for instance argued that learning is an active process in which a learner infers principles and rules, and consciously tests them. Piaget (Piaget and Inhelder, 1969) argued that before children can comprehend concepts or manipulate symbols such as words, they have to experience directly or physically the actions or events that are represented by abstract concepts or symbols. Piaget is not alone amongst psychologists in pointing out the importance of direct experience and the manipulation of objects for laying the foundations of logical thinking.

For those who believe that learning takes place through making inferences and testing them, it will be important to assess the extent to which a technology enables learners to develop and test their own inferences and to explore for themselves the underlying structure and assumptions of a subject. Also, to what extent does the technology enable feedback and criticism to be provided of learner-generated inferences and hypotheses? There is also the underlying question of the extent to which media and technology can substitute for direct, physical experience. For instance, in Piagetian terms, can media adequately substitute for direct experience in developing abstract concepts? (See Olson and Bruner, 1974, for an excellent discussion of this issue).

Humanistic psychology

Humanistic psychologists, such as Carl Rogers, are at the opposite end of the spectrum from behaviourists. Humanists argue that each person acts in accordance with his or her own conscious perception of the world, and hence each person is unique and free to choose his or her own actions. Rogers (1969) states that 'every individual exists in a continually changing world of experience in which he is the centre'. The external world is interpreted within the context of that private world.

Rogers, then, like Bruner, believes that knowledge is constructed by each individual interpreting and testing the meaning of external events in terms of the relevance to that individual's past experience. For Rogers, though, this is essentially a *social* process; inferences are primarily tested through feedback from and social contact with other people. Rogers then rejects the notion that learning is mainly about the absorption of information. Learning requires interpersonal communication between a learner and a 'facilitator' with whom the learner can personally and genuinely relate.

Constructivism

In recent years, this humanistic approach to learning has developed into a theory of social constructivism, by which learners 'construct' knowledge actively through dialogue and discussion. Certain features of the Internet, such as the ability to communicate over time and place with others, and the interactive nature of the medium, have coincided with the move towards more constructivist approaches to learning. However, we have already seen that many cognitive psychologists also believe that knowledge is constructed internally, by reflection, by testing inferences, and by integrating information about the same or similar contexts from different sources. In brief, 'constructivists' believe that knowledge can be constructed personally, through reflection and relating new knowledge to prior experience, or socially, through interaction and discussion with others, such as teachers, other learners or family and friends. Either way, knowledge becomes personal and embedded within a context that is relevant to the learner's own life and experience.

Taking a position regarding learning theories

The need to make a conscious choice of learning theory is a profoundly practical issue with respect to the selection of technologies for teaching. To what extent for example does a technology facilitate inter-personal communication at a distance? If it does not do this, what alternative strategies are needed, and at what cost? Can machine-based education represent the diversity of and differences between the experiences of individuals, and how those experiences lead to original or new thoughts or insights? If not, what will be the educational consequences of relying heavily on machine-based education? These questions cannot be answered solely in objective or scientific terms; they require value judgements to be made about what kinds of education and training we want.

Content and skills

When preparing for decisions about technology use, it is also useful to make a distinction between *content* and *skills*. Olson and Bruner (1974) argue that learning involves two distinct aspects: firstly acquiring knowledge of facts, principles, ideas, concepts, events, relationships, rules and laws; and secondly using or working on that knowledge to develop skills. *Knowledge* can be considered the appropriate application of skills to a particular content area.

The representation of content

Media differ in the extent to which they can *represent* different kinds of content, because they vary in the symbol systems (text, sound, still pictures, moving images, etc.) that they use to encode information. Different media are capable of combining different symbol systems. Books can represent content through text and still pictures, but not through sound or moving pictures. In this respect, computers in the past have been similar to books, although now they can also incorporate sound and moving pictures (i.e. multimedia). Television and film in the past have been the richest media symbolically. They were the only media which could encompass text, still and moving pictures, natural language, natural movement, music and other sounds, and full colour. Of all the technologies they are still the most able to represent closely 'real' experience in all its facets, although it is only a matter of time before computer-based technology surpasses television and film in this respect.

Differences between media in the way they combine symbol systems influence the way in which different media represent content. Thus there is a difference between a written description, a televised recording, and a computer simulation of the same experiment. Different symbol systems are being used, conveying different kinds of information about the same experiment. For instance, our concept of heat can be derived from touch, mathematical symbols (80° Celsius), words (random movement of particles), animation, or observation of experiments. A large part of learning requires the mental integration of content acquired through different media and symbol systems. Integration of content derived from a variety of sources leads to deeper understanding of a concept or an idea.

Media also differ in their ability to handle *concrete* or *abstract* knowledge. Abstract knowledge is handled primarily through language. While all media can handle language, either in written or spoken form, media vary in their ability to represent concrete knowledge. For instance, television can show concrete examples of abstract concepts, the video showing the concrete 'event', and the sound track analyzing the event in abstract terms. Well-designed media can help learners move from the concrete to the abstract and back again.

Media also differ in the way they *structure* content. Books, the telephone, radio, audio-cassettes and face-to-face teaching all tend to present content linearly or sequentially. While parallel activities can be represented through these media (for example, different chapters dealing with different events occurring simultaneously) these activities still have to be presented sequentially through these media. Computers and television are more able to present or simulate the inter-relationship of multiple variables simultaneously occurring, but only within closely defined limits. Computers can also handle branching or alternative routes through information, but again within closely defined limits.

Subject matter varies enormously in the way in which information needs to be structured. Subject areas (for example, natural sciences, history) structure content in particular ways determined by the internal logic of the subject matter. This structure may be very tight or logical, requiring particular sequences or relationships between different concepts, or very open or loose, requiring learners to deal with highly complex material in an open-ended or intuitive way. Even within a single curriculum area, subject matter may vary in terms of its required structure (for instance, social theories and statistics, within sociology).

If media then vary both in the way they present information symbolically and in the way they handle the structures required within different subject areas, media which best match the required mode of presentation and the dominant structure of the subject matter need to be selected. Consequently, different subject areas will require a different balance of media. This means that subject experts should be deeply involved in decisions about the choice and use of media, at least at a tactical level, to ensure that the chosen media appropriately match the presentational and structural requirements of the subject matter.

The development of skills

Technologies also differ in the extent to which they can help develop different skills. Gagné (1977,1985) drew attention to different levels or kinds of skills, as also did Bloom *et al.* (1956). Skills can range from intellectual to psychomotor to affective (emotions, feelings). I will concentrate here on intellectual skills. Table 3.5 compares content with skills.

Comprehension is likely to be the minimal level of intellectual learning outcome for most education courses. Some researchers (for example, Marton and Säljö, 1976) make a distinction between surface and deep comprehension. At the highest level of skills comes the *application* of what one has comprehended to new situations. Here it becomes necessary to develop skills of analysis, evaluation, and problem solving. In analyzing each technology, I shall attempt to identify the relationship between that technology and the development of certain specific skills.

Why teaching and learning is a weak criterion for media selection

Many might feel that teaching and learning considerations should be the first criterion to be considered. If the technology is not effective educationally, then no matter how cheap, or how convenient it may be for access, it should not be used. However, there are significant difficulties in using teaching and learning as a criterion for media and technology selection.

Motivated teachers will overcome weaknesses in a particular technology, or conversely inexperienced teachers will under-exploit the potential of a technology. Design decisions are critical in influencing the effectiveness of a particular technology. Thus a well-designed lecture will teach better than a poorly designed television programme, and vice versa. Similarly, students will respond differently to different technologies due to preferred learning styles or differences in motivation. Students who work hard can overcome poor use of learning technologies. It is not surprising then that with so many

Table 3.5 Distinction between content and intellectual skills

Content	Intellectual skills
Facts	Comprehension
Ideas	Analysis
Principles	Application
Opinions	Synthesis
Relationships (e.g. A causes B)	Restructuring and modifying
Criteria	Evaluation
Problems	Problem-solving

Source: from Bates, 1981.

variables involved, teaching and learning is a weak discriminator for selecting and using technologies. It is much easier to discriminate between technology on the basis of access or cost, than on the basis of teaching effectiveness.

The complexity of teaching and learning also helps to explain why it has been so difficult to relate specific technologies to learner performance. Research comparing media or technologies for teaching usually results in a finding of no significant difference statistically. This is because there are so many intervening variables that they tend to cancel out each other (in the jargon, variance within conditions is greater than variance between conditions). Unfortunately, the regular research result of 'no significant difference' has led many to conclude that media and technology do not matter as far as instruction or learning is concerned (see, for instance, Clark, 1983; Russell, 1999). However, instead of trying to make crude comparisons between different technologies, the question that needs to be asked is one posed by Wilbur Schramm as early as 1972, 'Under what circumstances and for what instructional purposes is a technology best used?'

In summary, teaching and learning requirements are weaker than access or costs as discriminators for choice of technology. Nevertheless, as research begins to identify what different technologies do best in specific circumstances, teaching and learning will become increasingly important as a discriminator for technology decisions.

INTERACTION AND EASE OF USE: THE LONELINESS OF THE LONG-DISTANCE LEARNER

Most theories of learning suggest that for learning to be effective it needs to be active; in other words the learner must respond in some way to the learning material. It is not enough merely to listen, view or read; learners have to do something with the learning material. Thus they may need to demonstrate (if only to themselves) that they have understood, or they may need to modify their prior knowledge to accommodate new information, or they may need to analyse new information in the light of their existing knowledge.

Feedback is considered an important component of interaction. Feedback provides learners with knowledge of results that indicate whether they have learned correctly. Feedback can take the form of a response from another person indicating how well the learner has learned, or from a computer or software program that analyses the student's activity and provides an appropriate response. As technologies differ considerably in the ways in which they encourage interaction, it is important to match the choice of technology to the kind of interactions required in particular learning contexts.

Particularly in higher education, *academic discourse*, that is, developing student skills of analysis, constructing and defending an argument, assembling evidence in support of an argument, and critiquing the work of scholars and fellow learners, is highly valued. (See Laurillard, 2001, for a discussion of technology and academic discourse.) Many professors consider the skills of academic discourse are best learned through small group discussions, led by an experienced academic (Plato's 'Socratic Method'). Although this kind of small-group, face-to-face interaction is quite rare in post-secondary education today, high quality interaction that supports academic discourse is possible at a distance.

Many arguments about the value of technology in distance education and e-learning, and the extent to which technology can or should replace face-to-face or human interaction, are often based on confusion and misunderstanding about the contexts in which interaction takes place. In effect there are two rather different contexts for interaction. The first is an *individual*, isolated activity, and that is the interaction of a learner *with* the learning material, be it text, television or Web site; the second is a *social* activity, and that is the interaction between two or more people *about* the learning material. *Both* kinds of interaction are important in learning.

Interaction with learning materials

For both conventional and distance education students, by far the largest part of their studying is done alone, interacting with textbooks or other learning media. The difference is that for distance learners, opportunities for interaction have to be consciously designed within the learning materials. The aim is to *simulate* a face-to-face conversation between teacher and student. Holmberg (1983) has argued that:

> the character of good distance teaching resembles that of a guided conversation aiming at learning ... the distance-study course and the non-contiguous communication typical of distance education are seen as the instruments of a conversation-like interaction between the student on the one hand and the tutor counselor ... on the other.

This simulated guided conversation is conducted through the interaction of learner and teaching materials, and is not dependent on (although may be enhanced by) the intervention of a human instructor. The simulated conversation is achieved through the design of the teaching materials (embedded questions and feedback). This is interaction between the learner and the learning materials.

Learning as a social activity

Social interaction may be of three types in e-learning and distance education:

- Interaction between the learner and the originator of the teaching material (often a tenured research professor).

- Interaction between the learner and a tutor (often a contracted instructor) who does not originate the learning materials, but who mediates between the original material and the learner, by providing guidance and/or assessment.
- Interaction between the learner and other learners.

The first kind of interaction with the originator of the material was relatively rare in distance education until the development of the Internet, but it is now becoming more common with Web-based teaching. The second kind of interaction, with a tutor, has in the past been mainly done through correspondence via the mail service, by telephone contact, or by local, optional face-to-face classes. With the growth of online learning, mediation of learning by a tutor is now quite common when student numbers reach the level where the originator of the teaching material cannot cope, and extra tutors or instructors need to be recruited. Interaction with other students is possibly the most important for many learners. The development of online discussion forums now makes student-to-student interaction in small or large groups much easier to organize.

Note that interaction of all three kinds can take place without face-to-face contact; in other words, even interpersonal interaction can be at a distance, via the mail service or through technologies such as the telephone or online discussion forums. In the area of social interaction, then, we need to differentiate between interaction that is remote or face-to-face, and also interaction that is in real time or asynchronous. In other words, social interaction is not necessarily time- or place-dependent, or even dependent on the teacher, if peer groups are used.

The quality of interaction

It is dangerous to assume that a technology like computing is automatically more interactive than one like television, because computers can force a learner response, while television is a 'passive' medium. The quality of the interaction and feedback is critical. Much of the most useful interaction between a learner and the learning material is covert – perhaps best described as thinking. A well-written book or stimulating television programme may well encourage high-level reflection in the learner, without any apparent overt actions. Similarly, learners can easily find ways to 'beat' a computer, not by thoughtfully responding to its questions, but by second-guessing the pattern of predetermined, multiple-choice answers, or by random guessing until the correct answer is found.

Feedback to learners can be very simple, merely providing correct answers to straightforward questions; or it can be much more complex, suggesting a variety of alternative responses and ways to evaluate between them. One way of evaluating a technology's capacity for feedback is to examine the extent to which it provides flexibility for dealing with the learner's response to activities. Does the feedback provide merely 'yes'/'no' information as to whether the learner has responded correctly? If the student answer is not rated correct or adequate, does the feedback provide remedial activities such as further information or reading? Does the feedback engage the learner in some form of discussion or dialogue about the quality of the learner's response? For instance, does the feedback allow the learner to develop or test an argument or a pattern of thinking? How does the feedback handle an original response not anticipated by the designers of the learning materials?

As we progress through these questions, the more easily is such feedback handled by the intervention of a teacher or tutor, or other students, and is less easily provided by machines. Nevertheless, with the development of simulations and of expert systems, computers are able to develop a much richer range of feedback and interactivity for learners than in the old days of computer-based training. Such a use of computers results in cost-effectiveness, reducing (but not entirely replacing) the time a teacher needs to spend with each student, and at the same time enhancing learner performance.

A perceived weakness of the older 'broadcast' technologies, such as print, television and radio, is that they are one-way technologies, good for delivering large quantities of high quality information to large numbers of students, but not good for interaction between student and teacher. 'Simulated guided conversation' is a good substitute, but not as flexible as interaction with a real person. Video-conferencing and audio-conferencing are relatively expensive, and time- and place-dependent. This is why the Internet, with its potential for two-way, asynchronous communication, thereby allowing the student to interact directly and flexibly with the teacher or other students, at a distance and at a time of their choice, is such an important technology.

Despite the in-built advantages of some technologies to facilitate interaction, it is important to separate the quality of the interaction from the technology through which it occurs. Some forms of interaction, such as academic discourse, are hard, but not impossible, to replicate through technologies such as print or broadcasting. Other two-way technologies, such as video-conferencing and online discussion forums have the capability of handling high quality interpersonal interaction, even if done at a distance. However, the mere attendance at a face-to-face seminar, or participation in a computer conference, does not of itself guarantee high quality interaction. Good design and effective moderation are critical. Nevertheless, it is more difficult or at least less common for 'high quality' learning activities and feedback to be handled through some technologies compared with others, and this will be explored further in the following chapters.

Ease of use

In general, technologies that are easy to use will be used more than those that are difficult to use. While this is hardly an earth-shattering revelation, it is often a factor overlooked by enthusiasts for the latest advanced technology.

Virtual reality may be of tremendous educational potential, but if designers find the whole process of creating high quality programme material difficult, or if learners cannot control adequately the learning environment, the technology will quickly lose its appeal. Furthermore, there is clearly a disadvantage in using a particular technology if it takes students several weeks to learn how to use it before they can start on the course content. Design of learning materials for distance education, and of the computer interface for e-learning, is critical. Students must be able to navigate easily and intuitively through online or distance education course material.

Reliability is another critical factor. If the technology breaks down or 'crashes', it can severely disrupt the learning process. If the software has a bug, all students will likely have the same problem at the same time, swamping help-desks. Given the reliability now of most commercial learning platforms, difficulties are likely to occur locally, either with the students' Internet service provider, or their own machines or software. It is important then that, where necessary, students are clear on what skills and what technical requirements are needed before beginning a course.

Although good design and reliable technology can greatly reduce student demand for help, the provision of a technology help desk is essential for any computer-based distance learning. Interaction and user-friendliness are therefore strong discriminators between different technologies, and these issues will be discussed in more detail against each technology in the following chapters.

ORGANIZATIONAL ISSUES

Successful technology applications usually require more than just the purchase and installation of equipment, hiring of technical staff, and the training of teaching staff. Successful implementation also requires some major structural or organizational changes within an institution. In addition, there are often powerful external factors influencing the decision to use a particular technology, such as government initiatives or high-profile marketing of services by the commercial sector. These can be seen either as distorting factors or as opportunities. The important questions then that need to be asked in this area are:

- What opportunities or threats exist in the external environment that may influence the choice of particular technologies?
- What are the internal organizational requirements, and the barriers to be removed, before this technology can be used successfully?

External factors

The existing technological infrastructure within a country is a major factor in influencing media selection. If Internet access is widespread in homes and the workplace, it can much more easily be used for distance education. However, if Internet services are expensive, unreliable, or focused only in certain large urban areas, it would be unwise to develop programmes that rely on the Internet. Most distance learning rides on the back of technologies already established for entertainment or business purposes.

Government initiatives, such as the development of a state-wide education and training network, or commercial vendors of services such as video-conferencing or fibre optic networks, will also generate potential technology-based projects. However, institutions need to be proactive rather than reactive to such initiatives.

It is essential then to develop a clear vision of the role of technology within an organization, so that when particular initiatives come along, there is a framework for project evaluation (see Bates, 1995b). Too often organizations find themselves involved with short-term technology-based projects, which, while successful in themselves, cannot be sustained because of lack of continuing funding or a clear idea of where such projects fit into the long-term plans of an institution.

Internal restructuring

A major implication of using technology is the need to reorganize and restructure the teaching and technology support services in order to exploit and use the technology efficiently (sometimes called 're-engineering the organization'). Too often technology is merely added onto an existing structure and way of doing things. Reorganization and restructuring is disruptive and costly in the short term, but usually essential for successful implementation of technology-based teaching (see Bates, 2000, for a full discussion of management strategies for supporting the use of technology for teaching in higher education).

The need to exploit an already existing technological infrastructure within an institution can be a major conservative influence limiting the application of new technologies. Thus if a heavy investment has already been made in a particular technology, with both capital equipment and permanent staff, it is likely that the head of the division responsible for production in that area has a senior decision-making role, because of his or her control over a large budget. However, introducing the use of a new technology may require the shift of funds away from 'traditional' cost centres into new ones. This though is likely to lead to opposition not just from those who control the budgets of traditional technologies, but also from those in the departments who fear for their jobs.

These organizational challenges are extremely difficult, and are often major reasons for the slow implementation of new technology. Thus there is often a bias towards those technologies that can be introduced with the minimum of organizational change, although these may not be the technologies that would have maximum impact on learning.

NOVELTY

It is often easier to get funding for new uses of technology than funding to sustain older but successful technologies. Although audio-cassettes combined with print materials can be a very low-cost but highly effective teaching medium, they are not sexy. It will usually be easier to persuade funding agencies to invest in much more costly and spectacular technologies such as satellite TV, learning objects or wireless networks.

On the other hand, novelty can be a two-edged sword. There is much risk in being too early into a new technology. Software may not be fully tested and reliable, or the company supporting the new technology may go bankrupt. Students are not guinea pigs, and reliable and sustainable service is more important to them than the glitz and glamour of untried technology. Thus it is better to be at the leading edge, just behind the first wave of innovation, rather than at the bleeding edge.

SPEED

In a society subject to rapid change, courses need to be put on quickly, and to be easily updated. However, in some distance education systems it can take over a year to develop a course, because of the high front-end development. Once produced, many courses have to remain unchanged, despite known errors or weaknesses in the material, or changes in the subject matter that make the material out of date, because funds are not available for maintenance, or production of new courses is always given a higher priority.

There are advantages then in using technologies that can enable courses to be developed quickly and be easily maintained. The importance of fast development and continuing maintenance though will be more important for some subject areas, such as microbiology and computing science, than for others, such as history or English literature, where the content base does not change so quickly

CONCLUSIONS

The **A C T I O N S** framework was first developed in 1988 for distance and open learning, and has been used successfully by a number of organizations as a framework for selecting, using and evaluating technology in distance education. More recently, the **A C T I O N S** framework has been amended for choosing technologies for campus-based learning, becoming **S E C T I O N S** (Bates and Poole, 2003). In **S E C T I O N S**, S = students, and includes student access to technology, and **E** = ease of use, with the rest of the acronym remaining the same. For distance and especially open learning, though, I prefer to keep the **A C T I O N S** framework, because access remains the most important decision-making variable for such learners.

The appropriate use and selection of technology will be very much influenced by local circumstances: context is all-important. Even between countries with similar levels of economic development, choice and use of technology will vary according to geography, local technological infrastructures (for instance, availability and pricing of Internet services), and educational structures. Even within a single institution, different decisions will be required in different areas of teaching, dependent on the needs of the target group and the academic requirements of a course.

One then should have no illusions that there are simple solutions to selecting and using technology in either conventional or distance education. Decision making about media and technology in e-learning and distance education is a complex process, requiring consideration of a great number of factors. In fact, decision making in this area is getting more difficult all the time, with the proliferation of new technologies and new teaching initiatives. It is also about personal choice, driven as much by values and beliefs as by technical considerations. These different factors cannot easily be related to one another quantitatively. In the end, an intuitive decision has to be made, but based on a careful analysis of the situation.

Fortunately, one of the great advantages of the human brain over computers is that the brain is far better than a computer at handling complex, value-based decision making, provided that people have the necessary information and an appropriate framework for analysis. Decision makers can then come to their own conclusions intuitively about the best mix and match of specific technologies to use. This requires taking into account not only the factors enumerated in the **A C T I O N S** framework, but also all the factors in the local context that only local decision makers can fully appreciate.

The following chapters identify the main media and technologies now available for e-learning and distance learning, and each of these technologies is analysed using the **A C T I O N S** framework.

4 Print

> ... the meaning of a text is enlarged by the reader's capabilities and desires ... This transmigration of meaning can enlarge or impoverish the text itself; invariably it imbues the text with the circumstances of the reader ... the reader re-writes the text with the same words of the original but under another heading, re-creating it, as it were, in the very act of bringing it into being.
>
> (Albert Manguel, 1996, p.211)

I am starting with what may appear to be an old technology for several reasons. Ever since the invention of the Gutenberg press, print has been a dominant teaching technology, arguably at least as influential as the spoken word of the teacher. Even today, printed materials, in the form of textbooks, dominate as the main technology of teaching in formal education, training and distance education. Why is this? What makes print such a powerful teaching medium, and will it remain so, given the latest developments in information technology?

First of all, we saw in Chapter 2 that there are many distance education organizations that are still using print as the main medium of communication, because the students they are targeting do not have access to computers or the Internet. We shall see that a combination of print and audio in the form of cassettes or CDs is in fact very cost-effective. Even fully online courses still make heavy use of printed materials, in the form of student readings from books, journal articles or duplicated custom course material. Furthermore, much of the research into the relationship between text, audio and video conducted on print-based distance education courses is relevant to design decisions for Web-based courses. Indeed, such research becomes more relevant as increased bandwidth allows for the development and delivery of material combining text, audio and video (multimedia). There are strong reasons then for beginning with print.

THE TECHNOLOGY

The changes that are occurring as a result of information technology make it necessary to define carefully what we mean by print, since it combines both technological and communications aspects. Books and other printed materials such as collections of readings distributed to students (custom course material) have broadcast and asynchronous technology characteristics.

Until recent times, print, in the form of words and pictures reproduced from blocks or plates, was the main method by which words and two-dimensional pictures or diagrams could be reproduced on a large scale. Print, however, took over from an already established hand-written medium of communication. Books existed long before the invention of the printing press. Printing did not make a fundamental difference to the representational qualities of books. Indeed, until lithography and engraving became established, the move to printing actually reduced the pictorial quality of books, compared with the manuscripts that were beautifully coloured and illustrated by monks. The main significance of the mechanization of printing was to make books available to a much wider public: in other words it made books more accessible.

With the invention of computing, though, both text (that is, words and other related signs, such as numbers) and pictures could be stored in the form of digitized data, and displayed on screens. Computer-generated text can also be printed as 'hard copy' on paper. This chapter is concerned primarily with 'hard copy', in the form of printed teaching texts, namely textbooks or correspondence texts, although much of the discussion regarding the representational qualities of 'print' will also apply to text displayed on screens.

ACCESS

One reason why you are reading this in book form rather than on a computer screen is because print is still more accessible, easier on the eyes, and more portable than computing. Another reason is that the business model for print-based publishing ensures reliable revenue returns for publishers and royalties for authors. However, a business model for electronic books that can match print-based publishing has not yet been developed. The technology for electronic publishing is now almost as portable as books, but a book is a true, stand-alone device, needing no electricity to power it, and no network connection to load it.

In most densely populated and reasonably affluent countries, the mail service is fast and efficient. Thus in many Western European countries, print can be directly delivered to every home within two or three days of mailing, using the general postal service. In these countries, delivery is reliable, very few packages going astray. Distance education students may complain about delays in the mail, but delays are in fact more likely to be due to organizational problems within the distance teaching organization.

In comparison with Western Europe, though, the postal services in Canada and the United States of America are relatively slow and unreliable, unless the more expensive courier services are used. In many developing countries, postal services to the home do not exist or are very unreliable. There is no doubt that the long-term trend will be away from the use of postal services, which have high costs in terms of labour, especially for residential and more remote areas, and towards the use of the Internet for mail and text delivery. In many countries, though, it will be many years before every home has the facility to send and receive text over the Internet.

Thus print has considerable advantages in terms of access, because of portability, the ubiquity of the mail service, relatively low delivery costs, and a well developed organizational infrastructure for marketing, publishing, and distribution. Print is particularly valuable for specific target groups, such as learners in remote or rural areas, learners in developing countries, learners with literacy but not computer skills, and the poor or socially disadvantaged.

TEACHING AND LEARNING

From a teaching point of view, print is by tradition a powerful medium. There is a common assumption by many academics that print is the intellectually superior medium – that television, by comparison, 'encourages children to be passive, mindless and unimaginative' (Greenfield, 1984). Indeed, some writers such as Postman (1994) have argued that print provided the necessary foundation for intellectual and scientific thought, but with the advent of television and computing, 'rational' thinking has been severely undermined, as witnessed for instance by the modern political process of electing a president, where image-building, rather than ideas, argument or logic, becomes paramount. Postman claims that it is no accident that with Ronald Reagan, the USA elected an actor as president. The problem with these kinds of statements is that they have a 'common-sense' plausibility that is at the same time difficult to prove or disprove scientifically.

If we examine its physical characteristics, print can present words, numbers, musical notation, two-dimensional pictures and diagrams. It can also, at a cost, carry full colour illustrations. It cannot directly present movement. Text is linear, although literary conventions, such as parallel developments being represented sequentially or in the form of 'flashbacks', allow for non-sequential events to be represented.

Illustrations and diagrams in texts provide an intermediate stage between direct experience and abstraction, because they can be used to give more concrete or physical representations of abstract ideas or concepts. Illustrations and diagrams give added flexibility to text, by providing alternative approaches to the representation of knowledge, thus adding variety to a student's learning.

Through text, print can precisely represent facts, abstract ideas, rules, principles, and detailed, lengthy or complex arguments. It is good for narrative or storytelling, and in the hands of a skilled writer can lend itself to interpretation and imagination. Because print can handle abstractions well, it can be a very dense medium, in that a single book can contain large amounts of 'coded' information. Print therefore appears to have major advantages for dealing with logical and rational thinking, which require precision, factual accuracy, clarity of thought, and the ability for arguments or ideas to be stored, reproduced and examined by others. Thus print lends itself both to consciously critical analysis and to intellectual, as well as emotional, persuasion by those that have learned the skills of communicating through print.

Print then has traditionally been the main means of presenting information and transmitting knowledge in education. Print can also be precise or deliberately ambiguous, remembering the point made by Manguel at the beginning of this chapter that reading is always an interpretative act. Alternative explanations or approaches can be handled, if only in a sequential manner. Print therefore should enable students to develop higher level skills of interpretation, synthesis and evaluation, as well as comprehension. Print is a medium that facilitates what Piaget calls the 'formal operational' stage of intellectual development, which is the manipulation of symbolic or abstract concepts. It is thus an appropriate medium for the intellectual activities expected in higher education.

Although many of the features of print-based teaching will transfer easily to the Web, there are likely to be some important differences that need to be identified and understood. For instance, the *structure* of the Web, with small chunks of discrete information displayed in non-sequential screen pages, is less conducive to the presentation of formal and lengthy arguments than printed books or articles. More research though is needed on the qualitative differences between books and the Web as instructional media.

INTERACTION AND EASE OF USE

All forms of reading require interaction between the reader and the text. Iser (1978, p.ix) states that:

> [Reading] sets in motion a whole chain of activities that depend both on the text and on the exercise of certain basic human faculties. Effects and responses are properties neither of the text nor of the reader; the text represents a potential effect that is realized in the reading process.

Iser points out that the meaning of the text is something that the reader has to assemble, leading to what Iser calls an 'aesthetic response': 'although it is brought about by the text, it brings into play the imaginative and perceptive faculties of the reader' (p.x). Thus a text is not a 'neutral' object; its meaning depends on the interpretation of the reader, whether it is a work of great literature or a car mechanic's manual. Therefore, if the reader is to obtain meaning from a text, there has to be an interaction.

What differentiates distance education texts from other kinds of printed material is a deliberate attempt to structure explicitly a student's response to the material. This may be done in one of several ways:

- Detailed objectives expressed in measurable outcomes ('advance organizers' for the student).
- A system of headings and sub-headings that make explicit the structure of the text.
- Organization of the text into discrete 'chunks'.
- Step-by-step explanations.
- Use of illustrations, diagrams and examples to illustrate concepts.
- Self-assessment questions within the text.
- Student activities – and 'model' responses.
- Heavy use of summaries.

Research on how students process text (see, for instance, Marland *et al.*, 1990) indicates that while such 'organizers' of student reading can be helpful, they have to be used with care if students are to process information at a 'deep' rather than a 'surface' level.

Print then can vary in how it is structured to encourage interaction. Highly structured, 'controlled' texts, interspersed with very frequent and explicit activities, would represent a more behaviourist approach to learning. Dense, loosely structured text, with few headings, would represent a more open, interpretive or constructivist approach to learning. Indeed, little guidance other than assessment questions, which may be few and require broad-ranging answers, may be given to the student as to how to interpret the material. The choice of approach will depend on the nature of the subject matter, the experience and previous level of education of the learner, and the type of learning that the teacher believes to be important. Print then is an extremely flexible teaching material, and can be designed to suit a wide variety of teaching approaches and purposes.

Nevertheless, a major weakness of print is its limitation in assisting students who have failed to understand parts of the text. Although good print design tries to reduce the extent of misunderstanding, there will always be occasions where alternative explanations or a different approach are required for those students who have difficulties. In other instances, students are often unaware of their failure to understand, and this is often where an intervention from a teacher is most necessary.

Another weakness of print is its difficulty in providing feedback for questions that have a variety of acceptable responses, or which require complex or elaborate responses. Print cannot challenge or 'discuss' the appropriateness of students' responses to in-text questions. Furthermore students can easily go to the printed 'feedback', where answers or 'discussion' of the activity is provided, without actively engaging in the exercise. 'In-text' questions or self-assessment exercises may be too frequent or too trivial to stimulate 'deep' processing. Feedback through print is also less appropriate for more practical forms of learning requiring the development of social or psychomotor skills.

Thus one important role of a teacher is to provide the necessary inter-ventions to assist students in learning from texts, and in particular to help students challenge the material where appropriate, and to challenge or clarify students' own interventions. To provide this kind of feedback and interaction for students studying at a distance, most distance teaching institutions have established an elaborate system of part-time tutors, who use correspondence by mail, the telephone, or regular local face-to-face sessions for interaction with students. However, such 'field' support for students is very expensive to provide.

Ease of use

Professionally printed text has many advantages over both screen-delivered text and text from printers linked to desktop computers. Print is self-sufficient: it does not need another piece of equipment to make it accessible to the learner. Because techniques such as content lists, page numbering, chapters, headings and indexes are well developed, even relatively inexperienced learners can quickly access information. Books are portable, easily accessible, easy to skim and search, relatively cheap to deliver, and can provide high quality graphics and design. Thus they are easier to read, compared with either materials printed on a home or office printer, or, even more so, screen-based text.

For these reasons, students in general still appear to prefer to read print, rather than text on a computer screen. For instance, a survey of over 2,500 computer-literate Canadian post-secondary students found that printed textbooks were still the single most popular choice of format, chosen by 49 per cent of those sampled. Computer disc was preferred by 22 per cent, CD-ROM by 14 per cent and access via networking by 15 per cent (Environics Research Group, 1994).

Technical developments such as the introduction of large-screen monitors, text messaging, and better quality low-cost colour printers, improved software, such as the printed document format (pdf), and the increased portability of computers may change students' preferences. However, there are still two main advantages in providing students with existing printed material, rather than transferring it for downloading by computer. First, it is still in most cases cheaper for students to buy printed material, rather than download and print the same material locally. Second, from the institutional perspective, copyright permission is often easier to obtain for print, although this is beginning to change. Nevertheless, more extensive research into students' preferences for print or Web-based text is needed, as the technology changes and develops.

One major disadvantage for distance education developers using textbooks as required readings is the difficulty in getting timely delivery from the publishers. Often a distance education unit must decide on textbooks up to six months ahead of the course opening to guarantee delivery to the students. Since now it can take less than three months to develop a Web-based course, textbooks may need to be chosen before the design of the course is known. Also, courses dependent on printed texts need to be completely redesigned if the required book goes out of print, which happens often.

If students are living in another country, it may be necessary to use more expensive courier services for delivery, so as to be able to track delivery (it is not unusual for customs officials to hold up required printed material until it has been inspected, which can take several months). The more international a programme, then, the more incentive there is to move delivery entirely online.

In order to exploit the benefits of text, a great deal of effort has to be put into developing learners' skills in reading and writing. In fact, these are extremely difficult skills to develop. Even in advanced, developed countries, up to 30 per cent of adults have difficulties reading tabloid newspapers – generally measured to require the level of reading achieved by the 'average' seven year old! So, despite its familiarity and pervasiveness, text is not so user-friendly, as far as learners are concerned, as it may at first appear.

Furthermore, intellectual development requires more than just the technique of reading. The ability to manipulate words and ideas is both facilitated by and dependent on print, but also requires a great deal of instruction to achieve. There is therefore heavy investment in the education industry to make print work. (However, the same also applies to the use of computers. Students need literacy and keyboarding skills, given the current graphical user interface and word processing software.) Despite the amount of education and training that goes into making people skilled in using print at school, for many people it remains a difficult medium to learn from. It is therefore an inappropriate technology for those with low or no literacy skills (unless literacy is the goal).

COSTS

Costs of print will depend on the complexity of the design and production process. Although costs will vary from institution to institution, and country to country, the relationship between costs should remain relatively stable. The focus here is on the direct print-related costs, in terms of cost per student study hour on print, so comparison can be made both between the costs of print for large open universities and smaller, dual-mode operations, and between the costs of print and other technologies. However, student support costs such as tutoring are included in the analysis of print costs, as they tend to be different between print and Web-based courses, and are an essential component of print-based distance education.

Cost is a function of design. Therefore the way a distance education course is designed will affect all costs. I will look at two different approaches to course design and production, to illustrate the cost differences.

The United Kingdom Open University model

The UKOU course production system is based on the course team, which may have up to 20 different people from a range of disciplines and job categories working on it. A typical course team for a large foundation course of 6,000 students a year will include the following:

- Four or five 'core' OU academic staff (one of whom will chair the team).
- Up to 10 other academic contributors (some from other institutions).
- A television and radio producer from the BBC.
- An educational technologist (concerned with pedagogic design).
- A print editor (concerned with literary style, typography and graphic design).
- A course administrator concerned with budgets, deadlines, and with arranging, recording and following up on course team meetings.

The course team will discuss the detailed contents and structure of the course, which is usually broken down into blocks of several weeks' study, or single 'units' of one week's study. Members of the course team will be allocated responsibility for the development of particular blocks or units.

Each printed text will usually go through three separate drafts. Each draft will be discussed or commented on by several members at least of the course team. Each course will have a paid external assessor from another university, who checks and comments on all the material, and who must give written, formal approval before the course can be offered to students. Additional external block assessors may also be used, especially where the course is inter-disciplinary. Typically, a course will take two to three years to be developed before delivery to students, then the course will be offered for an average of eight years before being withdrawn or remade.

Development costs

These are the costs of developing print materials from scratch. These are *fixed* costs, in that they are independent of the number of students who take the course. In a 'typical' open university, the specially designed print component (the correspondence text) usually takes at least half the total student study time. If the supplementary printed materials (the audio-visual notes, assignment questions and student assignment notes, and so on) are also included, print probably accounts for nearly two-thirds of student study time.

What is more difficult to calculate is how much time academics spend on print development, compared with their other activities, such as course maintenance and revision, tutoring, and research. However, Rumble (1986) has suggested a basis for dividing academic time at the UKOU, and building on that; the relevant estimates are given in Table 4.1.

Historically, over the 40 or so years that the UKOU has been operating, the academic staff have each averaged roughly one unit per year. Given that academics spend a notional figure of 145 days a year on course development, and assuming that they spend roughly a half to two-thirds of that time on print-related activities, the following estimates can be made:

- 75–100 academic days on print development for every unit produced.
- About 10 academic days for each hour of student print-based study.

As well as the academics, there are editors, photographers, graphic designers, educational technologists, course administrators and secretaries involved in the development of printed material. An editor's workload is about 20–24 units a year, and course administrators and educational technologists average about two courses a year. It would not be unreasonable to assume that the additional staff cost is at least as much as the academic time for each unit of print.

Table 4.1 Notional allocation of academic time at the UK Open University

	Days	%
Weekends and holidays	140	38
Research	40	11
Administrative duties (committees, etc.)	10	3
Sub-total	190	52
Teaching days:		
Course maintenance	16	4
Summer school	14	4
Sub-total	220	60
Developing new courses	145	40
Total	365	100

Distribution costs

Distribution costs for print, unlike development and production costs, are *variable,* in that they are dependent on the number of students enrolled in a course. Print costs per student vary considerably, depending on the number of students and hence the size of the print run: the more copies, the lower the average unit cost. For instance, in 1988, the average printing cost per student for 1,000 students was £14.32, but for 10,000 students the average cost per student was £6.27.

In addition to the costs of development and printing, there are warehousing, packaging and mailing costs to be added. Warehousing used to be considerable, but electronic publishing and the resulting 'print-on-demand' has helped reduce these costs, but the basic economics of printing still favours large runs over small runs. Packaging costs are also substantial. An average mailing to a UKOU student may include the following separate 'teaching' items:

- Course manuals: four different correspondence texts (= one 'block' of four weeks study).
- A block guide.
- Supplementary reader articles.
- Notes on the audio-visual materials.
- An assignment question, with notes.
- Two different audio-cassettes.
- A stop-press sheet, with amendments or corrections and course news.
- A contents list.

For each mailing of the course material (normally eight for a full credit course – 32 weeks – in the first year, then between two to three mailings in subsequent years), all these materials need to be collated, packed and mailed. With 150,000 students across over 300 courses, this is a major logistical exercise for the UKOU. Lastly, there is the cost of postage. The UKOU has special contracts that averaged out at between £5 to £8 per student per 32-week course in 1990.

Table 4.2, based on data originally published in the first edition of this book (Bates, 1995), converts these production and delivery costs into costs per student and per student study hour, assuming students spend 250 hours a year (7.8 hours a week) on the printed texts. Table 4.2 excludes the costs of course maintenance, which were not calculated but are probably substantial (see Table 4.4). Table 4.2 also excludes the costs of television and audio production and distribution, which account for roughly one third of the total costs of a UKOU course, and the costs of the textbooks. In Table 4.2, the data in Bates (1995) has been extended to include costs for courses with 30 and 3,000 students a year, at 1989 prices.

More recently, Hülsmann (2000) has published two case studies of costs of course development and delivery at the UKOU, one of which was for a

Table 4.2 Costs per course of printed teaching materials at an open university

Over 8 years	240 students (30 per year) £	1,000 students (125 per year) £	5,000 students (625 per year) £	10,000 students (1,250 per year) £	24,000 students (3,000 per year) £
Cost head					
Development	400,000	400,000	400,000	400,000	400,000
Printing	5,000	14,432	37,568	62,668	144,000
Storage	720	3,000	15,000	30,000	72,000
Packing	1,440	6,000	30,000	60,000	144,000
Mailing	1,560	6,500	32,500	65,000	156,000
Total for print	408,720	429,932	515,068	617,668	916,000
Average cost per student for print	1,703.00	429.93	103.01	61.76	38.17
Tutor costs	16,800	70,000	350,000	700,000	1,680,000
Total institutional costs	£425,520 US$638,280	499,932 749,898	865,068 1,297,602	1,317,668 1,976,502	2,596,000 3,894,000
Total per student	£1,773.00 US$2,659.50	499.93 749.89	173.01 259.52	131.76 197.64	108.17 162.26
Per student study hour (250 hours)	£7.09 US$10.64	£2.00 US$3.00	£0.69 US$1.04	£0.53 US$0.79	£0.43 US$0.65

largely print-based course. This was a second level undergraduate course in the School of Health and Social Welfare, requiring 220 hours of study, with eight specially designed print-based course manuals and five sets of supplementary printed material, seven audio cassettes each of 30 minutes, and one 25-minute video cassette.

One feature in the Hülsmann study missing in my 1995 analysis was the identification of the associated costs of tutorial support for a print-based course at the OU. Hülsmann calculated the total direct learner support costs (tutor-marked assignments, face-to-face sessions) for this course at £70 (US$105) per student, or 32 pence (48 cents) per study hour. This has been added to the print costs, as tutorial support is an essential component of print-based teaching.

It can be seen from examination of Table 4.2 that the cost per study hour drops from £7.09 (US$10.64) for a course of 30 students to 43 pence (65 cents) for a course with 3,000 students, demonstrating the impact of economies of scale for print-based teaching. The proportion of development costs drops from 94 per cent for 30 students a year to 15 per cent for 3,000 students a year. For courses with 10,000 students a year, the tutorial costs begin to exceed the print costs.

The UKOU now uses smaller teams for lower enrolment courses, but the impact of student numbers on print costs can be clearly seen from Figure 4.1.

The UKOU course team approach, with its extensive discussion of teaching materials, teaching approaches, and media design, is labour-intensive, and consequently has high development costs. The rationale for this process of discussion by a range of people with different skills and knowledge is to ensure that the material is comprehensive, well structured, accurate, clearly written and coherent. It enables the development of topic-based or inter-disciplinary courses, as well as the more 'traditional' single-subject based course, and enables new curricula to be developed, embracing and integrating a wide range of perspectives, theories or approaches. The UKOU justifies these costs by arguing that independent, isolated learners need high quality materials, and that the average cost per student is still low, because of the very large numbers served.

On the other hand, the process is lengthy and bureaucratic. Many academics feel they are driven by the course production system, with academic decisions subordinated to production decisions. The main academic weakness of this process has been the difficulty in altering texts once handed over for printing. The high cost of replacement means that courses tend to last beyond an acceptable length of time without major alteration or improvement. Also,

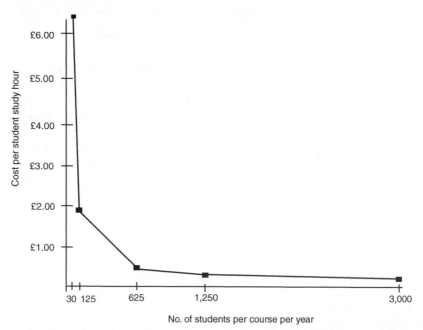

Figure 4.1 Cost per student study hour for print at the UK Open University, 1989

the process distances the teachers who originate the teaching material from their students, both in time and in interaction.

The University of British Columbia dual-mode model

It is not surprising then that dual-mode distance education institutions, which generally have courses with relatively low student numbers per course (under 200), have found less labour-intensive methods to produce course material.

In some dual-mode institutions, the on-campus teaching is carried over to the off-campus teaching, in that lecture notes are converted to duplicated or printed materials and reading lists are distributed to off-campus students. This is very much cheaper, but raises serious questions about the quality and appropriateness of the printed course material for distant, independent learners. For instance, many such courses have very low completion rates (around 30 per cent).

More commonly, in dual mode institutions, a course team process is followed, but more streamlined than the process at the UKOU. A typical dual-mode print-based correspondence course would have the following team:

- A tenured professor.
- A course developer, combining project management and instructional design skills.
- A print editor.

If audio- or video-cassette production is required, the course developer will contract this in as necessary. The course will still be independently assessed academically.

With regard to costing academic time, there are at least four models for funding the academic course author:

- The most common is to pay a professor an extra stipend to develop a distance education course. At UBC, the stipend for a 13 week, 100 hours of study, three credit course is C$6,000 (US$4,500). It should be noted that this is at a contract professor rate, even though the academic may be tenured. This model results in course development being treated as extra work for extra pay.
- Alternatively, the department head will assign time for distance education course development as part of regular teaching load. The Distance Education and Technology department (DE&T) will transfer C$6,000 to the department. This enables the head of department to hire a contract instructor to cover for the face-to-face class the professor would otherwise have taught. This is a preferable model for a tenured professor, who has a reduced face-to-face load instead of payment at a low rate. This model is now becoming more common for undergraduate distance education

courses at UBC, in that a distance education course is just treated as another 'section' of a large class.

- For full cost-recovery programmes, the university calculates the full cost of a senior tenured research professor, as these courses are seen as additional to the 'normal' government-subsidized undergraduate or graduate programmes.
- A fourth funding model is to contract an instructor from another institution or who is otherwise unemployed. UBC has tried to avoid this model for course development, for reasons of academic quality and control. (The aim is for all courses to be the responsibility of a UBC tenured or tenure track research professor).

For the purpose of this exercise, I will use the second method above.

Development costs

Distance education courses vary in length from three credit, 13 week (one semester) courses to six credit, two semester courses. In the traditional print-based dual-mode institution model, the professor will develop a course outline (usually identical to the on-campus version of the course) and write up in text format the lecture notes for the course. The text is then handed over to the course developer (who combines instructional design with project management).

Following discussions with the professor, the course developer then adds activities and overall course design features to make it suitable for independent study. A course developer would work on an average of two new courses a year, and would spend between a quarter and half of their time on course maintenance. I have estimated that they will spend roughly one-third of their time on one new course development (C$60,000/3 = $20,000).

Most course maintenance is done by the course developer. Course developers handled roughly 12 courses a year on regular maintenance, taking approximately one-third of their time, so I have estimated C$1,667 per year for time spent by course developers on maintenance of a single course. After initial course design, the academic plays a fairly minor role, unless they also decide to tutor the course (which they often do).

One editor covered all new course development (about six new courses a year) and all editing required for course maintenance. I have estimated roughly 10 per cent of an editor's time on editing one new course ($45,000/10 = $4,500), so with six new courses per annum, this allows for 40 per cent of their remaining time to be spent on maintenance, equal to C$1,500 per course. Thus the total development and maintenance cost of a print-based course over five years at UBC was C$43,667 (US$32,750).

Delivery costs

At UBC, printing is done by means of desktop publishing. In1996, new course production switched to Web-based teaching. Nevertheless, almost half the courses in the UBC distance education calendar in 2004 were still print based and needed to be maintained (and thus often reprinted every year). In 2003, the course manuals for print-based courses varied between 25 to 150 pages in length for a three credit course, and there were variations in cost depending on the size of the print run. Thus the printing costs vary from 6 to 16 cents a page. The average printing cost of a course manual though is around C$10 (US$7.50).

The reason for this relatively low cost is because the course manuals are study guides, directing and guiding students on readings from textbooks or collections of duplicated journal articles. The students buy these, and the average cost spent per course by students on textbooks and other printed material for UBC distance education courses is roughly C$100 (US$75.00) per course. Thus when calculating the costs of print-based courses, it is necessary to include both institutional and student direct costs.

In addition to printing costs, there are the costs of handling (packing and postage). The average cost for packing a full course package is C$6 per student, and mailing charges average another $5 per student package. In addition, because many undergraduate students take only one or two distance education courses, there is a learner guide sent to every student on every course. The cost of this is approximately $5. Printing and the associated costs of handling and postage are of course variable, depending on the number of students enrolled.

Most print-based courses had one or more part-time contracted instructor (adjunct faculty) hired by the department, whose main job was student assessment, but who would also help individual students if they had difficulties. They were paid C$181 per student who successfully completed the course. As the completion rate for print-based courses averaged around 85 per cent, instructors in effect were paid C$154 per enrolled student. Thus the cost of tutoring was also a variable cost, dependent on student enrolments (and completions).

Table 4.3 summarizes these costs, calculated at 1994 prices.

Direct costs for 30 students a year

It can be seen that the total cost of the course over eight years was C$120,367 (US$90,275), or C$501 (US$376) per student. At roughly 100 hours study for a total of 240 students (30 × 8), this averages C$5.01 (US$3.76) per study hour. This includes $100 per student for the cost of the texts ($1 per student study hour). Because of the high costs of textbooks, students were directly paying 20 per cent of the total costs (in addition to tuition fees). The cost of developing the course was $31,000 (32 per cent of the institutional

Table 4.3 Print-related costs for a dual mode correspondence course (C$)

30 students per year	Year 1	Year 2	Years 3–8 (Year 2 × 6)	Total
Development				
academic	6,000			6,000
reviewer	500			500
developer	20,000	1,667	10,000	31,667
editor	4,500	1,500	9,000	15,000
Development sub-total	31,000	3,167	19,000	53,167
Delivery				
course manual (30 × $10)	300	300	1,800	2,400
handling (30 × $6)	180	180	1,080	1,440
postage (30 × $5)	150	150	900	1,200
learner guide (30 × $5)	150	150	900	1,200
Delivery sub-total	780	780	4,680	6,240
Total print	31,780	3,947	23,680	59,407
Tutor costs	4,620	4,620	27,720	36,960
Total institutional costs	36,400	8,567	51,400	C$96,367 US$72,275
Institutional cost per student (240 students)				C$401.53 US$301.15
Institutional cost per study hour (100 hours per student)				C$4.01 US$3.01
Student books	3,000	3,000	18,000	24,000
All costs	39,400	11,567	69,400	C$120,367 US$90,275
Total cost per student (with text books)				C$501.53 US$376.15
Total cost per study hour (with text books)				C$5.02 US$3.77

Table 4.4 Costs per course of printed teaching materials at a dual-mode institution

Over 8 years	240 students (30 per year) C$	1,000 students (125 per year) C$	5,000 students (625 per year) C$	10,000 students (1,250 per year) C$	24,000 students (3,000 per year) C$
Cost head					
Development	53,168	53,168	53,168	53,168	53,168
Printing	3,600	15,000	75,000	150,000	360,000
Packing	1,440	6,000	30,000	60,000	144,000
Mailing	1,200	5,000	25,000	50,000	120,000
Total for print	59,407	79,168	183,168	313,158	677,168
Average cost per student for print	247.53	79.17	36.63	31.32	28.22
Tutor costs	36,960	154,000	770,000	1,540,000	3,696,000
Total institutional costs	C$96,367 US$72,275	233,168 174,876	953,168 714,876	1,853,158 1,389,868	4,373,168 3,279,876
Total per student	C$401.53 US$301.15	233.17 174.88	190.63 142.98	185.32 138.99	182.22 136.67
Per study hour (100 hours)	C$4.01 US$3.01	2.33 1.75	1.91 1.43	1.85 1.39	1.82 1.37
Per study hour with textbooks	C$5.01 US$3.76	3.33 2.50	2.91 2.18	2.85 2.14	2.82 2.12

costs), and the maintenance cost over seven years was $22,167 (23 per cent). The costs of tutoring were $36,960 (38 per cent). Other delivery costs made up the remaining 7 per cent.

These costs provide the basis for Table 4.4, which looks at the direct costs over an eight-year period for the print component of a print-based correspondence course at a dual-mode institution. Not included in Tables 4.3 or 4.4 are indirect or student administration costs (which apply to all courses, and would have to be included in a business plan – see Chapter 8).

It can be seen from examination of Table 4.4 that the cost per study hour drops from US$3.76 for a course of 30 students to US$2.12 for a course with 3,000 students. Because initial development costs are less in the dual-mode institution, the economies of scale for print-based teaching are less than in the open university model. The proportion of development costs drops from 55 per cent for 30 students a year to 1 per cent for 3,000 students a year. For courses with more than 100 students a year, the tutorial costs begin to exceed the print costs. Thus tutoring costs become an increasingly high proportion of institutional costs as enrolments increase, from 38 per cent for a class of 30 per year to 85 per cent for a class of 3,000 per year.

Also, it is worth noting that the cost of textbooks becomes an increasingly higher proportion of the total costs as numbers increase (from 18 per cent for 30 students a year to 35 per cent for enrolments of 3,000 per year). Indeed, it is not really appropriate to use this low cost development model for very large enrolment courses (over 600).

Lastly, we can compare the print related costs of an OU with those for a dual-mode institution, by looking at the average cost per student study hour (Table 4.5). This examines just the direct institutional print related costs (that is, excluding tutoring costs and student textbook costs). To enable comparisons, both British pounds and Canadian dollars have been converted to US dollars.

It can be seen that the print costs per student study hour spent on institutionally funded print materials are substantially lower for the dual-mode institution for courses with 1,000 students or fewer. For the smallest course, the open university model is over three times the cost. It is only when courses reach over 4,000 students a year that the OU model becomes cheaper.

The development process and the price of quality

Although the UKOU print costs per study hour, particularly for large courses, are not high when averaged over a course life of eight years, their print development costs are substantial (US$18,750 per week's study compared with US$3,427 per week for the dual mode example). Does high-quality university-level printed distance teaching material have to cost so much to develop? Is it five times the quality of the dual-mode material?

Table 4.5 Comparison of costs for print between an open university and a dual-mode institution

Over 8 years	*240 students (30 per year)*	*1,000 students (125 per year)*	*5,000 students (625 per year)*	*10,000 students (1,250 per year)*	*24,000 students (3,000 per year)*
	US$	*US$*	*US$*	*US$*	*US$*
Print cost per study hour (without textbooks)					
Dual-mode	3.01	1.75	1.43	1.39	1.37
Open university	10.64	3.00	1.04	0.79	0.65

There are three different aspects to quality in printed distance teaching materials:

- The quality of the academic content, in terms of comprehensiveness, balance and accuracy (content).
- The quality of the educational design, in terms of clarity of objectives, the way the content is organized and structured, and the quality of student activities and assessment (instructional design).
- The quality of layout, graphics and print presentation (print design).

The OU considers that the process of peer-group analysis and discussion prior to course delivery is essential for courses that are likely to have well over 1,000 students a year. If poorly designed, such a course could have damaging effects on many students long before changes could be implemented, for once a printed course is finalized and delivered, it is extremely difficult and expensive to correct or change. In an integrated course, changes in one part of a text often have knock-on effects in other parts of the text or television programmes.

Having worked in both types of institution, I find it hard to believe that the quality of instructional design and graphics is any higher at the OU. However, although the quality of individual academics is also as high, if not higher, at UBC than the OU, the OU courses definitely benefit from the extensive peer review and discussion to which they are subjected. The printed course manuals are more extensive, more richly illustrated, and are less dependent on required textbook readings at the OU.

Also, one must be careful in comparing dual-mode institutions with the OU. UBC distance education students are highly selected with top grades from high schools. It is not surprising then that the completion rates and grades for UBC's distance students almost match those of their fellow students taking face-to-face classes (85 per cent compared to 90 per cent). The OU though has decided to take any student who wishes to study, irrespective of their previous experience or qualifications. The OU believes that printed teaching materials must be of exceptionally high quality because of the particular circumstances of their distance education students. These students cannot be assumed to have independent study skills nor do they have strong peer-group support in their learning context. They are therefore much more isolated, and therefore need materials that are clear and easily understood.

The fear is that by lowering the costs of development the quality of the print materials may also deteriorate. However, dual-mode institutions such as UBC have shown that using lower cost methods, standards for print-based distance education courses can still be high, while lowering costs.

Other costs

It must be remembered that print is rarely the only medium or technology used in distance education correspondence courses. Most print-based courses include other activities, such as broadcasts, audio or video cassettes, written assignments, optional local face-to-face classes with contracted part-time tutors, or week-long summer schools, and may also have e-mail as well as print communication with students. Increasingly, even print-based courses aimed mainly at those without computer access are including 'optional' Web activities for those who do have computer access. Thus students may spend a good deal of their time working on activities other than reading. Thus the total cost for such courses usually increases as other activities are added.

Finally, print needs to be supplemented by some form of tutoring, in order to provide two-way interaction. As well as the costs of paying part-time tutors for student counselling, feedback, and assignment marking, there are substantial costs for the support required to administer the tutorial system.

Summary of cost issues

It is important not to get too exercised by the actual costs of the two institutions used here as examples. The aim of this section has been to identify the various stages of the development and delivery of print materials, to look at the relationship between the costs of different stages of the process, and the relationship between costs and student numbers. In addition, I wanted to compare two different methods of course production. As a result of this analysis, the following conclusions can be drawn:

- The major costs are for course development and maintenance, tutoring and student-purchased textbooks, rather than for printing and distribution.
- The major development costs are academic time and instructional design; these costs can be reduced but at the risk of reducing the quality of instruction.
- The direct costs of print are relatively low for courses with more than 100 students per annum (below US$2.50 per student study hour).
- There are economies of scale, but these diminish for courses of over 120 students per year due to the increasing proportion of tutor and textbook costs.
- Print requires substantial support from part-time tutors; such learner support costs are a significant cost factor.
- High quality print-based materials can be produced at lower cost in dual-mode institutions, by working to a smaller course team model than the large open universities.

ORGANIZATIONAL ISSUES

With regard to the production and distribution of print, book publishing is a highly organized industry, because of its long history. Consequently, the human skills and the procedures necessary for the production and distribution of print materials are well established. There is a very strong organizational infrastructure supporting the distribution of print material, from educational publishing companies, through high street bookshops and public libraries, to comprehensive coverage by postal services. Furthermore, there is a highly formalized system of education and training for people working in publishing and printing. Specialist colleges provide training in the more 'vocational' aspects, such as printing and graphic design, while managers and editors are usually drawn from graduates in literature, classics or history.

One common feature of technology-based systems is the demarcation of skills and professional boundaries. For instance, each of the following jobs concerned with the production of print materials may be found within a distance teaching institution:

- Subject expert (author, consultant, academic).
- Instructional designer (course developer, educational technologist).
- Editor.
- Librarian.
- Graphics designer (illustrator; lay-out consultant).
- Proof-reader (copy editor).
- Printer.

Several approaches have been adopted with regard to the organization of these jobs. At open universities, most of these jobs exist separately, resulting in considerable division of labour, and with it a clear differentiation of salaries between different jobs, and the creation of different departments concerned with each function (for example, Faculties, Institute of Educational Technology, Publishing). Subject experts and even educational technologists may have full academic status, including tenure, while editors and graphic designers have less favourable salaries and conditions of service.

In smaller institutions, one person may combine several of these jobs. Sometimes, particularly in dual-mode institutions, the job of converting academics' lectures or previously published text-books into distance-teaching material is seen primarily as a 'technical' job and therefore something to be left to the print shop or media resources centre to do. Instructional designers may be seen as nothing more than glorified editors.

However, a major difference between traditional publishing and publishing for distance education is the role of the instructional designer. This distinction has arisen because in distance education, learners may need to be totally independent, and cannot necessarily fall back on a teacher for help in understanding or motivation. Thus distance education texts have to combine both information giving and direct teaching. The responsibility therefore for learning is shifted away from the face-to-face teacher to the teaching material itself. Converting the 'texts' handed over by subject experts into printed material suitable for distance education requires more than just the traditional skills of a publishing editor.

The skills needed to design good quality print material for distance learners are specialized. They include organizing and structuring the whole course, setting realistic learning objectives, identifying accurately the level of ability and knowledge of the target group, assessing realistic study loads for students, selecting appropriate media and technologies, and designing appropriate student assessment and course evaluation procedures. These are in addition to skills in advising on writing style, illustrations and page lay-out, and avoiding unclear or confusing prose. These latter skills may or may not overlap with those of a traditional editor.

Because of the need to work as part of a team, and the problems of status within the teams, social and communication skills are equally as important as technical skills for such instructional designers. However, finding people with the appropriate instructional design skills is not easy. With the increasingly rapid expansion of e-learning and distance education projects, especially as part of in-house company training, there is a growing need for properly trained people in this area.

Even in institutions where each job is clearly demarcated, there is often a good deal of overlap in the areas of work, and academics with experience of designing distance learning material often acquire many of the skills of the educational technologist and editor. This can and does lead to conflict and organizational jostling between the different departments responsible for these different jobs. Academic staff sometimes find it difficult to subordinate their autonomy to the needs of a production process or to working in a team of professionals. However, a well-defined and disciplined operational process is essential for the timely production of high-quality print materials for distance education.

NOVELTY

With the advent of the Web, printing is no longer considered a leading-edge technology, although it is a medium that continues to develop technologically. In particular, improvements in printers, scanners and copying machines now enable high quality print material to be developed at low cost even for small runs.

SPEED

This is probably the major weakness today of print as a teaching technology. It takes a long time to develop high quality printed material. Print-based distance education courses can take from nine months to over two years from approval to the first opening of the course. Once produced, a print-based course is difficult to change. Often, supplementary printed material has to be produced and distributed to students to accommodate errors (especially where this may affect assignments) and any major changes since the material was originally produced (for instance, new laws, new developments in a particular field). Textbooks going out of print can be a major problem for print-based courses, especially where the course manual has been written around a particular textbook.

CONCLUSIONS

Despite the growth of the Internet and the Web, print will continue to be a major teaching medium, and is likely to remain so for well into the twenty-first century. This is because print will remain more accessible and convenient for learners than digitized text, since no special equipment is needed to learn from print. Also, it will remain more accessible than computing to many target groups in both developed and developing countries for some time to come.

Print is an extremely valuable teaching medium, able to carry large amounts of information in a condensed form, and is ideal for courses requiring high levels of abstraction, and where logical thinking or argument is required. However, learning from print at a distance requires high levels of skill from both the learner and the designers of print material. The teaching material itself has to be designed specifically to help people who may not have strong literacy or study skills, and who have to study for the most part independently.

The main limitation of print is the time required for the development of high quality text, and it is difficult to see how this can be reduced substantially without affecting quality. Print unit costs for courses of 100 students or more a year are still very low as far as higher education is concerned. Good quality distance education print materials can cost less than one (US) dollar per study hour per student, including delivery. However, because of the weakness of print in terms of student interactivity, print needs to be complemented by a teacher. This requires the establishment of a costly and comprehensive tutorial system.

There is substantial differentiation of labour in the production and delivery of distance learning materials. In both open and dual-mode universities, a project management approach has proved to be a crucial mechanism for harnessing and integrating the various skills required, and for controlling the costs of development and delivery. Instructional design skills are particularly important. Institutions often have difficulties with the structural organization of the various groups of staff concerned with the design of distance education materials, because of the overlap of professional roles, the added costs of non-faculty staff concerned with design, and the perceived threat to faculty autonomy. Nevertheless, despite the major inroads of the Internet and the Web into distance education, print is, and will remain, a most important technology.

5   Television and video

TELEVISION: PROMISE, DIVERSITY AND MISUNDERSTANDING

Of all the media available to educators, television and video come in the most diverse forms, have arguably the greatest potential for teaching and learning, and are probably the least well used. Following the definitions in Chapter 3, 'video' describes the generic features of the medium, such as moving pictures combined with audio. 'Television' refers to a particular form and organization of communication that is dependent on the medium of video.

There are many different forms of educational video: for example, educational broadcasting; instructional television; video-conferencing; video cassettes; DVDs; digital video clips; and video streaming via the Internet. In this chapter, the focus will be on educational television and recorded forms of video such as video cassettes and DVDs. Although video-conferencing and Web-conferencing are also dependent on or can include video, these technologies are discussed in Chapters 9 and 10.

Educational video can be delivered using synchronous technologies (broadcast television, video-conferencing) or asynchronous technologies (video cassettes and DVDs). Video can be incorporated into 'one-way' technologies (for example, broadcasting, DVDs) or 'two-way' technologies (for instance, video-conferencing).

Video can also be created or used in a wide variety of production formats. These include lectures, studio discussions, drama, documentaries, case-studies, digital video clips, or as an audio-visual data-base. The production and delivery of video can be managed through a variety of organizations, particularly in terms of who controls production and delivery. Such organizations include national or regional broadcasters, educational institutions, satellite or telecommunications companies, or training organizations. Lastly, video varies enormously in the different technologies used (for example, satellite, terrestrial broadcast, cable, video cassettes, DVD, and video streaming over the Internet).

Every one of these differences has a significant implication for technology selection and educational design. However, while the diversity of video applications makes generalization difficult, a good deal is known about how to use video successfully in education, even if this knowledge is not often applied.

A complex medium

Perhaps of all the media available for learning, video is the least understood and most underrated by teachers and learners, and 'television' has been the technology probably most overrated by educational policy makers (at least until the arrival of the Internet).

It is important to be clear about the different kinds of television available for educational purposes. There is a big difference between educational broadcasting and instructional television, the former concentrating more on the unique presentational features of video, the latter on the delivery of lectures.

Broadcast educational television is found in one form or another in most countries. Programmes produced by broadcasting organizations have a different purpose and target audience from those produced by educational institutions. Although the organization, objectives and operation of educational broadcasting are extremely diverse (for a full description of broadcasting in education, see Hawkridge and Robinson, 1982 and Bates, 1984), there are certain common general characteristics.

The oldest and most established form of educational television is the programming transmitted by major public broadcasting organizations, such as the BBC in the United Kingdom, the Public Broadcasting System in the United States and TVOntario in Canada. This kind of educational television is designed for specific if broad target groups, such as pre-school children, pupils in schools, or adults with a curiosity about the world of arts or science. It is an 'open-access' service, available to anyone interested enough to tune in and watch, and usually designed with this general audience in mind. Educational broadcasting organizations provide a particular kind of programming, characterized by high production standards, relatively high production budgets, exploitation of the presentational characteristics of the medium and certain prevalent styles and formats, such as documentaries.

With the advent of the Open University in Britain in 1971, and its unique partnership with the BBC, educational broadcasting also became associated with credit programmes leading to nationally recognized qualifications, such as a degree. This pattern of partnership with a national or local broadcaster has been followed by a number of other open universities, such as the Open University of Hong Kong, the Bangladesh Open University, and the Korean National Open University.

Many teachers do not see television as a 'serious' instructional technology; indeed, often they are openly hostile to it, seeing it as trivializing the educational process. At the same time, decision makers, and particularly politicians, often underestimate the costs and overestimate the educational potential of television. It costs money to exploit fully its presentational qualities, and television requires a great deal of training and expertise to use well as an educational tool. To understand better the complexity of video, we need to understand the technologies behind it.

THE TECHNOLOGY

Video can be delivered through a wide variety of technologies.

Terrestrial broadcast transmission

With terrestrial transmission, broadcasts are radiated from a ground transmitter, with programmes often relayed between different transmitters to form a network perhaps covering a whole country. The frequencies within which television (and radio) can be broadcast terrestrially are limited. This means in effect that in many countries, radiated terrestrial transmission is restricted in practice to four or five national networks at a maximum, and local services are also restricted in number. Individual governments allocate bandwidths to broadcasting organizations, either directly, or through national commissions established by government, e.g. the Home Office in the UK, the Federal Communications Commission in the USA and the CRTC in Canada. These bodies also allocate other television services, such as cable and satellite frequencies.

Cable services

Cable television is essentially a local distribution facility, but usually linked to national networks through the relay of satellite or microwave signals. There are two main kinds of cable television: co-axial and fibre-optic. Co-axial cabling uses copper wires, but configured differently from telephone wiring. Up to 30 or so television channels can be delivered by co-axial cable into any one site. Fibre-optic cabling is installed mainly on 'trunk' routes, although it is increasingly being used for connecting individual sites with large telecommunication requirements, such as tower blocks in downtown city centres. Fibre-optic cabling can handle very many television channels.

Satellite

A satellite is like a mirror in the sky, allowing telecommunication signals of various kinds (television, radio, voice, data) to be sent up from the ground (up-linked) then re-transmitted down again. A satellite is likely to carry several transmitters (called transponders). Each transponder can usually carry the equivalent of one analogue television channel and several radio channels or over a thousand telephone channels or very large quantities of digital information, such as words, computer programs, still pictures.

Since the footprints of several satellites are likely to overlap, and since there are also terrestrial-based radio, television and microwave signals, it is important that satellites broadcast at frequencies that do not interfere with either those of other satellites or of other ground services. This means that there has to be international agreement about the power and the frequencies at which satellites will operate, and where they must be placed in the geo-stationary orbit. They need to be spaced apart to avoid interference with one another. Because there is a limit to the number of satellites that can be placed in the geostationary orbit at any one time, there also has to be international agreements on how many satellites (or rather satellite channels) each country can have.

Digital transmission

A full analogue colour television signal requires the equivalent of approximately 1,000 telephone lines to transmit at the same speed as a voice-only communication, and thus needs a very wide transmission bandwidth. Analogue television signals are transmitted, or stored and played back from recordings, at 25 frames ('still' pictures) per second in Europe, and 30 frames per second in North America.

Digital compression techniques enable cable, satellites and the terrestrial networks to carry several television transmissions simultaneously, thus increasing the overall television channel capacity (see Chapter 9 for a fuller description of digital compression techniques). However, many domestic television sets are currently analogue. Thus if the signals are originated in digital format, conversion equipment is required, either at the cable head end or in the home. Digital formatting allows not only the number of television channels to be increased significantly, but also for the integration of television with computing and telephone technologies. Bandwidth still restricts digital video transmission over the Internet. Eventually, though, all video transmission is likely to be digital, whether it is broadcast, recorded on DVD, or sent through the Internet.

In summary, there are several different technologies that can deliver broadcast television. However, they are all synchronous, largely one-way technologies.

Video cassettes

Television material can be recorded on and replayed from electromagnetic tape. Video cassette machines can record and playback, enabling both 'time-shift' recording and playback from broadcast television. Educational programmes can also be pre-recorded and copied to video cassette for direct distribution via the mail. Video cassettes are standardized on one format for domestic and educational playback purposes (1/2" VHS), although there are still difficulties when moving between different international television standards (NTSC, PAL, SECAM).

Video cassettes store images in a linear, analogue form. This means that to access information in the middle of a cassette, the machine has to wind through the cassette to reach the desired point. Even with fast wind mechanisms, it can take up to a minute to locate the right segment. Furthermore, searching usually requires an element of trial and error.

There are several technological advantages of video cassettes: the widespread availability of the technology, the ability to record as well as replay, the low cost of the recording format (video tape), and standardization of format.

DVDs

There has been a long journey in moving to digital recording of video, through large laser discs down to the current small, CD-ROM sized digital video discs. DVDs operate differently from video cassettes.

> DVD is essentially a bigger, faster CD that can hold cinema-like video, better-than-CD audio, still photos, and computer data. It has replaced laserdisc, is well on the way to replacing videotape and video game cartridges, and could eventually replace audio CD and CD-ROM.
> (DVD Demystified (http://www.dvddemystified.com/dvdfaq.html#1.1))

A single DVD can provide over 2 hours of high-quality digital video and sound (such as in a full movie). Each 'frame' has its own digital code number, allowing any single frame to be accessed almost immediately. Each single frame can be held steady and for as long as desired. Picture quality is higher than that on cassettes or broadcasts. As well as video, DVDs can also store sounds on several different audio tracks, and huge quantities of text and graphics in the form of digital data.

Production of DVDs requires digital recording (or conversion from analogue to digital) of video, audio, graphics and text. While programmes made for broadcasting or video-cassette distribution, once digitized, can be transferred straight over to DVD without further editing, this will not exploit the control characteristics of DVD; producing for educational disc replay can be a complex and highly specialized job. The complexity increases considerably when production exploits the linking of a computer or the Internet with the DVD.

Most DVDs are now standardized on the MPEG-2 format. Although the number of discs suitable for educational purposes is growing slowly, there is still a shortage of appropriate learning material on DVD. Video cassettes and DVDs are asynchronous, one-way technologies.

The technological trend

There are two paradoxical trends with regard to video technology: convergence of the technology and the fragmentation of services. The digitization of video means that it is no longer a technologically distinct medium; it can be closely integrated with text, audio and graphics within the same technological format. Secondly, with the ability now to deliver hundreds of different digitally-based television channels, the television industry is fragmenting into more and more specialty channels. In theory, this should be good for educational television, in that it can have its own 24 × 7 distribution. In reality, the increasing commercialization of television makes it more difficult to finance and support a specialty channel for education, although several organizations have tried.

Video is an extremely valuable medium for education. However, new methods of designing video for delivery in a flexible, integrated and user-friendly manner are needed in order to exploit the educational potential of new digital technologies.

ACCESS

Homes

Television is one of the most accessible technologies, in terms of equipment. Nearly every home in many countries has at least one television set. Programmes may be delivered through a variety of technologies. From an educational point of view, the distribution method is very important, particularly if the teaching institution has an open access policy.

Most economically-developed countries have comprehensive and technically high standard national terrestrial transmission systems for television, with some regional services as well. Thus the UK Open University was able to deliver its television programmes into 98 per cent of United Kingdom households, using one of the BBC's two national terrestrial transmission networks (BBC2). Television programs for the UK Open University frequently attracted audiences of up to 400,000, which 'suggests that the OU philosophy of "openness of instruction" extends well beyond its cohorts of students formally registered in the undergraduate and CE areas' (Open University, 1988, p.13). Thus for every registered student watching, there were about 100 general viewers in the late 1980s.

In North America, educational broadcasting is delivered primarily through local cable stations or direct reception of satellite transmissions. TVOntario, the provincially funded educational television station, has two channels dedicated to educational programming (one in English, one in French), and is able to cover the whole of a very large province through a combination of cable and satellite distribution.

Video cassette home ownership has increased in more economically advanced countries, where more than 70 per cent of all homes now have video cassette recorders. Video cassettes illustrate the difficulties caused when not all potential students have access to a particular technology. Despite clear instructional and cost advantages, there was considerable reluctance to use video cassette distribution or production methods at the UK Open University, until home penetration reached 80 per cent, on the grounds that this would discriminate against those without a video-cassette recorder, and thus restrict access. This was despite the fact that fewer than 50 per cent of the students were watching broadcast transmission of the programmes. DVDs now present the same kind of problem for open institutions. In 2004, about 40 per cent of homes in North America had either a stand alone DVD player or a computer capable of playing a DVD.

Access at work sites

A number of education and training systems use cable and satellite transmission to deliver instruction into the workplace. Stanford University has for many years offered masters' courses in engineering by cable and satellite television to employers in California and beyond. The National Technological University, with headquarters in Fort Collins, Colorado, has used satellite transmission to relay post-baccalaureate engineering and management courses from universities across North America to business and other sites. These programmes specialize in bringing the latest research developments to the workplace. NTU uses digital transmission requiring special reception equipment, which ensures that its transmissions are limited to those end users that have paid for the service.

Access at local centres

In developing countries where not everyone has a television set, the use of community or local centres for educational broadcasting is quite common. For many years, the INSAT project in India delivered programmes by satellite to community sets in schools and villages, although the cost of maintenance and security was always a major problem. The Central Chinese Radio and Television University (CCRTVU) delivers programmes through a combination of satellite and terrestrial transmission. Although its programmes can be received on domestic television sets, it also delivers through hundreds of local centres around China, through its partnership with state RTVUs.

Until recently, many universities and colleges in the USA delivered instructional television through local campuses across a state, in an attempt to meet local legislation requirements for equal access to higher education, irrespective of a student's location. As the students attended a local campus for face-to-face teaching in some subjects, it was attractive to deliver other subjects through instructional television when enrolments in these subjects at the local campus were low.

However, there are challenges in using local study centres to provide alternative access for students who do not have particular technologies at home. In 1982, the UK Open University, worried about the loss of viewing due to a deterioration in broadcast transmission times, set up a central copying facility to make video cassette recordings available of selected television broadcasts. Students applied to the University's headquarters for a copy of programmes in the scheme, and a cassette was sent to the student's home address. At the same time 311 VCR machines were located in local centres. It was then up to the student to decide where to use the cassette, before returning it, so the cassette could be used at home, if the student had a machine, or at a local study centre.

In practice, the main student usage was at home. Very few students used the facilities in the study centres, although the provision of rented equipment in the study centres cost more than half the whole project. Consequently, the machines were eventually withdrawn from centres, although students could still borrow cassettes. Thus this scheme failed to solve the problem of access to television for those without their own VCR machines, although it substantially improved access to those who were unable to watch the broadcasts (see Brown, 1983).

The importance of quality of delivery

Because of competition between limited numbers of television channels, minority programming, such as education, has tended to be pushed into off-peak times. The UK Open University had access to over 35 hours a week on the national BBC television network at its inception in 1971. In theory, it should have been able to access all students at home in this way. However, as competition from commercial channels increased, the quality of transmission times allocated by the BBC for Open University programmes progressively deteriorated from 1979. In 2004, the bulk of the Open University transmission times are in the middle of the night, although selected programmes are available as general broadcasts during daytime at weekends.

Many studies (Bates, 1975; Gallagher, 1977; Grundin, 1978, 1980, 1981, 1983, 1985) showed the adverse effect that poor transmission times had on the proportion of students who watched the programmes. By 1984, barely half of Open University students were watching off-air transmissions. Fortunately, the advent of video cassette machines reduced the impact of poorer times on Open University students to some extent, but the average viewing figure (viewing on transmission combined with viewing recordings) was still down to 60 per cent by 1984. Given the cost of television to the University (13 per cent of its budget that year), a 40 per cent loss of viewing on each transmission was extremely inefficient.

The use of a particular medium must be questioned if it cannot deliver learning materials to most of the target students. Course designers are reluctant to teach essential content or skills through a particular technology if substantial numbers of students are disadvantaged in this way.

Competition for mass audiences between broadcasting organizations, new and cheap recording technologies, and the popularity of the Internet in education have all reduced the use of educational broadcasting and instructional television in more economically advanced countries. However, in many less economically advanced countries, national broadcasting is still the best way to deliver education and development programming to many millions of people.

TEACHING AND LEARNING

What is special, if anything, about the role of television and video in learning? What can it do that can't be done by other methods, such as print or face-to-face lectures? To answer such questions the unique educational characteristics of television must be examined.

General arguments for educational broadcasting

There are five general reasons that are frequently used to justify the use of educational broadcasting in open and distance learning.

Personalizing the teaching

The argument is that television allows the student both to identify the individuality of the teacher(s) responsible for the distance teaching material, and to provide a public image and awareness of the university's presence, a sense of belonging and community for the otherwise isolated student. The feedback collected from UK Open University students over a number of years indicated clearly that students appreciate seeing the people responsible for their courses on television.

The general reaction of students was to be reasonably tolerant towards nervous or slightly 'camera-shy' lecturers who made small verbal fumbles or dropped things. One student commented: 'It's important to me to know that the materials are created by human beings who are not always perfect, but do care about what they are doing.' In any case, many lecturers became very proficient with practice.

Improving learning efficiency

By using some of the unique presentational features of television, understanding can be better facilitated through television than through reading alone. In the next section, evidence will be examined that suggests that television programmes can improve learning efficiency for many students.

Pacing

Do scheduled broadcasts keep students working regularly, and break the inertia of beginning to study? The evidence on pacing is less conclusive. A study by

Ahrens *et al.* (1975) showed that what influenced students' pacing was not the regular television programmes (students were often several weeks behind with their reading when the programmes linked to the reading were transmitted) but the regular monthly assignments, which counted towards their end-of-course grade.

Student recruitment

When the UK Open University started in 1971, its association with the BBC, and the controversy over using broadcast television for university-level teaching, contributed to publicizing the Open University. In its first year, there were over 50,000 applicants for the first 25,000 places. The Open University now has over 150,000 students. Although it is difficult to separate the influence of television from general marketing, most of the initial staff at the Open University believed that the association with the BBC was extremely important for recruiting students in the early days (Perry, 1976).

Academic credibility

One factor that clearly led the UK Open University to be accepted by the rest of the academic community in Britain, despite initial scepticism, was the academic quality of the television programmes, which were publicly available and easily accessible. As a result many lecturers and students in regular universities began to use the UKOU's course materials in their campus courses.

However, the availability and prominence of the Open University's teaching through public television has been a two-edged sword. The Conservative education minister, Sir Keith Joseph, strongly objected to a particular social science television programme that he had seen on Marxist economics (on a foundation course that was based on examining similar social phenomena from three different ideological perspectives, including Marxism), and the following year the university's operating budget was reduced by £2.5 million, against the trend of previous and subsequent years. This incident indicates that there is a particular pressure on open learning institutions using public television to ensure that their courses have academic credibility and are free from bias; the corollary is that there is inevitably a pressure towards safe and uncontroversial teaching.

In general, both research and experience suggest that with the possible exception of pacing, the claims for the general benefits of using public television have held true at the UK Open University.

Educational broadcasting or instructional television?

Television is a rich technology, in that it can combine all the major forms of symbolic representation: words, pictures, movement, sound, and representation of events as they occur over time. Television can of course be used merely to relay a lecture or a talking head. It is important then to distinguish between television that exploits its full range of presentational qualities, and television that is merely another way of delivering the lectures.

Usually one can make a clear distinction between the use of television by educational broadcasting organizations and the use of television by educational institutions (instructional television). Programming can vary along any of the following dimensions:

Instructional television	*Educational broadcasting*
lectures/discussion panels	unique presentational characteristics of television
low cost	high cost
live, interactive	pre-recorded
programmes to classes/groups	programmes to individuals
sole medium	mixed media
'narrowcasting'	'broadcasting'.

In between is a whole variety of different programme styles or approaches, for example 'enhanced lectures', using specially prepared graphics, or drama 'dropped into' a conventional lecture (e.g. a History course at the University of Saskatchewan), or relatively low-cost productions which nevertheless fully exploit the presentational features of television (e.g. laboratory experiments or demonstrations). In general though, educational broadcasters better exploit the unique presentational features of television, while educators emphasize the transmission of content through lectures.

There are several reasons why broadcast lectures are the preferred mode of television for university professors. There is very little need to change their normal campus-based approach to instruction. There is plenty of evidence (see Clark, 1983; Moore and Thompson, 1990) that live, televised lectures can be as effective as face-to-face lectures. Exploiting the presentational features of television is usually more expensive – and requires more training and specialist production – than does using it for relaying lectures. Professors and administrators therefore need to be convinced that more expensive production techniques lead to better teaching.

There are arguments though for trying wherever possible to break away from the lecture format. Unless there is a great deal of interaction between individual students and the lecturer, lecture-based instructional television tends to result in what Marton and Säljö (1976) call 'surface processing', that is, learning focuses on recall and reproduction of what has been taught, rather than on analysis, questioning or reworking of the learning material: 'deep processing', in Marton and Säljö's terms.

In order then to assess the appropriateness of the televised lecture, the question that needs to be answered first is: what are the teaching objectives? If the teaching objective is to achieve more than just the efficient transmission of information, then it is likely to be worth making the effort to exploit the unique presentational characteristics of television.

Unique presentational characteristics of television and video

As well as the ability of television to deliver learning material to large numbers of students, to sites far removed from the classroom or lecture hall, there are *presentational* characteristics of television and video that are important for education. Perhaps the most obvious is the ability of video to bring resources to home-based learners that would not be possible through any other medium, or even through direct experience, such as, for instance, scientific experiments, case-study material of social and technological events, field-visits (particularly to foreign countries), and dynamic presentation of ideas through animation and graphics.

This feature of video is particularly important for learners who cannot get to institutions, or who cannot access resources available in, for example, larger universities or urban areas. However, even for students in the best resourced universities, there are often phenomena or experiences that are not easily available to them through campus-based provision. (See Appendix 1 for a full listing of the unique teaching characteristics of television).

From the concrete to the abstract

For many students there are often times when words are not enough; they need to be able to see to understand, and video is one way in which this can be done. A major presentational characteristic of video is its ability to provide an illustration or a concrete example of an abstract principle or generalization. Examples or illustrations can be given in texts, but the power of the moving picture, combined with the ability to synchronize such pictures with words and sound, is to create striking audio-visual images symbolizing important concepts or ideas. The learner can use these images in the same way as keys to a room. One function of video is to generate appropriate audio-visual images linked to otherwise difficult abstract concepts.

It is extremely valuable to be able to provide students with powerful audio-visual concrete examples, especially, but not exclusively, in higher education, where abstraction and generalization are important aspects of learning. Abstract ideas are usually stored and communicated in words. However, cognitive psychologists such as Bruner and Piaget have argued that full understanding and internalization of abstract concepts need to be preceded by some form of concrete experience. It is often difficult to provide this physical experience directly for distance learners, but video can act as an effective substitute.

Some help is often needed to move learners from the concrete to the abstract, or from the specific to the general. Because television can combine and integrate concrete images with words, it can act as a bridge between the operational (concrete) and formal (more abstract) stages of learning. One of the major limitations of both text and computers is their inability (at least until recently) to synchronize natural voice with full moving pictures, yet the importance of being able to link words and pictures to develop this higher level of abstract thinking cannot be too strongly emphasized.

For instance, Gallagher (1977) found that in Open University Mathematics courses, it was the borderline students (i.e. students getting Grade C or D for the course – E and F were fail grades) who tended to rate the television programmes as very helpful (50 per cent of C/Ds, compared with only 24 per cent of A/Bs). The higher achieving Mathematics students (A and B grades) were able to follow the course primarily from the text. In other words, they were already able to work at a high level of symbolic abstraction, and hence needed less help from television; but for those struggling with the course (C and D grades), the television programmes were able to provide extra help in understanding concepts, mainly through the use of concrete examples.

Video then can be of particular value to those students on a course who are struggling with difficult concepts. Video seems to be of particular value to 'high risk' students, and can help to reduce dropout resulting from the difficulty of a course. It should also be noted that the presentational advantages of video just described are independent of whether video is broadcast or distributed on cassettes, discs or over the Internet, although we shall see that video delivered asynchronously has other advantages.

Content or skills?

Much of the educational media research conducted in North America has been concerned with measuring to what extent a particular medium leads to *comprehension*. Are the students able to reproduce accurately and with understanding what they have been taught?

However, comprehension is not the only learning outcome that may be desired. To what extent can the learner *apply* what has been taught to new situations? Can the learner *evaluate* evidence or arguments, on the basis of what he or she has been taught? Can the learner *analyse* a new situation on the basis of previously taught concepts? Can the student bring new or unanticipated *insights* to the situation portrayed?

One major criticism of print-based distance education is that the evaluation of what it is important to learn and the analysis of issues to be studied are all decided by the professors, not the students (Harris, 1987). Knowledge is packaged in texts by the teacher, then studied and churned back by the learner. The structuring of the print material makes it difficult for students to impose their own order or structure on the subject matter, or to restructure it for themselves.

Television, on the other hand, can be designed to encourage interpretation, by presenting situations or cases that have to be analysed or classified using concepts taught in the texts. As early as 1967, Trenaman found that television encouraged viewers to analyse for themselves real-life situations, and what they themselves might do in similar circumstances. When used in this way, television can provide an opportunity for students to make their own interpretations, and to develop skills of analysis and application of principles taught elsewhere in the course.

There are many areas of study, not only in the humanities and social sciences, but also in science and technology, where it is important to develop students' skills in handling open-ended situations, or to encourage students to bring not only their learning from the printed materials, but also relevant life experiences, in order to analyse situations and suggest possible courses of action.

A particular form of television programme that can encourage skills of analysis and application of knowledge is the documentary-style programme. While documentaries encompass a wide range of production styles and approaches, they tend to have a loose semantic structure (that is, there is not usually a strong, continuous narrative line), and they tend *not* to build in explicit guidance or interpretation in the sound track. 'Open-ended' documentary style programmes can be a valuable teaching resource, if used to encourage students to interpret, analyse and problem-solve.

However, far too often the educational purpose behind a documentary-style programme is not articulated or recognized by the teacher using the material or by those who designed the program, nor, more importantly, do the students themselves understand how they are expected to use such material. Because television is such a familiar medium, it tends to be taken for granted that students will know how to learn from it. This is not the case, particularly where comprehension is not the main purpose.

After a lifetime in some cases of using television as a 'relaxing' entertainment medium, it is hardly surprising that many adults, as well as children, have great difficulty in learning from television; nor, in most cases, do they even believe it to be a problem. For instance, UKOU students often complained that the programmes were 'too easy' or 'irrelevant' (because they were seeking factual information or comprehension) yet they were unable to use the programmes in the ways intended by the course designers and TV producers, which was often for analysis or interpretation.

Most students will approach an educational television programme as if it were a lecture, unless the programme is made in such a way as to encourage them to question and analyse what is being presented to them. Students may need a 'bridge' between the concrete and the abstract through the commentary. Without explicit links, students may not see concrete examples in a television programme as illustrators of ideas or principles learned in the text (Salomon, 1983). In fact, there is strong evidence that these kinds of programmes are often ineffective in developing students' skills of analysis and interpretation, even when this purpose is made explicit.

A number of studies of such programmes were carried out at the UK Open University (Bates and Gallagher, 1987). From the results, Bates and Gallagher identified a 'one-third rule'. One-third of students watching this kind of programme knew what they were supposed to do with such material in their course, and were able to do so successfully. These students tended to get high grades in the end of course examination. Another third knew that this type of programme was not meant to be didactic, and that they were meant to analyse and interpret it, but were unable to do so. The last third of students not only failed to approach the programme in the way intended, but were also totally unaware that they were meant to do so. This group of students was highly instrumental in their approach to studying at the Open University. They wanted didactic programmes, and were often furious that they were expected to watch, in the words of one student, 'this irrelevant rubbish'. This group tended to get relatively low grades over the course as a whole.

It is also important to relate the use of different media to assessment of students. If television is used for developing skills or providing knowledge not available elsewhere in the course, but these skills are not assessed in the examination, then students are unlikely to make the effort to learn from television. Also, if students, rightly or wrongly, perceive the television programme as optional, and the source of examination success resides in reading the printed material, for instance, then they will not watch the programmes.

Comparing the educational benefits of video with other media

In the end, what do learners get from video? Do they learn just as well as from, say, print or face-to-face lectures? Media differ in the *kinds* of learning they encourage. Thus in general, print is best for teaching in a condensed way, dealing with abstract principles, where knowledge of detailed facts or principles is important, and where knowledge is clearly defined. Video, on the other hand, is much better for presenting complex or ambiguous 'real-world' events, for providing concrete examples to illustrate abstract ideas or principles, and for encouraging students to make their own interpretations and to apply to new situations what they have learned in an abstract way.

The extent to which video is successful in doing this depends on how programmes are made. Video is rarely best used as the prime medium for delivering large quantities of information (print is best for this); instead, video is much more valuable for providing deeper understanding and for developing skills of analysis and application of ideas presented through other media, particularly print.

Despite the difficulties and the extra costs incurred, there is no doubt that video that exploits the unique presentational characteristics of the medium has an important and valuable role to play in learning. A well-designed video component can help not only to reduce dropout and increase comprehension, but can also assist the development of higher-order learning skills. In other words, video can increase the *quality* of learning – but only when the unique presentational characteristics of video are combined with a well-defined instructional approach.

INTERACTION AND EASE OF USE

While the presentational qualities of broadcast television make it valuable to learners, its main instructional weaknesses are its lack of interactivity and its inconvenience. Students often have great difficulty in interacting with television, for a number of reasons

Prevailing broadcast professional ideologies about what constitutes 'good' television can conflict strongly with educational approaches that encourage interaction. For instance, to keep viewers watching, broadcast television is continuous, and uses techniques that discourage the 'interruption' of the flow of the program. By its nature broadcast television cannot be interrupted unless recorded. Even educational or training programmes that are never intended for broadcasting, however, are often made in a continuous sequence, using broadcast formats such as documentary style.

In a situation where television is a regular component of a course, a strategy can be used of gradually moving from highly didactic to more open-ended programmes, with guidance within earlier programmes on how to use or interpret the television material. This strategy was adopted on D102, a remake of the UK Open University's Social Science foundation course. The students rated the programs on this course much more highly than students on the first foundation course (D100).

With regard to instructional television, interactivity is related to student numbers. The opportunity for any individual to participate in questioning or discussion decreases in proportion to the number of students viewing a live interactive programme. Another factor influencing interaction is the style of presentation. There is no real need for a live programme if the instructor takes up most of the time delivering information.

Viewing behaviour for educational television materials in a pre-recorded form is still dominated by general 'broadcast' television viewing habits, or by the 'lecture' mode of talking and listening. However, once recorded onto cassette or DVD, television can be used quite differently from viewing a broadcast. The tape or disc can be stopped, some parts can be selected for use, and not others, and the same television material can be used as many times as required.

However, even when such techniques are built into the production of the programme, it is still difficult to provide good feedback on learners' responses within the video medium itself. Indeed, Durbridge (1982) found that learning best occurred from video materials in a group context, where students could test out their interpretations on tutors and other students.

Production techniques to increase learner interaction

It is perhaps unwise to assume that viewers are passive if they do not overtly respond during the act of watching a programme. As with a good book, play or film, the programme may stimulate deep thought, imagination or fantasy, raise awareness, provide new information that is easily absorbed, or challenge the values or attitudes of the viewer. This of course depends on the ability or motivation of the viewer, and the quality and purpose of the programme.

However, although educational broadcasts tend to be continuous and non-didactic, they do not have to be. It is possible to design even broadcast programmes so that they encourage interaction. This can be done in a variety of ways:

- By 'wrapping' programmes with a prologue (giving viewers 'advance organizers' on what to look for) and a conclusion, summarizing some of the points or issues raised.
- Using 'voice-over' questions, or questions to camera by the narrator/presenter, during the programme.
- 'Interruption' of the narrative by the studio presenter, asking questions, indicating what to look for, summarizing points.
- Repeating a segment of film, with perhaps an additional comment.
- Use of captions, animations, or still frames to highlight a concept being illustrated.
- Using a still frame (or black screen) to give time for a viewer response to a prompt or question, possibly followed by feedback 'on screen'.
- Use of a telephone 'call-in' from viewers at the end of a programme, with an expert, or panel of experts, responding to the calls.

The less able or less educated the target viewers, or the more instrumental the learner (in the sense of being 'exam-driven', rather than by subject interest), the more viewers are likely to require this 'interventionist' style of programme, if they are to learn from television.

Many of these techniques will seem strange or artificial to producers working primarily in an entertainment medium; the effectiveness of these techniques also depends on fine judgement of the needs and ability of the audience. They do illustrate the point though that educational video needs a style appropriate to the teaching function, and that the style of the programme is an instructional as well as a television production decision.

In summary, despite the various techniques available for increasing interaction with a broadcast programme, and the ability of skilful producers to stimulate thoughtfulness and emotional involvement, the continuous and 'seamless' nature of broadcast television makes it a difficult learning context for most students.

Students differ in their ability to analyse and learn from video materials. The less familiar they are with a subject area, the more help they need to move from concrete to abstract thinking, and the more instrumental they are in their learning, the more video needs to be broken up and tightly integrated with other media. As students become familiar with the core concepts and skills needed in a subject, have greater facility in dealing with abstractions, and become more engaged with the subject matter, the better they will be able to handle documentary-style television programming as a learning resource.

Interactive video technologies

For most learners, it is essential that they can access video material at the appropriate point in their studies. There are learning benefits from stopping and reflecting on what they have just seen before moving on to the next part of a programme, and from watching the same scene as many times as necessary to interpret it.

New technologies such as DVDs, computers and the Internet enable carefully selected video produced in small chunks to be integrated with other media such as audio and text. When video is integrated in this way with computer technology, and made available asynchronously or in a recorded format, the learner can more actively respond to the video material. Educators (and broadcasters) have generally been slow to appreciate the significance of this difference between broadcast and recorded video.

COSTS

Probably no other teaching medium varies so much in its costs. Educational broadcasts produced by national broadcasting organizations such as the BBC tend to be very expensive compared with programmes produced by universities for limited distribution on local cable channels. Some BBC–Open University drama productions (co-produced with other broadcasting organizations) have cost over £100,000 (US$150,000) an hour to produce and transmit when overheads are included; the 'direct' costs of producing and relaying a lecture to a few off-campus sites may be under $300 an hour.

Nevertheless, the cost *structures* of the different video technologies are clear and consistent. The first edition of this book (Bates, 1995a) provided detailed analyses of costs for educational broadcasting, instructional television, and video-cassettes. The analysis of these costs will be briefly summarized here.

Educational broadcasting

The example used in Bates (1995a) was the BBC-Open University Production Centre. The main cost categories identified were:

- Capital costs (studios, transmission network).
- Fixed costs (overheads).
- Production costs.
- Transmission costs.

The BBC estimated that 85 per cent of its costs were fixed, because the BBC had invested in a full production centre for the Open University that had to be staffed at a certain level, if staff were to be regularly employed. The capacity of the studio centre to some extent determined the level of production. In essence this meant that the optimal level of production was about 230 × 25 minute programs a year.

Within this somewhat inflexible business model, costs were calculated for the production year 1983/4, chosen because the BBC–OUP Production Centre was operating at optimum capacity that year. The annual operating cost for television programming at that time was £5.5 million. The average production cost per hour for a television programme was £60,353 (US$90,000) (including overheads), and the average cost of transmission per programme was £660 per hour for a single transmission, or £1,320 (US$2,000) for two transmissions (which were necessary for optimum viewing figures for OU students).

The marginal television cost per student, that is, the cost of adding one additional student, was nil, since neither the cost of production nor transmission is determined by the number of students. Thus the more students per course, the lower the average cost per student. A typical course would have 16 × 25 minute television programmes, and each programme would be broadcast twice a year, over an eight-year period (the average life of a programme). Table 5.1 summarizes these costs.

Figure 5.1 shows more clearly the large economies of scale for broadcasting. To show the difference in costs, the print costs from Figure 4.1 have been drawn to the same scale.

Over the years since this study, production costs will have dropped, and inflation will have increased. However, the basics will not have changed. These can be summarized as follows:

- Broadcast television requires large investment and high operating costs, and unit costs (cost per student hour) will generally be high, especially if utilization is taken into account (only 65 per cent of students viewed the programmes in 1983/84).
- A dedicated broadcast television production system requires high levels of production to maximize fixed costs.
- Once a dedicated television production system is established, the marginal costs of producing each extra programme is relatively small; conversely, a small reduction in overall resources will lead to large reductions in output, unless fixed costs are slashed.
- Transmission (delivery) costs are less than 20 per cent of production costs.
- There are very large economies of scale for broadcasting, provided very large numbers of students are enrolled in the courses.
- To bring costs down to a reasonable level, 3,000 students or more per course per year are needed. The largest courses at the OU were the

Table 5.1 Cost per study hour per course for television (BBC–OU, 1983/4)

Over 8 years	1,000 students (125 per year)	5,000 students (625 per year)	10,000 students (1,250 per year)	24,000 students (3,000 per year)	48,000 students (6,000 per year)
Cost per study hour	£73.25 US$110.00	£14.65 US$22.00	£7.33 US$11.00	£3.05 US$4.58	£1.53 US$2.29

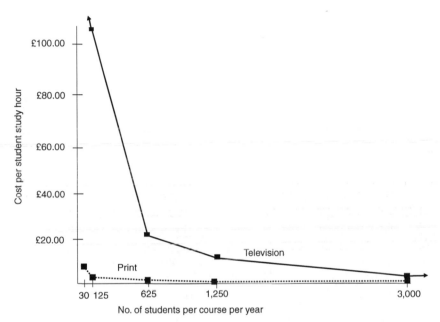

Figure 5.1 Cost per student study hour for television at the UK Open University, 1983/4

foundation courses, with 6,000 students a year. For these courses, the average cost per student study hour was approximately £1.50 (US$2.30).

- The high investment and high fixed operating costs of providing dedicated production facilities can be justified only if production levels are kept high, i.e. studios and ancillary facilities are used at least 75 per cent of normal working times for 'in-house' programming; if production levels are less than this, it is almost certain to be cheaper to contract out production to other organizations, thus reducing overheads.
- The high fixed costs of maintaining a dedicated television production capacity results in enormous pressure on teachers within the organization to utilize fully the production capacity, *irrespective of the appropriateness of educational use.*

- The investment in dedicated television production facilities also reduces the flexibility of an organization to change to new technologies.

Technological advances in recent years have not only reduced dramatically the cost of equipment required for television production, but also have reduced the previously high levels of staffing needed, thus allowing for still quite sophisticated production for considerably less cost. Nevertheless, location shooting, computerized graphics and other special effects often needed and used in educational broadcasts are still expensive. Thus, television production costs are still relatively high even today, because of the standards required by broadcast-quality educational television.

Although actual costs will be lower for organizations using less expensive production facilities than the BBC–OUP, nevertheless their cost structures, i.e. the ratio between different types of costs (production, transmission, etc.) and the shape of their cost curves will be very similar and broadcast television will remain much more expensive than print, except for very large course enrolments.

Video cassettes

In terms of cost, video cassettes impact mainly on distribution, rather than production. Studies at the UK Open University (Open University, 1988) established at what point it became cheaper to distribute television material on cassettes through the mail, rather than through broadcasting. The Open University determined that it was more economical to distribute on cassette than to pay for two transmissions when there are 350 students or fewer on a course (Open University, 1988). In fact, in 1988, 40 per cent of all Open University courses had 350 students or fewer. The Open University did not give video cassettes to the student, but loaned them for the duration of the course; the student returned the cassette after the course ended. (Less than 10 per cent of the cassettes loaned were lost or damaged per annum.)

The cost structure for the distribution of video-cassettes can be seen in Figure 5.2.

Thus although broadcast transmission (delivery) costs are fixed in terms of student numbers, video cassette distribution costs are variable.

Low-cost, non-broadcast digital video

Low-cost digital cameras, digital editing suites, and distribution of video on compact discs, DVDs or over the Internet now enable video to be produced and distributed much more cheaply than before. DVD players now cost under US$250, and discs can be copied at around US$4 per copy, including labels and box. (This excludes production costs.) Digital production suites can be set up for under $10,000. One hour of material can cost less than $100 to produce, using a single cameraman who may also be the subject expert. Digital

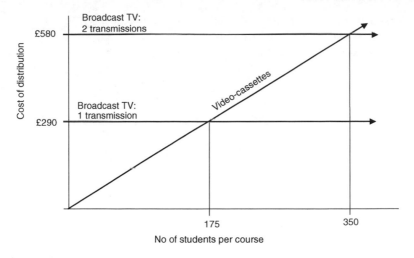

Figure 5.2 Structure of television delivery costs: broadcast TV and video cassettes

video may not look anything like broadcast television, but when used selectively to exploit its unique characteristics, it can be a very useful and relatively low-cost enhancement to other digital materials such as a Web site or a CD-ROM based text.

ORGANIZATIONAL ISSUES

Broadcasting organizations tend to have an ideology or a professionalism that is often markedly different from that of educational institutions. This is both an organizational strength and weakness. Schramm (1972) claimed that broadcasters bring a different set of professional criteria to educational television: 'Most educational broadcasters tend to talk of a "good" program in terms of *quality*; most scholars, in terms of *effectiveness*.' Trained and experienced television producers are able to think visually, and have learned ways to attract and hold an audience. Teachers, on the other hand, especially in higher education, often have difficulties in thinking 'visually' or in concrete terms, or have settled into approaches to teaching that are not appropriate for a broadcast television format (e.g. lecturing).

However, broadcast television works best in education when there is active follow-up or integration with learners' other studies or with other media. Thus a team approach is often needed, with a teacher and producer working together to exploit the medium. This is not always an approach that is readily accepted by television producers (or academics).

The most common finding in research into educational television is that, whatever style of programme is used, teachers need to adapt their teaching to the medium. There are many studies that indicate that if television is to be used successfully for instruction, it takes more time, and a different technique to lecturing or classroom instruction is required.

It will also be evident by now that curriculum design, in terms of identifying the various roles of video, the accompanying print or Web-based materials, tutorial support, and assessment strategy, are essential for effective teaching at a distance. Instructional designers can play an invaluable role in helping subject experts define the various teaching and learning needs of a course, and making sure they are assigned to the most appropriate media.

NOVELTY AND SPEED

Broadcast educational television is neither novel nor speedy. It has been around for about 40 years, and in comparison to the newer technologies of the Internet and DVD, television is not seen as terribly exciting by decision makers, a perception reinforced by the belief that it is an expensive medium.

Nor is it fast; while news or current affairs programmes can be developed at great speed, educational broadcasting tends to be much slower. A programme can take anything from six weeks to six months from conception to transmission. Educational broadcasts are also expensive to change. Thus programmes at the UK Open University are often broadcast for eight years. Nevertheless, good material can be relatively timeless; a computerized animation of a mathematical function, film of aboriginal dance rituals, or a production of Macbeth are not time-dependent and can be used many times in many contexts.

Instructional television, in the form of televised lectures, certainly has little novelty value; such programmes have been available in North America since the mid-1940s. Novelty comes from the use of video-conferencing, satellites or Web-casting. However, merely replacing one technology with a newer technology does not necessarily bring learning benefits if the teaching method remains the same.

The one real advantage of 'live' instructional television is that content can be changed quickly from year to year, or experts brought in quite late to such kinds of teaching. This can be important in areas where the subject matter rapidly becomes dated. However, with instructional television, programmes are remade each time a course is offered, and there are very high costs associated with this.

CONCLUSIONS

Broadcast television has been theoretically one of the most accessible media for education. In the past, broadcast television has been limited to major broadcasting organizations, but increasing deregulation, and access to cable and satellite channels, are making it easier for educational organizations or systems to access and use broadcast television. Nevertheless, competition for audiences and the increasing commercialization of broadcasting have forced educational broadcasting into inadequate transmission times for most students in countries with free market economies.

For developing countries, national broadcasting remains a major resource for education, able to reach millions of potential learners. The airwaves are a public resource under government control, and a country that places mass education as a national priority should not hesitate to allocate broadcast transmission frequencies for educational use. Educational broadcasting can deliver mass education at a low unit cost, but nevertheless needs substantial total investment. In order to ensure that the context in which television is used is appropriate, collaboration and partnerships between educational and broadcasting organizations are important, but not always easy to achieve.

The major strengths of high-quality television are its unique teaching characteristics. Broadcast television has its own way of stimulating thinking and interaction, which while 'covert' can still be powerful. Broadcast styles however tend to be influenced by a desire to catch the much larger 'caves-dropping' audience. This tends to militate against instructional approaches that encourage active learning or integration of the programme with other learning materials.

For learning to take place, video materials have to be carefully designed, following sound instructional as well as 'good' television production principles. Learners need help in understanding how best to approach video materials, especially when their use is not just informational, but to facilitate the development of higher-order learning skills. In other words, educational video needs to develop its own styles and formats, and above all needs to be integrated with other media.

Despite the past popularity of instructional television, particularly in campus-based institutions, this technology has severe limitations in terms of cost, instructional design and learner convenience. The popularity is more with the instructor, who does not have to radically rethink teaching strategies, than with the learners. Also, the apparent cost advantages are deceptive. For a single institution with small numbers of students using instructional television, the total cost may seem relatively small, but when aggregated across institutions, or when cost per student study hour is calculated, the costs are very high.

Even the advantage of interaction between student and teacher is deceptive with instructional television. Unless the teacher is particularly skilled, and the numbers per class low, the level or quality of interaction is usually poor, confined to a small number of questions from a small minority of participating students. Thus instructional television, particularly where it fails to exploit television's unique presentational characteristics, is not likely to be a cost-effective technology.

In recent years the Internet has replaced educational broadcasting and instructional television as the flavour of the month in education. The synchronous nature of broadcast television, the associated passive viewing, and the failure of teachers (and students) to understand the unique role that video can play in learning have resulted in television being seen generally as a 'weak' teaching technology. The decline of educational broadcasting, concerns about the high cost of television, and early limitations in using video over the Internet due to lack of bandwidth, have led to the educational benefits of video as a medium being overlooked. This is a pity. Digital video, specially designed to integrate with the Internet, can add powerful learning benefits to Web-based teaching, as long as the lessons from the use of educational broadcasting are absorbed.

6 Radio, audio cassettes and compact disc players

AUDIO: THE ORIGINAL LOW-COST, FLEXIBLE TEACHING MEDIUM

Audio is perhaps the most undervalued of all the media. When I am pressed to say what I think is the most cost-effective teaching medium, I tend to answer: CDs + print. Radio is the most accessible of all technologies for distance learners. Audio technologies are cheap, easy to use, accessible, and generally educationally effective, they are not exotic, though, and as a consequence tend to be ignored or undervalued by educational decision makers. For this reason, Schramm (1977) called audio-based technologies 'little media'.

Many of the educational uses of audio centre around the human voice. Durbridge (1983) noted that, compared with print, the human voice can have an informal quality that is not so easily transmitted in academic print. The human voice can be modulated, that is, it contains variations in pitch, tone, pace, volume and emphasis, and these cues are invaluable to the learning process.

Although in economically advanced countries audio cassettes have been replaced more and more by compact discs (CDs) and DVDs, the audio cassette has the advantage of being able to both record and replay at low cost. Audio is becoming less and less a separate medium as it becomes digitized. It is being combined more and more with data, print and video, to the point where it will soon be difficult to discuss audio separately from other media as a teaching medium. Nevertheless, there is much to learn from earlier uses of audio in education.

ACCESS

Radio

Radio is accessible to more people than any other single technology. Millions of people around the world who cannot read or do not have access to television have a radio set. In developed countries, almost all households have at least one radio set (UNESCO, 1986). Even in many less economically developed countries, access to radio is widespread, and increasing year by year. In Mongolia, for instance, 74 per cent of households had radio in 2003.

One problem of access is ensuring that students are able to listen when the programmes are actually broadcast. Research similar to that on television transmission times was carried out on the accessibility of radio programmes at the British Open University (Grundin, 1981). The research found that there were always students who were unable to listen at any particular time, because they were at work, travelling to or from work, or had other unavoidable commitments that prevented them from listening. Recording for subsequent replay can alleviate the problem, but radio is less easy to record 'remotely' than television, because most radio/cassette machines do not have timers as standard equipment (unlike video cassette machines).

Despite these difficulties, radio is generally an extremely accessible technology for teaching, and can reach certain target groups, such as the illiterate and very poor, better than other technologies.

Audio cassettes

A survey of British Open University students' access to audio cassette machines in 1985 showed that 95 per cent had audio cassette machines at home suitable for study purposes (Grundin, 1985). Most of the few students without an audio cassette machine said they would purchase one if they felt it was necessary for their studies.

Even in developing countries, audio cassette machines are common. For instance, in Afghanistan in 1977, I was surprised to find audio cassette players more common among the Kutchi nomads than radio receivers. The reason for this was that the radio airwaves were controlled primarily by government, and used for official information and 'cultural' programming, while the Kutchis used the audio cassettes for playing popular music. However, audio cassette machines are gradually being replaced by CD players, so they are now becoming less accessible a technology.

Compact disc players

It is difficult to obtain figures on access to CD players, but in more economically advanced countries, 50 to 70 per cent of homes are likely to have a CD player, especially if there are teenagers in the home. CD players with a set of headphones are self-contained and portable. CD players are often integrated with a portable radio. The technology is now standardized, in that the same disc will play on nearly all brands of CD player. One disadvantage, compared with cassettes, is that low-cost CD players cannot record. In general, CD players are now slightly more accessible than audio cassette machines in most countries.

TEACHING AND LEARNING

Radio has been used in education for over 70 years. It has in that time been used in many different ways (see Bates, 1984, for a full review). Its uses include school broadcasting, informal general education, social action programming, and adult basic education and literacy.

There are more than 20 radio literacy schools in Latin America, largely sponsored by the Catholic Church, which use radio, combined with specially prepared print materials, and face-to-face classes, often run by the local priest. These radio literacy schools have been very successful in teaching literacy to the 'campesinos', the poor farmers of Latin America (see Fuenzalida, 1992).

Radio has also been used for direct teaching in Australia, where the Radio Schools are used to link children in isolated farmsteads in the outback together with a teacher located many hundreds of miles away. Two-way radio is used (the farmsteads having short-wave receive and transmit radios), enabling the children to participate directly in the lesson (parents provide the 'back-up' support). Thus the teacher operates very similarly to a classroom teacher, except that the children are at a distance.

A $20 million USAID programme advocates a direct teaching approach through radio that, it claims, 'offers hope for 100 million children in the poorest nations who cannot attend school' (Agency for International Development, 1990). The approach is based on the use of 'interactive' radio instruction (IRI) for teaching core curricular subjects (e.g. Maths, Spanish, English, Science and Health Education), and has been applied in 18 developing countries over a period of 25 years (Bosch, 1997).

Distance teaching universities in Spain, Thailand, Sri Lanka, and Indonesia all use a significant amount of radio as part of their course provision, as do to a lesser extent distance teaching universities in Britain, Israel and Pakistan. Distance teaching universities often use radio for its publicity and recruitment value, as well as for teaching. It should be noted though that radio's publicity value is not high when transmissions are restricted to late at night or early in the morning.

One use of radio is for relaying lectures by professors. In the British Open University, though, at the peak of its use of radio, this format was used for only about 20 per cent of the programmes, even though students often wanted or expected this use of radio (Meed, 1974; Bates *et al.*, 1981). More frequently it was used for:

- Discussions of course material or issues covered in the printed materials.
- Alternative viewpoints to those contained in the printed material (e.g. guest speakers).
- Source material for analysis (e.g. children's speech patterns).
- 'Performance', including poets reading their own poetry, dramatization of literature, musical performance.

- Providing aural experiences: music, language learning, analysis of sounds.
- Collecting the views or experiences of specialists, experts or witnesses.

More examples of radio use can be found in Appendix 1. However, as audio cassettes became more popular at the British Open University at the beginning of the 1980s, radio's role became more restricted to relating course material to current events and updating a course over its eight-year life, providing corrections or course 'news' (such as information on examinations or help with examination technique) and overviews or summaries of units or blocks.

Audio cassettes can be used in a variety of ways. One is to record radio programmes. Because broadcasts often come at times that are inconvenient, or do not fit the times when students want to study, the programmes are recorded and played back at the time that suits the learner ('time-shift' recording). Students at the British Open University tended increasingly to record radio programmes for replay at a later time to coincide with the rest of their study pattern, and they rated the radio programmes as being much more useful when listened to as recordings, rather than live, on-air (Bates *et al.*, 1981). However, when using cassettes to record radio transmissions, the programme format and style are of course those of a continuous, uninterrupted radio programme.

A second use, and the one which is more cost-effective, is where the cassettes are deliberately designed to exploit some of the control features available to users of cassettes, such as stopping, re-wind, and repeat. This can lead to a format that is very different from a radio programme. Thus the cassette can be broken up into a number of discrete, non-continuous segments. Activities can be built in, which require the student to stop the cassette and return to it later. Most important of all, the cassette can be tightly integrated with other learning material. Some of these roles are summarized below:

- Talking students through parts of the printed material:
    - text (e.g. analysis of arguments);
    - formulae and equations (explaining and discussing);
    - illustrations, graphs, diagrams and maps;
    - technical drawings;
    - statistical tables.

- Talking about real objects that need to be observed (e.g. rock samples, reproductions of paintings, metal fatigue in examples sent as part of a home kit).
- Talking students through practical procedures (home experiments, computer operations, etc.) so their hands and eyes are free for the practical activity rather than needed for written instructions.
- Analysing human interaction (e.g. decision-making; personal experiences; conduct of meetings): here the roles of print and audio are reversed, in that the text is used to help analyse the audio material.

- Providing feedback on student activities: cassettes allow answers to be more easily tucked away, thus encouraging students to make more effort to answer the questions themselves rather than search for the answers.

Many of these functions of radio and audio cassettes can be replaced by digital technologies such as CDs, computers and the web. However, for those students without computer access, audio and print combined provides an easy, cheap and accessible alternative.

INTERACTIVITY AND USER-FRIENDLINESS

Perhaps one of the greatest advantages of radio is that it is an easy and familiar technology for most people. No special skills are required to operate a radio set, and even people with low levels of literacy can learn from radio. Nevertheless, there is some evidence that there are listening skills that need to be developed, if students are to get the most from radio as an instructional medium.

One of the main weaknesses with radio is the difficulty of two-way communication between the teacher and the learners. In theory, 'phone in' radio programmes provide an opportunity for interactivity between students and the teacher, but the level of interactivity and participation rates are often low when this format is used. Also, where phone-in programmes were tried at the Open University, feedback showed that they are not usually popular with enrolled students (Bates *et al.*, 1981). The questions generated did not usually relate to the individual problems that other students had or students were not interested in the views of other students. Thus radio phone-ins appear to be a less acceptable form of participation and interaction to students than, for instance, audio-conferencing via telephone.

Also, there are strong cultural differences that influence the student's ability to respond effectively to radio programming. Brown (1980) for instance found that students' use of radio at the Open University was strongly correlated with their previous use of general radio. Before they enrolled with the Open University, Arts students, for instance, tended to listen to radio drama and documentaries, while Science and Technology students tended to listen primarily to news bulletins and pop music. Once enrolled, Arts students listened much more to the Open University radio programmes on their courses than the Maths, Science and Technology students. Arts students apparently brought general skills in listening to radio that they were able and willing to transfer to the similarly-formatted Open University programmes. Science and Technology students were not accustomed to listening to extended 'talk' programmes, and were less willing to accept 'enrichment' programmes. It is also likely that radio is a more acceptable teaching medium for cultures with a strong oral tradition.

A major weakness of radio is that it is ephemeral. Many distance education students find it difficult to be available at a fixed time on a regular basis. The advantage of being able to listen to recordings of programmes, at times that suit the learner, in comparison with listening to a radio transmission, is substantial. In a survey of student listening on 88 different courses (Bates *et al.*, 1981), programmes that were listened to on transmission received an average student helpfulness rating of 3.42 (on a 5-point scale, where 5 = very helpful). When the same programmes were listened to as a recording, the average helpfulness rating was 3.79. (Given the size of the sample, and the narrowness of the rating scale, this difference was highly significant statistically.)

Nevertheless, one should not underestimate radio's power to stimulate the imagination or provoke strong student support. Those students at the British Open University who did listen to the radio programmes on a regular basis tended to rate them highly. The Open University research clearly indicated large individual differences between students in their reactions to radio, with Arts students in particular showing strong positive reactions.

The importance of audio cassettes and CDs as teaching media is far greater than just the additional convenience of 'time-shift' recording. Audio cassettes and CDs increase the *control* that both students and teachers have over the medium. Table 6.1 compares the control characteristics of broadcasts (audio and video) with those for cassettes, and the implications for learners.

One of the characteristics of broadcasts is that because they are open to everyone, there is a tendency to make them understandable to the general public, in an 'entertaining' style. This is especially important if one of the main rationales for using broadcasts is to 'market' courses. Cassettes on the other hand can be much more narrowly targeted, designed to meet just the needs of enrolled students, or to encompass a specific teaching approach.

One of the constant findings from the research on radio and television at the British Open University was that registered students wanted very different styles of programmes from 'general' listeners (or viewers) interested in watching or listening to educational programmes. Enrolled students wanted the programmes to deal with specific areas of difficulty, or to provide help or an approach that was not available through other media used in a course. They did not like, or in the end use, programmes that adopted more entertaining styles, if they could not see an educational purpose beyond mere interest or general relevance; in the most part, registered students wanted didactic programmes (Bates *et al.*, 1981). The replay facility is extremely important where the teaching intention is to go beyond mere comprehension and to develop 'higher level' learning skills of analysis, evaluation and so forth.

Perhaps the most interesting finding of the research comparing radio and audio cassettes though is that the ability to design cassettes differently can enable learners to interpret and analyse material more easily than through broadcasts, as was pointed out in the previous chapter with respect to television. The combination of all these features means that well-designed audio cassettes and CDs, when combined with print and other materials, can

Table 6.1 Control characteristics of broadcasts compared with cassettes

Broadcast characteristics	Learner implications	Cassette characteristics	Learner implications
fixed schedules	time and place dependent/ sets pace for study	available when required	convenience/ use when appropriate
mass audience	poor quality times/popular appeal/recruitment	targeted audience	learner specific
ephemeral	non-retrievable non-interruptible	permanent	repetition/ analysis
continuous	thinking 'on the run'/made for the 'average' student	stop-start facility	reflection/ activities/ individual pacing/ mastery
holistic	synthesis/ overview/ summary	segmented	integration with other media/ restructuring

result in high levels of interactivity between the learner and the learning material. The learner is not limited to a narrow range of pre-determined responses, but can be encouraged to think individually and interpretatively, although feedback on the learner's responses is still limited to what is already in the materials.

The advantages are not all on the side of cassettes or CDs. The continuous format of radio programmes can be useful for 'advanced' students who can 'think on the run', and since such programmes tend to be complete in themselves, or holistic, they are excellent for presenting a summary or an overview of a topic, where the broader picture is more important than the detail. On the other hand, the ability to stop a cassette and do an activity, and to design a cassette in discrete segments, allows students to move easily between the cassette and other learning materials, thus tightly integrating the cassette in the study process.

Another reason for the popularity of the audio cassette at the British Open University was the greater control academics felt they had over the design of the material. The production of a radio programme was more of a separate event from the design of the textual material, involving a producer who controlled the process. Audio cassette design though could be developed in parallel with the development of the textual material. Professors sometimes used a cassette recorder at home to 'rough out' the interplay between cassette and textual material. Even in this situation, it is important to produce a polished script and have the cassette properly recorded in a studio, but the 'producer' here is more of a technician than in the case of a radio programme.

COSTS

The first edition of this book (Bates, 1995a) provided detailed analyses of costs for radio and audio cassettes. These will be briefly summarized here.

Radio

Radio has the same kinds of cost variables as television, although the amounts are much less (radio has overall roughly one tenth the costs of television, according to the BBC). These variables are fixed costs or overheads, production costs and transmission costs. Once again, looking at the BBC example analysed in Bates (1995a), the BBC in 1981/82 spent £746,000 (just over US$1 million) on radio production for the Open University. The average production cost per hour for a radio programme was £5,721 (US$8,500) (including overheads), and the average cost of transmission per programme was £225 per hour for a single transmission, or £450 (US$675) for two transmissions.

As with television, the marginal radio cost per student, that is, the cost of adding one additional student, was nil, since neither the cost of production nor transmission is determined by the number of students. Thus the more students per course, the lower the unit costs for radio. Table 6.2 provides a summary of the costs of radio for a course with 32 programmes, each broadcast twice a year, over an eight-year period (the average life of a programme).

Account also needs to be taken of the utilization (listening) rate. The average listening rate for OU radio was consistently under 50 per cent. In other words, for any single programme, less than 50 per cent of the students on that course would listen to it in any fashion. In 1981 the listening rate was 47 per cent. Furthermore, it was found (Bates *et al.*, 1981) that of those that did listen, only about 20 per cent listened to more than a single transmission of the same programme.

BBC radio production costs are not the cheapest that can be found. However, the sharp separation of costs between the Open University and the

Table 6.2 Cost per study hour per course for radio (BBC–OU, 1983/4)

Over 8 years	240 students (30 per year)	1,000 students (125 per year)	5,000 students (625 per year)	10,000 students (1,250 per year)	24,000 students (3,000 per year)
Cost per study hour	£40.00 US$60.00	£9.92 US$14.88	£1.98 US$2.97	£0.99 US$1.49	£0.40 US$0.60

BBC does allow the full costs of radio, including administrative overheads, to be fully identified in this example. What is important here is not the actual costs, which will vary from institution to institution, but the relationship between the different costs, which are likely to be more consistent across institutions.

Audio cassettes

The BBC–OUP claimed that the production costs of audio cassettes are exactly the same per hour as for radio. However, as well as having access to the BBC production facilities, the Open University also operated a small audio studio, with its own technical staff. Audio production costs in 1981 through this studio averaged approximately £1,840 (US$2,760) an hour. This was about three to four times below the cost of BBC–OUP radio production (£6,321 per hour).

Even so, the two services are difficult to compare. The OU/AV services were able to produce only about 60–100 'radio programme equivalents' per year, and their production costs did not usually include fees to external speakers, use of copyright material, or overheads for buildings, heating or administration (which could amount to another 10 per cent of production costs), all of which are included in BBC–OUP costs. The technical staff in the OU–AV service were also on much lower salary scales than BBC producers and technicians. Student ratings of BBC-produced cassettes were higher than those produced by OU/AV services (3.89 compared with 3.66). Basically the two production facilities were providing different services. What it does illustrate though is that audio cassette production costs will usually be a good deal less than radio production costs.

The cost of copying, labelling, packing and mailing a 60-minute (C60) audio cassette, and the cost of the cassette itself, was calculated by the Open University to be 50 pence (75¢), including handling and clerical costs (cassettes are normally included with the mailing of the correspondence texts, which keeps down the mailing costs). Despite inflation, this figure of 50 pence remained stable between 1980 and 1988, as copying equipment and packing techniques improved. At the British Open University, students kept the cassettes, as it cost more to recover them.

As with video cassettes, audio cassette distribution is a variable cost, while the variable cost for radio transmission is nil. In other words, an extra cost of 50 pence is incurred for each student who receives an audio cassette, while for radio, the transmission cost is the same, whether one or a million students listen. The result is a graph similar to that for video cassettes in Figure 5.2 in the previous chapter.

The point at which radio becomes cheaper than audio cassettes for distribution is simply calculated by working out the number of students who could receive audio cassettes for the same cost as a radio transmission. At the Open University, it was cheaper to use one transmission when there were

Table 6.3 Comparison of costs per student study hour between radio and audio cassettes

Over 8 years	240 students (30 per year)	1,000 students (125 per year)	5,000 students (625 per year)	10,000 students (1,250 per year)	24,000 students (3,000 per year)
Radio	£40.00 US$60.00	£9.92 US$14.88	£1.98 US$2.97	£0.99 US$1.49	£0.40 US$0.60
Audio cassettes (BBC)	£26.84 US$40.25	£6.82 US$10.23	£1.76 US$2.65	£1.13 US$1.70	£0.76 US$1.15
Audio cassettes (OU–AV)	£8.17 US$12.25	£2.34 US$3.50	£0.87 US$1.30	£0.68 US$1.00	£0.58 US$0.86

225 students or more in a course, and for two transmissions radio was cheaper when there were 450 students or more in a course. Table 6.3 shows the difference between radio and audio cassette costs.

While costs for audio cassettes made by the BBC are much lower than for radio for smaller student numbers, by 1,000 students a year per course, radio starts to become cheaper. It is not surprising then that eventually audio cassettes replaced radio at the Open University. Both the cost and pedagogical advantages were too great to be ignored. It should be noted though that neither radio nor audio cassettes are usually used to replace print, but are an additional cost. Also student support costs of approximately 28 pence per student study hour should be added.

Compact discs

Production costs of compact discs will be similar to those for audio cassettes, although digital audio production has brought down production costs a little. The main costs though of scripting, collecting sound material (interviews, etc.) and editing have not changed a great deal. In addition, there is the cost of cutting the 'master' disc, which for professional recording standards can be around US$1,000 per disc. In North America, 'raw' discs can be bought for under US$1, and their light weight enables discs to be included with print materials at almost no extra cost. However, by the time the discs have been recorded, and the labels designed and printed, the distribution cost per disc is likely to be around US$3 (£1.67) each.

ORGANIZATIONAL ISSUES

In many European countries, it is the public broadcasting organizations that provide the educational radio programmes. Some public broadcasting organizations go to considerable efforts to involve the educational system in the planning and utilization of the educational radio programmes. For instance, the BBC has advisory councils for both schools and continuing education radio, and also regional education officers who liaise with schools and colleges. In a number of developing countries, educational radio is directly funded by relevant government ministries.

There are instances in some countries, particularly in Latin America, where educational institutions have negotiated access via a commercial channel, but this is rare. The Latin American Radio Literacy Schools and some universities in the USA have negotiated licences for their own radio stations. In several other countries (e.g. Thailand) the Ministry of Education has its own radio channel. In general, though, educational institutions or organizations, including Ministries of Education, have had great difficulty in directly accessing radio transmission facilities and this has been a major inhibitor to greater use of radio in education.

Even when educational institutions do obtain access via public or commercial broadcast services, the educational programmes are often relegated to a ghetto of poor transmission times. For instance, in 1988 the majority of the British Open University's radio programmes were being broadcast after 11.30 pm or before 7.00 am.

It should however be noted that the most convenient times for Open University students (between 6.00 pm and 9.00 pm) is one of the least used periods by general radio listeners (in the UK, less than 2 per cent of the general population listen to radio between 8.00 pm and 11.00 pm). In general, educational radio (as distinct from public service programming) has more or less disappeared in North America; in Europe, increased competition from commercial channels has resulted in some public broadcasting organizations dropping educational radio altogether, while in others it has become increasingly marginalized.

Audio cassettes or CDs can easily be designed and distributed without the need for 'high-tech' facilities. If a simple recording studio is not available on campus, many cities have audio recording studios that can be hired for little cost. Similarly, while the British Open University had its own high-speed cassette duplication facilities, it is not usually difficult to find commercial companies able to copy from master tapes at similar costs to those cited in this chapter. While it obviously helps to have technical support in the form of an on-campus audio-visual service, most teachers should be able to organize the production of their own material without a great deal of cost or effort.

It is the design of the accompanying printed material that is likely to be more demanding, since considerable care is needed to ensure that the students can easily find the appropriate places in the text or tape, and can move from one 'segment' to another, and from cassette to print and back again in a smooth and obvious way.

NOVELTY AND SPEED

Radio is unlikely to attract much external funding or interest, except for unusual applications, such as narrowband satellite transmission and reception. Despite the fact that few institutions make heavy use of audio cassettes, they have little novelty value, and certainly not enough to excite funding agencies. In any case they are now being replaced by CDs, which surprisingly have caused little excitement or interest in distance education, but are in fact a very low cost technology.

Speed is a major advantage of radio. Programmes can be produced and transmitted to large numbers very quickly, often within 24 hours. Thus radio can be used to link contemporary events, such as strikes, international incidents, and political events, to the course materials, as they happen. Radio can be invaluable for an institution when corrections or last-minute changes of plan are necessary in the delivery of materials.

Although cassettes and CDs are not difficult to design, their production is determined to some extent by the speed of print design and development, which can be slow. Changes will also incur additional reproduction costs.

CONCLUSIONS

Radio is extremely accessible and can be used to reach even poor people in the least developed countries. It is also likely to be of interest where low average cost per user is considered essential, although even in less developed countries, production and transmission costs can be quite high. Although print is usually substantially cheaper per student study hour, it can be combined with radio. Radio has also been used for a very wide range of educational applications and radio is a quick and easy medium for students and teachers to use.

However, newer technologies such as television (for visual presentation), compact discs (for student control), and Web-based learning are stronger instructionally. Thus in deciding to use radio, a very careful assessment needs to be made of its benefits and weaknesses for the particular target group it is to serve.

Audio cassettes or CDs integrated with print are a low-cost, highly effective one-way teaching technology, especially where access to other technologies is difficult for the groups being targeted for distance education. Audio cassettes and CD players are easy for both teachers and students to use. One or two distance teaching institutions, such as the Open University of Sri Lanka, have used audio cassettes extensively in an integrated manner and have fully exploited the control characteristics of audio cassettes. In a period of less than five years, radio transmission at the British Open University dropped from 28 hours a week to just over 6 hours a week, while the amount of audio production actually increased, but almost entirely for cassette distribution.

The British Open University distributed more than 750,000 hours of audio cassette material to students each year up to the 1990s. Perhaps the most telling comment though on the value of cassettes used in this integrated way comes from a comment made by a student during an evaluation by Durbridge (1981): 'It's like having your tutor in the room with you.' However, audio cassette or compact disc design that achieves that 'tutor over your shoulder' feeling is still comparatively rare in most institutions.

7 Web-based learning: access and teaching issues

INTRODUCTION

Given that the first courses over the Web did not really start to emerge before 1995, there has been a rapid expansion of online learning. According to a survey of universities and colleges in the USA in 2002 (Allen and Seaman, 2003), over 1.6 million students in degree-granting higher education institutions in the USA took at least one online course in the autumn semester of 2002 (11 per cent of all US higher education students), and over 500,000 (3.4 per cent) took all their courses online. These figures were expected to increase by 20 per cent by autumn 2003.

This rapid growth in online learning is not limited just to technologically advanced countries such as the United States of America. Li Chen *et al.* (2003) reported that in 2003, 1,373,000 university students in China were studying via modern 'information and communications technologies', involving a combination of satellite and terrestrial communications, and including in most cases some elements of Web-based teaching.

At the time of writing, the major use of the Web for both e-learning and distance education is asynchronous, in that materials can be accessed at any time by learners, and teachers do not have to be present while students are learning. However, we shall see in later chapters that the Internet and the Web can also be used synchronously. This chapter though will focus on the potential and limitations of the asynchronous use of the Web for teaching and learning, or 'online learning'.

THE TECHNOLOGY

The first teaching online using asynchronous communications technology started in the early 1980s, based on computer conferencing software developed by Murray Turoff in 1970 (Hiltz and Turoff, 1978, p.43). Computer conferencing or computer-mediated communication (CMC) enables asynchronous communication between dispersed individuals. Early computer conferencing depended on local area computer networks, usually within a single institution. These early developments required special software programmes such as Virtual Classroom or CoSy, and were limited to short, typed online communication between students, and similar communications between teachers and students.

Although the ability for distance students to communicate with each other asynchronously was a major advance, the lack of common technical standards, the need for core content to be handled mainly by other media such as print or broadcasting, the need for distance students to network over slow and expensive long distance telephone lines, and the lack of user-friendly tools meant that computer conferencing was limited to a relatively few enthusiasts and pioneers until the mid-1990s (for a good overview of this period, see Harasim, 1990).

The big breakthrough for online learning came with the development of the World Wide Web, and the consequent rapid spread of the Internet into many homes, offices and higher education institutions in more economically advanced countries. The first Web-based university courses started appearing around 1995. The University of British Columbia, in Vancouver, Canada, offered its first credit courses delivered entirely over the Internet to distance education students in 1996. At the same time, Murray Goldberg, a young computer science professor at the University of British Columbia, developed a software package called WebCT, specifically designed to enable Web-based courses to be offered over the Internet.

WebCT rapidly became popular. In 2000, WebCT, which by then had been bought by an American company, had sold over one million student licences in 80 countries. WebCT and similar tools are easy to use by both students and teachers and are highly reliable. Now there are many other course management/course authoring tools on the market or developed by institutions for their own use.

At the same time, the development of the Web and increasing competition between telecommunications companies across North America resulted in the creation of local Internet service providers (ISPs). Increased competition, free local calls and flat rate pricing for Internet access has led to low charges for Internet services, especially in North America, where Internet charges can be as little as US$30 a month. It is not surprising then that by 2003, more than two-thirds of homes in Canada and the USA had Internet access.

Nevertheless, bandwidth has been a constraint on the use of the Internet for teaching. Most homes were originally limited to modem speeds of between 28 and 56 kilobits (kbs) per second. The development of DSL or ADSL (asynchronous digital subscriber line) and cable modems has enabled speeds of up to 2 megabits to be delivered over standard telephone or cable TV services. This in turn enables relatively good quality streaming of audio and not so good quality streaming of video. In countries such as Canada, USA, Hong Kong, South Korea, Singapore and the United Kingdom, at least half of the homes with Internet access had ADSL or cable modems by 2003.

Although the use of fibre optic backbones and wireless networks are rapidly increasing, especially on campuses, widespread high-speed access (1 gigabit = 100 mbps per second) to the desktop is unlikely to be widely available in homes and offices until at least 2010.

Audio and video can be streamed (i.e. downloaded) or stored on CDs and DVDs. However, two-way audio and video communication over the Internet will be relatively limited until high-speed access is widespread, although mobile telephony is increasingly integrating with the Internet. (Chapters 9 and 10 discuss synchronous Internet technologies in more detail.) These technical constraints have resulted in most uses of the Web for teaching being limited mainly to the use of text, still graphics and simple animations. It is this asynchronous use of the Web that has provided most experience in online learning, and it is this particular use of technology that will be discussed in this chapter.

ACCESS

One reason for the widespread use of online learning in many institutions is that most students now have access to the Internet and their own computer. However, one must be careful in making this assumption. The University of British Columbia, for instance, is a large public research university in Canada that requires very high grades from high school before students are admitted. Most of the students come from relatively affluent families. Consequently, over 90 per cent of students entering UBC already have a computer and Internet access at home. UBC is a public but not an open university, and can therefore require students to get a computer, if necessary, and there are bursaries and scholarships available to students admitted to the university who could not otherwise afford a computer and Internet access.

On the other hand, Vancouver Community College, across town, is also a publicly funded institution, but many of its students come from the poorer part of the city and home computer ownership and Internet access amongst its students is much lower compared with UBC. Although Vancouver Community College does a good job in ensuring computer and Internet access for students on the college premises, it cannot assume that all students will have Internet and computer access at home. Thus compared with UBC, it is much more difficult for Vancouver Community College to require students to provide their own computer.

Furthermore, home ownership of computers breaks the general trend for domestic electronic equipment. In general, low-income working families have been relatively early adopters of 'entertainment' technology such as colour and satellite TV, video cassettes, CD players, DVDs and mobile phones. With respect to computer technology though, ownership is almost linearly related to income: the higher the income, the more likely there is to be a computer and Internet access within the home.

Concerns about computer and Internet access in the home have slowed the adoption of online learning at a number of open universities. Although the first institution to offer online teaching to fully distance students (in 1988), the British Open University has very cautiously adopted online learning, despite its claim to be the British e-university. Even in 2002, students were *required* to access a computer in only 17 of its 500 courses (mainly in the technology area), although online components were optional in many more courses. The concern to offer open access to all students has proved more important to the British Open University than the benefits claimed for online learning. Thus it has offered predominantly optional use of online learning in its courses.

The appropriateness of online learning therefore will depend very much on the groups being targeted. If the target groups are mainly young entrepreneurs, people working in technologically advanced companies, IT professionals, or relatively affluent middle class students (in for instance private colleges or universities), then online learning may be practical in even relatively less economically advanced countries. If on the other hand the target groups are adults with low levels of literacy, industrial or agricultural workers, teachers in remote rural schools or in schools with no or unreliable electricity, or unemployed or low-income workers, then online learning is not an appropriate choice, unless special arrangements can be made to provide such learners with low cost or free access to computers and the Internet.

Caution though is needed in jumping to conclusions about computer and Internet ownership. Of all technologies, this is the most dynamic. The number of Internet users in Canada who were female rose from 27 per cent to 51 per cent in one year (1997). Based on data collected in the US census in September 2001, the US Department of Commerce (2002) reported that 54 per cent of the population were using the Internet – an increase of 26 million in 13 months – and 66 per cent used computers. More significantly, the same report indicated that 90 per cent of children between the ages of 5 and 17 (or 48 million) used computers. Computer ownership amongst blacks and Hispanics and those in lower income households was increasing at a faster rate than for whites, Asians and those in upper income families, although from a lower base. The study also found that computers in schools substantially narrowed the gap in computer usage rates for children from high and low income families. Thus it appears that the digital divide is narrowing in the USA. The next big jump forward in terms of technology access is likely to be in broadband Internet access and mobile computing.

The general tendency of post-secondary teachers is to *underestimate* public access to Internet technologies, based on their own generally slow adoption of entertainment technologies. The clear lesson is that anyone considering using Internet or Web-based technology for teaching needs to obtain reliable figures about access specifically *for the target groups that they are intending to serve,* before making decisions as to whether this is an 'accessible' technology. As it can take up to two years from the time of making a decision to offering the first Web-based course, it is also important to observe the trend in access over time.

TEACHING AND LEARNING IMPLICATIONS

There are several important educational features that distinguish asynchronous computer mediated communication from other technologies. The first is that the learner can be in regular (but not necessarily continuous) contact with teachers and other learners, even though the teacher and other learners are not physically present. Second, communication is not synchronous, but forwarded, stored and accessed at the learner's (and teacher's) convenience. Third, a vast array of digital resources can be accessed through electronic networks, and downloaded into the learner's or teacher's own computer, and stored for later use. The interaction is not so much *with* the computer, as *through* it, to other people or sources of information.

Types of online learning

With the rapid expansion of online learning has come a rapid expansion of different forms of online learning. We saw in Chapter 1 that there is a continuum of online learning, as set out by Bates and Poole (2003). Even this categorization oversimplifies the possible combinations of e-learning and face-to-face teaching. For instance, Royal Roads University in Victoria, Canada, combines sessions on campus with long periods when students are off-campus, studying online. In this section, the various ways in which online learning has been used for teaching will be explored.

Supplementing classroom teaching

From about 1996 onwards, when the World Wide Web was first applied to teaching, classroom teachers started to incorporate the Internet into their regular classroom teaching. Hybrid, blended or mixed mode are all terms used for integrating the Internet into regular classroom teaching. This is still by far and away the most prevalent form of online learning.

There are several ways to supplement classroom teaching. The teacher may bring in resources from the Internet to illustrate a lecture or provoke discussion. These resources may be downloaded live during the lecture, or may be images downloaded previously and stored on the teacher's computer (thus avoiding the need for Internet access in the room, or slow downloading). In order to use the Internet to supplement classroom teaching, there must be an LCD projector, and of course the teacher must have a computer in the room.

Online discussion forums can be used to continue discussion after lectures, using software such as WebCT, Blackboard or dedicated computer conferencing software such as First Class. Students may be asked to do Web searches (see for instance: http://webquest.sdsu.edu for a structured way of doing this) or students may be asked to review recommended Web sites as part of their studies. Textbooks have started to appear with dedicated Web sites, or accompanying CD-ROMs, which provide video clips, animation, student activities and tests based on the textbook.

The next step in supplementing classroom teaching is to require the students to use computers during class time. Software such as Silicon Chalk (www.siliconchalk.com) allows students using wireless-connected personal computers to download the teacher's words and any illustrations from an electronic whiteboard used by the teacher. In this way, students can store and edit each 'class'. In addition, each student can communicate electronically with the teacher during the lecture in several ways. For instance, students can indicate on their computer when they do not understand something, and this will appear as a blinking sign on the lecturer's screen while the lecturer is talking. This use of technology, however, is still supporting just the 'transmission' mode of teaching and requires all students to have a computer with wireless facilities and dedicated software.

A different approach to teaching with computers in the classroom is to enable students to do individual or collaborative work in class by going online, finding resources, and assembling a report, which they then present and discuss with the rest of the class. This is a more learner-centred, active approach to learning, and is a good way to introduce students to more independent learning methods within nevertheless a controlled environment. Again, this requires students to have access to computers in the class, and multiple access points to the Internet (usually through a wireless network). This approach may also require special software to be purchased or leased, and students to be skilled in using the software. The teacher also needs to be well prepared, with clearly structured activities, and must be aware of suitable online resources for the projects.

The most common way though of supporting classroom teaching is to create a course Web site, for use by students outside of classroom time. The development of software platforms such as WebCT and Blackboard has encouraged teachers to create their own Web-based learning materials that can be added to the course Web site. Such sites can range from the very simple to quite elaborate. The following are some of the resources that can be made available on a course Web site:

- PowerPoint presentations used in lectures (very popular with academic departments as it reduces the costs of copying and distributing lecture notes).
- Course reading lists.
- Selected links to discipline related Web sites, including online journals and readings, and library holdings.
- Course schedules, including due assignment dates.

- Assignments, exam questions.
- Self-assessment tests.
- Online discussion forums, for post-lecture discussions.
- Biographies of the course teacher or teachers.
- Student biographies.
- Original materials created by the teacher or colleagues not yet in published form (e.g. research data, digitized photographs, personal reflections).

Although a teacher can build up such resources over time, there comes a point where the management and maintenance of a course site can become extremely time consuming. Furthermore, student workload can be increased to the point where few students are using much of the material available. Students may need to be given guidelines as to what is essential and what is optional in terms of the resources available online. As both teacher and student workloads increase, the teacher should start considering alternative approaches to course design, including a reduction of classroom time, sharing or joint creation of learning resources with colleagues, redesign of the course, and obtaining more technical and instructional support. An even better approach for the teacher would be to sit down with instructional design and Web programming staff to consider options and strategies before creating any online materials.

Supplementing print- or broadcast-based distance teaching

At the same time as classroom teachers were moving to online components of their teaching, so too were many print-based 'correspondence' distance education operations. Most distance education programmes began their use of the Internet by adding online elements to existing print and broadcast-based materials, such as e-mail communication between teacher and students, submission of assignments as e-mail attachments, and online discussion forums. Because of the concern about access, the use of the Internet was in such cases usually optional, an extra resource for those who could afford to use it.

However, there are some problems with the strategy of adding e-learning to existing print-based distance teaching materials (the same arguments incidentally apply also to creating optional online components for classroom based teaching). Students at universities with the same course offered both face-to-face and by print-based distance education will have been successfully taking the same examination by distance without these online additions. Because the print-based courses are designed as self-contained, integrated packages, the additional computer-based activities become extra work for teachers, design teams and more importantly, for students, who often do not see the added benefits for the extra work, particularly if the online part is optional.

Print-based courses often have open start and complete dates, but adding a discussion forum means that students will be at different points in the course at the same time, making it difficult to organize adequate discussions. Ruhe and Qayyum (2000) conducted a study of 14 courses from five institutions in British Columbia using a variety of learning technologies. They found that when online learning was added to pre-designed print-based courses, students often rated the value of the new online technology low, a term they coined as 'value-reduced'.

Also, the optional use of any kind of technology or medium raises questions about costs and effectiveness. Adding online learning as an option increases costs for both the institution and for students, and students often make the decision to avoid the extra time and costs involved if they can manage without the online component. This in turn makes it difficult for an institution to justify investment in resources that are by and large not used by students.

More importantly, the print-based and broadcast-based distance programmes were designed to achieve their objectives without the use of the additional online components. Although e-mail communication has the immediate effect of speeding up communication between student and teacher compared with the mail service, the other elements, such as online resources and discussion forums, are in most cases just bolted on as optional components. Thus they are not fully integrated with the course design, and in particular, the unique functions of these additional resources cannot be fully exploited if they are to remain optional. There is also an equity issue in making some components of a course optional. If there is any value in the optional components of a course, those who cannot access the optional components will be at a disadvantage to those who can.

It was for these reasons that the Distance Education and Technology unit at UBC decided not to add online functions other than e-mail and the submission of assignments to existing print-based courses, but to concentrate resources on creating new online courses from scratch. However, even courses designed from scratch as fully online may also include heavy use of printed materials such as textbooks and printed collections of journal articles. The difference is that students at UBC could not take the newly designed distance courses without using the Web site.

Mixed mode

In general, Internet-based activities have been incorporated into regular face-to-face classes as an added resource, without reducing classroom time. However, in what are still a few rare cases, teachers have actually reduced (but not eliminated) the number of face-to-face classes to allow for more online learning.

It would seem that given the extra work for both teachers and students in creating and using additional online materials, and the need to maintain personal contact in campus-based institutions, a mixed mode approach would be more common. Research conducted at the University of Central Florida found that although fully online students did just as well as students in regular face-to-face classes, students in mixed mode classes did better (Dziuban *et al.*, 2001). There appear though to be major logistical and philosophical barriers to greater use of mixed mode teaching based on reduced classroom time.

Many departments allocate teaching load based on hours of teaching related to time in the classroom. The North American semester system is based on a credit load for instance related to classroom time (three hours per week = three credits). Some funding agencies even base student financial aid solely on the hours spent in class. Classroom space is allocated often on formulae based on three or six credit sections. If one of the three classroom times per week is dropped, the classroom space cannot easily be reallocated. Thus there are strong logistical and administrative reasons for supporting the status quo.

However, probably the most significant barrier to combining reduced classroom presence with increased online activity is the lack of strong and tested pedagogical models for this form of teaching. It is not just a question of considering the design of the online teaching time; considerable thought also needs to be given to the best way to use the time when students are in class with the teacher. This raises the fundamental question as to what is unique or educationally advantageous in face-to-face teaching, and when can face-to-face teaching be replaced with gain or without loss by online teaching.

There is now some experience emerging in the use of mixed mode teaching that may help answer these questions. The Pew Foundation in the USA launched an important initiative between 1999 and 2003, focused on a particularly prevalent problem in North American universities, the very large first and second year courses with often over a thousand students per course. Traditionally, these courses tend to be broken up into smaller sections with young teaching assistants (usually graduate students) responsible for each section. As a result the teaching is often of a poor quality.

The Pew Foundation programme, under the leadership of Carol Twigg of the Center for Academic Transformation at Rensselaer Polytechnic Institute, New York State, worked with professors and teachers in over 30 participating institutions across the United States to redesign such large classes. Each institution received grants of US$200,000. Typically, many labour-intensive activities, such as presenting content and grading exams and papers, were transferred to technology such as Blackboard or WebCT. The subject matter was broken up into modules, with full-time faculty members working with a course co-ordinator and a group of 'preceptors' (usually graduate students), moving across each of the modules. The faculty members provided intellectual leadership for the course, and the course coordinator oversaw the course management. Preceptors were responsible for interacting with students, monitoring student progress and occasionally grading assignments (http://www.center.rpi.edu/PewGrant.html).

Twigg has claimed major successes for the programme. For instance, she claims improved learning outcomes in 20 of the 30 projects and generally improved course completion rates, better student attitudes, and increased student satisfaction (Twigg, 2003). Twigg also claimed cost savings averaging 40 per cent per institution (with some wide variations between institutions). There are some doubts about the savings, as some of the institutions claim that the analysis omitted some key hidden costs, and the infusion of $200,000 a project adds a further twist to making cost comparisons. Nevertheless, Twigg provides convincing evidence of the benefits of the redesign of traditional classes using technology, and outlines several different 'mixed mode' design models (supplemental, replacement, emporium, fully online, buffet).

There are still many contexts in which face-to-face teaching is likely to have advantages over technology-based teaching. Particularly important are teaching contexts dealing with emotional topics, such as counselling, or where children have deep psychological problems that need to be addressed by a caring and loving teacher. Young children often need the security and confidence provided by a teacher acting *in loco parentis* in order to learn well. Many face-to-face teaching contexts can be replaced by technology only at great expense. For instance, if a school is already equipped with laboratories and equipment, creating a simulated experiment digitally is probably not justified. On the other hand, if many schools in a district have no such physical laboratory facilities, it may be cheaper and more effective to buy computers and off-the-shelf simulated experiments.

Therefore the answer to the question about whether face-to-face teaching can be replaced by technology will vary according to context. It will depend on the needs of the students, the nature of the subject matter, the chosen perspective on teaching, and the resources and organizational support available. In other words, the **ACTIONS** model will need to be applied within each teaching context. Decisions need to be taken at two levels: what is the best alternative between the different modes of teaching (face-to-face, Web-supplemented, Web-dependent, mixed mode, fully online), and within the classroom model, what should be done online and what done in class?

Fully online

These will be online courses with no classroom contact, although in most cases the online component will be supplemented by or dependent on other media such as textbooks.

In a few cases, some whole institutions have gone or are going fully online. The Open University of Catalonia in Spain and the privately owned University of Phoenix Online in the USA have between 20,000 to 40,000 students each, and the University of Maryland University College has 85,000 students. Most of the courses from these institutions are fully online. These are truly 'virtual universities' in that not only are they fully distance, but also fully digital. Other universities – or university programmes – moving fully online are the Virtual University component of Tec de Monterrey in Mexico, the graduate programme of Athabasca University in Canada, and the World Campus of Penn State University.

Several 'dual-mode' institutions have also moved over to fully online development for all new distance courses, although such institutions often carry a large backlog of older print-based courses at the same time. Thus the Distance Education and Technology unit at the University of British Columbia has been creating all its courses fully online since 1997. Nevertheless, by 2003 only 60 of its 110 courses were fully online, with still a large backlog of print-based courses, especially for courses with higher enrolments (200+). In general, even by 2004, very few higher education institutions had moved all their teaching to fully online.

A typical fully online course will consist of one or more of the following:

- A Web site that acts as a study guide, including an orientation to the course, course objectives, list of contents, recommended readings, course schedule, assignment questions.
- Course modules or blocks, consisting of periods of study ending with an assignment, that contain content, readings, student activities and feedback.
- Original material posted by the teacher(s), including text, research papers, and raw data in the form of digital photos, etc.
- Online discussion forums.
- Access to web-based resources, such as urls for related Web sites, online journals and library resources.
- Computer-marked tests or essay assignments submitted online.
- Print-based readings, such as textbooks or collections of printed journal articles.
- Other media, such as audio or video clips, animations or simulations, embedded in the Web site, or sent separately on an accompanying compact disc.

Although there are variations on such standard designs, and different platforms used, this approach to Web-based teaching has become fairly standard for fully online courses.

THE RATIONALE FOR WEB-BASED LEARNING

In most North American universities, increasing access to higher education has not been the main reason for adopting online learning, especially in distance education. The main driver has been to improve the quality of learning. Part of the popularity of Web-based teaching is that it can to some extent automate traditional approaches to teaching based on information transmission and testing. However, online learning can also be used to develop new approaches to learning that better reflect the needs of a knowledge-based society.

The same but better

There are two ways to improve the quality of learning. One is to enable more students to achieve the same learning goals to a higher level. Thus for instance if 75 per cent of students pass a multiple-choice Mathematics examination with an average grade of 75, and the introduction of online learning results in 80 per cent of students passing the same multiple-choice examination with an average of 80 per cent, then it could be argued that online learning has improved the quality of learning (provided the second group of students was a matched sample with the first group).

Certainly, Web-based online learning using platforms such as WebCT do allow for self-assessment, multiple-choice testing, and continuing revision, thus providing students more opportunities for self-study than in a traditional classroom. Where careful comparative studies have been made, students learning at a distance through online learning do as well as students taking the same courses face-to-face. Also, experience at UBC is that course completion rates improve by between 5 to 10 per cent when moving from print-based courses to online courses. This was due mainly to moving to fixed start and completion dates for a course offering (with print-based courses students could spread their studying over several semesters). Fixed start and completion dates were necessary because the discussion forums require the students to keep working roughly at the same pace through the course. Online distance education compared with print-based distance education seems to provide more structure and study discipline, but this is not a unique feature of online learning – the same would apply to classroom teaching.

Although online learning seems to improve completion rates compared with print-based correspondence courses, it is much more difficult to find evidence that it leads to greater efficiency in meeting traditional learning outcomes. It seems to do no better and no worse than classroom teaching in this respect, following the well documented results of 'no significant difference' when media are compared.

Different and better

However, the main educational rationale for online learning is that it enables students to learn in a different way from traditional classroom teaching (or print-based distance education). In a knowledge-based society, there is a need for skills such as seeking, analysing and applying information, independent and lifelong learning, problem-solving, creative thinking, and teamwork. The education of knowledge-based workers requires an approach that enables them to learn both inside and outside conventional higher education institutions. Such learners must be encouraged to analyse and criticize, to offer alternative solutions and approaches and to take risks. This kind of learning cannot be easily done in large lecture classes or through mass communications such as broadcasting (see Bates, 2000, for more discussion of this issue).

As a result, in North America particularly, there was a growing reaction in the 1990s to objectivist approaches to teaching and learning that were then predominant, at least at an undergraduate level. It is no coincidence that online learning arrived at a point in time when constructivist approaches to teaching were being advocated in North American universities (see for instance, Jonassen *et al.*, 1995). For constructivists, reflection and discussion are key activities through which knowledge is constructed.

The asynchronous nature of online teaching, enabling students to control to some extent the pace and timing of their learning, allows for and encourages reflection. Online forums provide the opportunity for students to test ideas and build and construct knowledge through collaborative learning. Thus online learning became seen as a valuable tool for furthering constructivist approaches to teaching and learning; online learning was seized upon as a way of teaching *differently.*

THE CORE EDUCATIONAL CHARACTERISTICS OF WEB-BASED LEARNING

Web-based learning has certain core educational characteristics associated with the technology. These can be considered under presentational features, structure, and skills.

Presentational characteristics

Web-based learning is primarily text- and graphics-based. There are obvious cost reasons for this, as it is relatively easy to create text as PowerPoint, html or pdf files, and creating graphics, animation or video is more time-consuming, technically challenging, and thus more expensive. Furthermore, audio and video require at least medium network speeds (DSL or cable connections) for streaming, although CD-ROMs or DVDs can be combined with a Web site where digital files are large. The Web enables considerable presentational enhancements compared with print. Greater use can be made of colour and illustration (colour printing is expensive). Relatively simple animation, using off-the-shelf software, can be done.

The need to keep information, including graphics, to the size of a computer screen has both positive and negative design implications. Information needs to be presented in relatively small chunks, thus facilitating the absorption of information. However, it is more difficult to present complex or detailed information on a single screen, or a sequence of screens, compared with a textbook. There is though an underlying concern that Web-only learning may lack the integration, depth and coherence of print-based learning. This is an important area for research.

Sometimes, papers or articles are loaded onto the Web as pdf files, then printed by the student, or read on screen. My preference in general has been to use the Web more as a study guide, with detailed reading done outside the environment of the computer, using printed textbooks that students purchase, and collections of journal articles that are copied, collated, printed and physically distributed to students. This is usually cheaper for students than the students printing pdf files at home (and copyright clearance is easier).

In general, audio-visual media have been underexploited in Web-based teaching to date, mainly due to the cost of production and limitations in Internet bandwidth. However, with modern digital video-cameras, it is not expensive or difficult for instance to interview experts, record and explain experiments, record field visits, or observe naturally occurring phenomena, all of which can be recorded, edited and streamed at the appropriate point in a course. Such use of video or even audio would enrich the learning process, and in particular would help students move from the concrete to the abstract, and vice versa.

However, audio and video for the Web need to be designed differently from their use in broadcasting. Digital compression, and the need to break the material into tightly focused and relatively short clips integrated with Web-based text, demand a particular style of production and editing, and require some specialist equipment, such as video compression software, digital editing suites, and possibly CD-ROM or DVD copying facilities. Creating digital audio-visual material from scratch therefore does add cost to course development, but once produced, digital materials can be used in many different contexts.

The main presentational limitation of Web-based teaching is the high level of literacy and keyboard skills required. Asynchronous text-based communication lacks the spontaneity and the non-verbal communication signs that can help personalize the teaching and learning process.

Structure

A Web site can be structured in a linear manner, in the same way as a textbook. Thus, a narrative text or lecture can be accessed sequentially through a Web site. The media used in the Web site could be text, audio or video, but the structure would still be linear. A linear sequence though does not fully exploit the possibilities that a Web structure offers.

For instance, the World Wide Web is based on hypertext, which links Web 'pages' together. Different pages may rest on different servers around the world. Thus while a learner may start to work through the Web materials in a linear manner, at various points they can 'take off' to other sites, and explore these, then return to the main or 'home' site. In educational terms, the home site acts as a study guide, with links to many other sources of information. The learner retains more control over the links to follow up, and indeed, the teaching may be designed to encourage Web exploration, so that the teacher cannot predict where the learner will go.

For instance, a History teacher may spend some time discussing with a class the criteria or principles of historical research, using examples that the teacher draws from the Web. Using such criteria or principles, students can then be asked to explore in small groups the history of different cities, using Web- and print-based sources, resulting in group-constructed Web sites that provide the history of each city. The results could then be critiqued by the other groups and by the teacher, using the criteria discussed at the beginning of the course.

Learning objects enable other structures for courses on the Web. A learning object can be anything from a single graphic or paragraph of text, a single slide of a physiological cell, a self-assessed test, a simulated laboratory experiment, or a short module of teaching (see for instance, http://www. reusability. org/read/). As well as the object being created in a digital format, a whole set of other data can be digitally 'tagged' to the object, such as verbal descriptors, transaction software for charging a small fee for accessing the source, copyright holder information, links to similar objects, etc. The importance of the 'tags' against each object is that they enable Internet search engines to locate appropriate learning objects matching the descriptors used by the person searching for the object. A course designer then could build a teaching programme with many such links integrated within the overall teaching context, without having to create those objects from scratch.

However, this would merely be placing learning objects in a linear structure constructed by the teacher. A more innovative design would be to place more responsibility on the learner to find and analyse learning objects in such a way that the collection and ordering of learning objects helps the learner better to understand a subject area. Thus the teacher or course designer would provide a framework for the course, in the sense of defining the overall topic of study, possible criteria for success in learning, and possible 'starting points' for finding information, but would allow the learner to 'construct' their own course, by assembling learning objects and providing interpretation, analysis and conceptual links between objects. In other words, the learner would need to find and structure subject content (see McGreal, 2004, for a more detailed discussion of learning objects).

Thus one characteristic of Web-based teaching is that it enables a variety of ways to structure knowledge and to organize learning, thus providing teachers with more choice in design, but also adding complexity to the design process. Also, the structuring of knowledge and learning that the Web enables raises many questions about the nature of learning, the role of the teacher, the role of the learner, and methods of assessment. These questions will be discussed further in the final chapter.

Skills

Web-based learning can be used to develop a wide range of academic skills and to accommodate a variety of approaches to teaching and learning. At the same time, certain approaches to teaching have tended to be given greater attention in Web-based teaching.

Rote learning, comprehension and understanding

Those teachers wishing to take a more behaviourist or objectivist approach can give students tasks that are broken down into small units of work. Using a course platform such as WebCT or Blackboard, each unit of activity can be accompanied by immediate feedback according to the learner's response to the online materials. Feedback can take the form of test results or automated responses. Tests may require the student to click on multiple choice answer options on the screen. The computer will respond with the words 'correct' or 'wrong', or sounds such as cheering or boos. Feedback can include remedial activities to be repeated until the student has mastery over the item (defined usually as 100 per cent correct performance). Behaviourists particularly value this use of technology, as it allows for repetition, for 'objective' assessment and for tight control and management of the learning activities. This use of Web-based learning is found mainly in empirical sciences or engineering.

Knowledge construction

However, these more objectivist approaches to teaching are not in fact the ones where the most interest has been shown in e-learning in schools, colleges and universities. Most publications on Web-based learning focus on helping learners to 'construct' their own meanings of concepts and ideas presented in the course or offered by other learners.

Harasim *et al.* (1995) provide a good description of knowledge construction:

> Understanding ... grows out of interacting with information and ideas – for example, reconstructing ideas, setting ideas within frameworks, viewing multiple perspectives on ideas, questioning implications of ideas, and posing theories or hypotheses about ideas ... the learner actively constructs knowledge by formulating ideas into words, and these ideas are built upon through reactions and responses of others to the formulation (p.98).

A lot of the literature implies that just by creating the 'right online environment' these skills will be developed. However, this does not fit my experience. When well designed, online discussion forums can enable learners to construct their own meanings, increase their depth of understanding of key concepts and principles in a subject, and apply concepts and ideas to new contexts. It is less clear though from the literature on online knowledge construction whether learners develop new knowledge that has not been constructed and validated before (although it may be new to them). It is also dangerous to assume that knowledge construction will always lead to better understanding of a subject area.

Students need to be aware of the epistemological requirements of a subject and ensure that their understandings are consistent with the rules for validating knowledge in the subject area. Indeed there is increasing evidence that even good general moderating does not automatically lead to the development of knowledge construction in ways that are important within a particular subject domain.

Moderators of online discussion forums then need to work to ensure that students are meeting the necessary academic standards and values in their online discussion, such as evidence-based argument, setting argument within a conceptual framework and relating discussion to the concepts and ideas covered in the course materials. If not, the discussion can easily deteriorate into a swapping of unsubstantiated opinions among students.

Critical thinking

The development of critical thinking skills is another argument put forward for Web-based learning. There are several reasons why educators favour asynchronous computer conferencing for more reflective, critical thinking. The opportunity for students to challenge course materials, to challenge other students' conceptions and arguments within a course, and to find and compare multiple and perhaps conflicting sources of information should all help promote critical thinking.

Because computer conferences can be archived and analysed later, it is easier to evaluate these discussions than those that occur in the classroom. Despite this, once again it is difficult to find in the literature studies that relate specific design features of online teaching to the development of empirically validated critical thinking skills, although Scardamalia and Bereiter (1999) and MacKnight (2001) provide some guidelines on facilitating critical thinking skills and knowledge construction online within school settings.

Thus for guidance to teachers on how to develop critical thinking skills online, we need to go outside the literature of Web-based learning. Meyers (1986) and Garrison (1991) provide some general guidelines on developing critical thinking. Brookfield (1987) provides guidance on developing critical thinking in adult learners. Researchers at Washington State University have developed a critical thinking rubric that improves the teaching of critical thinking skills (http://wsuctproject.wsu.edu/ctr.htm). The following site provides a list of over 200 techniques for improving creative thinking: http://www.mycoted.com/creativity/techniques/index.php. In most cases, though, these findings need to be adapted to and validated within the online learning environment. Thus Web-based learning provides the *potential* for the development of critical thinking skills, but there is still a need for active intervention by moderators and designers to ensure that critical thinking skills are actually developed.

Problem-based learning

Another major trend in education is the move to problem-based learning, and this is an area where Web-based learning has been used successfully. In a UBC course on forest ecology, students take a 'virtual' walk through the forest (a digital video). As they move the cursor across the screen, different questions pop up, such as 'Why is this plant growing here but not over there?' To answer such questions, students were given partial clues, by clicking on the question, then searched a database of information on soil mechanics, botany, weather effects, etc. and also conducted some virtual experiments in order to answer the questions. Students bring their solutions to classes where they are discussed with the teacher and other students.

Collaborative learning

One great advantage of online learning is the opportunity for students separated by time and place to work together on a common task. Learning to work together online is an increasingly important workplace skill, but it also provides opportunities for students to share experiences, to learn how to work collaboratively, and to test and develop their own ideas, without being physically present. It is particularly valuable for courses where students are from different countries or cultures, and for continuing professional development, where participants have relevant professional experiences to share and draw from.

There is evidence that using the Web for collaborative learning is not without its own problems. The teacher must pay particular attention to ensure that students are clear as to their tasks, that they have adequate resources available for the tasks, and that there are clear guidelines for working collaboratively. There must be procedures in place to deal with conflict resolution within groups, and for dealing with students who do not participate fully, or at all, in group assignments. Assessment of individual students can be particularly challenging when they are working in groups. In this respect, once again, the general literature on collaborative learning applies just as strongly to online as to face-to-face teaching (see the journal *Distance Education*, Vol. 23, No. 1, for several articles on online collaborative learning).

A paradigm shift?

Does Web-based asynchronous learning then represent a true 'paradigm shift' in education, as claimed by Harasim *et al.* (1995) and more recently by Peters (2002)? Harasim *et al.* argues that online learning leads to knowledge construction, and Peters argues that online learning promotes self-autonomy in the learner and lateral rather than linear thinking. Peters lists ten 'functions' of 'virtual learning spaces' (p.87):

presentation of information	storing
retrieval	communication
collaboration	browsing
multimedia	hypertext/hypermedia
simulation	virtual reality

He then argues that these ten functions lead to specific educational activities:

- The computer is a universal multimedia teaching/learning medium.
- Learners can compile and access files of 'knowledge'.
- The computer enables rapid access to distributed knowledge.
- Computers can require interaction with learning materials.
- The computer enables collaboration and communication.
- The computer enables the simulation of dynamic models.
- The computer enables and simplifies discovery learning.

This is why Peters stated earlier (p.85) that:

> The teaching and learning situations in ... virtual spaces are structurally different from those in corresponding real spaces. Corresponding teaching and learning behaviour can be derived from [the educational benefits of virtual spaces] which in some points deviate decisively from that experienced in real learning spaces.

I believe that Peters is overstating the argument about virtual learning being a paradigm shift, at least in terms of current practice. In the first example he gives of a pedagogical shift, Peters argues that virtual environments create self-autonomous learners. However, does this occur merely by immersing students in a virtual environment? It is more likely that students need to develop the skills of self-autonomy gradually, with considerable guidance from a teacher, and this is no different in virtual space than in a classroom.

Six of Peters' ten 'functions' of virtual spaces (presentation, storage and retrieval of information, communication, collaboration and browsing) are not unique to virtual spaces. Computers may make these functions more efficient, but they do not necessarily change the quality of the experience. Similarly with respect to his 'six activity fields', computers again may make these activities more efficient or convenient, but most of these activities are also 'experienced in real learning spaces'. For instance, discovery learning is not dependent on a computer (ask any parent of a young toddler).

Peters, discussing the communications functions of e-mail, electronic noticeboards, and computer conferences states (p.98) that 'the innovations here go far beyond the forms of communication in traditional studying'. Again, though, on close examination of his argument it could be argued that *in educational terms* these electronic functions merely replicate what happens in real space in schools and campuses. They do not provide a new learning experience. For instance, if we have face-to-face classes of one teacher to twenty students, could not all the functions of online communication be easily replicated in a real classroom? Or is there for instance a *qualitative* difference between asynchronous written communication online and spoken discourse in a classroom? If so, what is gained and what is lost in educational terms? Peters is silent on this issue.

Peters raises some fascinating questions about the *potential* of the space behind the screen. He clearly believes that virtual space has the potential for new and educationally useful forms of learning, but if so, these new forms of learning still remain to be identified and validated. As he points out, one common technique for 'anchoring' the learning experience in virtual space is the use of metaphors, such as discussion forums, mailboxes and other icons. However, the danger of transferring metaphors from face-to-face experience is that we do not exploit the differences of virtual space. Until we reach the point of creating unique formats and approaches to learning that cannot be replicated in the classroom, the claim that online learning is a *pedagogical* paradigm shift remains to be validated.

At the same time, I would agree that there is a paradigm shift in the *organization of teaching* resulting from the use of the Web. Students and teachers no longer need to be in the same time or space for effective learning to occur. This leads to greater flexibility and convenience for both learners and teachers, and probably more effective use of time on task, therefore enabling more effective learning.

Summarizing the core educational characteristics of online learning

It can be seen then that online learning can be used to support a wide range of learning objectives, and there appear to be some clear advantages over print-based distance education in terms of content presentation and structure, and in terms of skills development, provided that the course design fully exploits such features. It is more difficult though to identify unique educational characteristics of online learning that cannot also be found in face-to-face teaching.

INTERACTION

Web-based learning provides several kinds of interaction. Asynchronous computer conferencing is quite different from the temporal, non-linear, spontaneous nature of synchronous environments (which will be discussed in Chapter 9), and communicating through typing is quite different from communicating orally.

Interaction with the learning materials

Students can interact through the screen using forms and interactive software such as multiple choice testing. Feedback can be hidden and provided on 'cue', encouraging students to be actively engaged. Self-administered tests provide feedback to students on their comprehension or coverage of a subject area, feedback to teachers on topic areas where students are having difficulty, or assessment of students on their comprehension. Using standard test software built into course development platforms, students can be automatically assessed and graded on their comprehension of course materials.

Student activities could include doing readings and responding to questions about the readings posted on the course Web site. Software such as WebCT and Blackboard provides a 'notes' tool that allows students to record their typed responses to questions on the Web page. These notes are automatically linked to the relevant Web page, facilitating student revision.

Other student activities might include conducting a structured approach to finding and analysing Web-based materials, reviewing Web-based content in the subject area, or downloading and editing information from the Web to create students' own e-portfolios of work. More advanced activities might include composing music using software that converts musical notation to audio, entering data to test concepts through simulations, or participating in games or decision-making scenarios controlled by the computer.

In other words, with good design and adequate resources, Web-based instruction can provide high levels of student interaction with the learning materials. There are strong economic advantages in exploiting the human-machine interaction possibilities of Web-based learning, because intense student-machine interaction increases the time students spend on learning, and reduces the time spent by the teacher on teaching. Once again, though, this aspect of Web-based learning tends to be underexploited, due as much to a lack of imagination or vision as to a lack of resources.

Interaction between students and teacher

Asynchronous online communication enables several important interactions between students and teachers (see Salmon, 2000, and Bates and Poole, 2003, for more detailed discussions of this issue).

Student counselling and help via e-mail

Students may want to contact the teacher for a number of different academic or personal reasons. Much potential e-mail can be headed off by providing easily accessible and clearly communicated information on the course Web site. Nevertheless, direct e-mail access to teachers is often necessary when students have pressing personal or study issues that act as a block to their further progress on the course.

Students may need to be able to extend the time for completing an assignment, to withdraw from a course and take it another time, or to ask advice on what other courses they need to take to achieve their academic goals. E-mail is a quick and convenient way for dealing with these issues. However, for more emotional issues, such as a death in the family, or serious illness, personal contact, if possible, is usually better, although often this is not possible for fully distance students.

Academic advice

Students may have difficulties in understanding the reasons for the particular approach to teaching and learning, or may not be familiar to learning in this way. They may be blocked by a lack of understanding of particular concepts or ideas in the course. In such cases they may need personal and individualized help from the teacher. However, if there is high demand from most students for personal and individualized help from a teacher, this is usually an indicator of design faults in the course, such as lack of clarity regarding course objectives, content presentation, or assignment questions.

Student assessment

Automated tests are good for testing comprehension and certain procedural skills, such as mathematical operations, but often more qualitative forms of assessment, such as written essays or multimedia assignments, are necessary. Some course development platforms provide a virtual space for the submission of assignments, but often assignments can be created by students in standard word-processing formats (e.g. Word or Word Perfect) and submitted to teachers as e-mail attachments. Teachers can then give not only a quantitative grade but also qualitative comments on the assignment, either as a separate e-mail or as annotated comments on the original word-processed document.

Cultural and epistemological issues

Online text-based environments can present real challenges to students when a constructivist approach to the design of online learning activities is adopted. We have found major cultural differences in students with regard to participating in online discussion forums that in the end reflect deep differences with regard to traditions of learning and teaching.

In many countries, there is a strong tradition of the authoritarian role of the teacher and the transmission of information from the teacher to the student. In some cultures, it would be considered disrespectful to challenge or criticize the views of teachers or even of other students. In an authoritarian, teacher-based culture, the views of other students may be considered irrelevant or unimportant. Other cultures have a strong oral tradition, or one based on story-telling, rather than on direct instruction.

Students from less economically developed countries may choose to take courses from institutions in advanced economies because of the prestige of the institution or the hope of getting better jobs or eventually emigrating to that country. They may take courses from an institution in another country without being aware that teachers in such an institution take a completely different approach to teaching and learning from the one to which the student is accustomed.

Even within a country, students come to the educational experience with different expectations and backgrounds. Thus teachers need to be aware that there are likely to be students in any class who may be struggling with language, cultural or epistemological issues, but in distance classes, where students can come from anywhere, this is a particularly important issue. For a fuller discussion of this, see the journal *Distance Education*, Vol. 22, No. 1 (2001). The whole edition is devoted to papers on this topic. For guidelines on how to manage such differences, see Bates and Poole (2003, p.245).

In summary, for most students, e-mail is a faster and more convenient way to communicate with their teacher, compared with the long time delays in correspondence, or the inconvenience of meeting teachers at limited times. However, if the course is poorly designed – for instance, if students are not properly guided to find the information they need on the Web site or in the reading materials – the dependence on e-mail for communication between student and teacher can lead to work overload for the teacher.

Student–student interaction

Although student–computer and student–teacher interaction can be greatly facilitated by Web-based learning, its main pedagogical advantage is the opportunity provided for high quality student–student interaction, and in particular the opportunity for discussion and dialogue between students. This is the strongest benefit compared with print-based correspondence teaching, where student–student interaction must be provided through usually optional face-to-face sessions at local study centres or at summer schools, which many students cannot attend, or can attend only at great personal and social sacrifice.

The quality of student–student interaction, and particularly the quality of discussion and argument, can be heavily influenced by the design of the course management software. In particular, the ability to create threaded discussion forums is essential. In a threaded discussion forum, when a student posts a comment to a previous posting it is placed close to that previous posting, thus allowing a thread of postings on a topic to be followed; an unthreaded discussion forum will post in chronological order, making it more difficult to follow a thread of argument. The software should allow both the teacher and any student to start a new topic, or to link their comments to any other previous comment. Ideally, a teacher should be able to go into a discussion and remove or rearrange individual postings, to improve the flow of the discussion. However, clear directions and an occasional intervention by the teacher to suggest alternative places for the posting of a comment will quickly train students to use a threaded discussion forum in the most appropriate manner.

Once again, the total design of an online course will strongly influence the participation of students and the quality of the discussions. This will be driven primarily by choosing discussion topics that engender controversy and that link to the teaching materials and in particular to the assignment questions.

Costs and organizational issues

These aspects of asynchronous online learning will be discussed in detail in the next chapter.

CONCLUSIONS

The situation continues to improve with respect to access to Web-based learning. In economically advanced countries, there appears to be a narrowing of the gap in the digital divide, although as in many other aspects of life, the poorest in the community are still likely to be the most disadvantaged. For those considering distance delivery, the critical issue is to obtain accurate information on access to computers and the Internet for the specific groups being targeted, given the dynamic nature of Internet access.

In general, there is strong evidence to suggest that asynchronous online learning has considerable educational advantages over print-based distance education, provided that students have access to the technology. Certainly, the weakness of print-based or broadcast-based distance education is the difficulty of providing opportunities for student discussion. Expensive and optional arrangements have to be made through local study centres for face-to-face interaction, and in practice these are often used by local tutors for more lecturing, rather than for group discussion of the printed material. Although the concern of open universities about access with respect to Web-based learning is understandable, in most economically advanced countries it would now seem to be overcautious (and costly) to make the use of the Web and the Internet optional, and educationally suspect to ignore them altogether.

Print-based or broadcast-based distance education has tended to take primarily an objectivist approach to learning. Online distance education programmes designed to constructivist principles start from a completely different premise. The online discussions are the 'core' of the course. The content is merely fodder or material for the discussions. Web-based learning offers the opportunity to achieve academic goals such as creative and critical thinking, knowledge construction, problem-solving and collaborative learning.

The choice of where on the time and space dimension to locate the teaching and learning experience is a critical design decision for campus-based institutions. The needs of the learners, the nature of the subject material, the learning goals, and the resources available are all factors that will influence the decision as to whether to use technology to enhance classroom teaching or to replace it entirely. In general, it is possible, with sufficient resources, to replicate probably far more learning activities than most people would anticipate through 'virtual' education. Thus campus-based organizations have the luxury of deciding what to do online and what in class. Nevertheless, the need to change methods of teaching to exploit the advantages of technology in a cost-effective manner presents a major challenge for conventional campus-based universities and colleges.

Given that the Web was not applied in any systematic way to education until 1995, it may be too early to decide whether an actual paradigm shift is occurring in education due to the development of the Internet and the Web. In epistemological terms, constructivist approaches to teaching existed long before the Internet. Project-based learning and knowledge construction were being used in many primary schools in England in the early 1960s (although it wasn't called constructivism in those days). Online learning does not lead automatically to constructivist approaches to learning. Traditional pedagogical approaches to teaching and learning, such as information transmission, questions and answers and assessment are still common in Web-based learning, especially when it is used to support classroom teaching,

The potential for an educational paradigm shift clearly exists, but this requires the design of new approaches to teaching that fully exploit the 'space behind the screen', independently of classroom metaphors. Thus there is still a long way to go before Web-based learning becomes a *pedagogical* paradigm shift. We shall see though in the next chapter that Web-based learning represents a major *organizational* paradigm shift in teaching and learning.

8 Web-based learning: costs and organizational issues

Currently in higher education ... we individualize faculty practice ... and standardize the learning experience ... Instead, we need to do the opposite: individualize student learning and standardize faculty practice ... What higher education needs is greater consistency in academic practice that builds on accumulated knowledge about improving quality and reducing costs.

(Twigg, 2003, p.38)

COSTS

A good deal of work has been done on measuring the costs of web-based learning (see for example, Potashnik and Adkins, 1996; Bartolic-Zlomislic and Bates, 1999; Jewett, 1999; Ortner and Nickolmann, 1999; Young, 1999; Bates, 2000; Finkelstein *et al.*, 2000; Hülsmann, 2000; Whalen and Wright, 2000; Boeke, 2001; Jones, 2001). There is a good deal of agreement about what direct costs to measure, and often about how to assign costs across different cost variables. There is also general agreement about the methodology of analysis, such as differentiating between fixed and variable costs, the importance of student numbers, as well as the methods of course development and the media used, and there is a general recognition of the importance of overhead or indirect costs (although little agreement on how to treat them).

There is though less information about actual cases where costs have been carefully measured and analysed under operational conditions. Most importantly, there has been a lack of business models built on the experience of running Web-based programmes in a cost-effective manner. Business models should investigate likely revenues from student tuition fees and/or government funding, the number of students required to break even at a given level of income, and the costs of sustainable operations that avoid teacher and student work overload. Business models should also include market research and risk assessment.

BUILDING A BUSINESS MODEL: THE UBC MASTER IN EDUCATIONAL TECHNOLOGY

Bartolic-Zlomislic and Bates (1999) and Bates (2000) detailed the costs for developing and delivering a single online course (EDST565f) first developed in 1996 at the University of British Columbia for the post-graduate certificate in technology-based distributed learning, offered in partnership with Tec de Monterrey in Mexico. The study identified that there were three main variables that determined whether or not a course or programme could break even or make a profit over a five-year period: the costs of developing, delivering and administering a course; the number of students enrolling in the course each year; and the fees charged to students (or the subsidy received from the university).

The study also identified that if the information for any two of these variables was known, the information for the third variable could be calculated. Thus for instance if the level of student fee was already determined either by government regulation or by what the market would bear, and the costs of developing, delivering and administering a course were also known, then the number of students that would need to be enrolled in the course each year could be calculated. However, this study looked at a single course, not a whole programme, and the study calculated only direct and some administrative costs, but not overheads and some other indirect but essential costs.

The UBC/Tec de Monterrey joint Master in Educational Technology

A better example therefore would involve a whole programme, including indirect or overhead costs, and one that did not require cross-subsidy from another organization. At the end of 2000, Tec de Monterrey approached UBC with a request to convert the post-graduate certificate into a full joint Master's degree, aimed at both the school and the post-secondary sector. The programme was approved by the universities, then by the government of British Columbia in June 2002. The first two courses in the new programme opened in September 2002 and the first students graduated in 2004.

Students needed to complete ten courses to obtain the masters. They could do the programme entirely in English or Spanish. Despite the complexity of the partnership arrangement (four jointly developed core courses available in English and Spanish versions, and electives developed independently by each institution), the programme was set up in such a way that each institution's activities were developed under two distinct business plans. In this way, if either party withdrew, the other institution would still have a full programme of courses in place. This chapter focuses solely on the UBC business plan. Although there were some costs (and savings) due to the partnership arrangement, the business model assumed that all courses offered by UBC (including the core courses) would have the normal full academic input for course development and delivery. This has proved to be a realistic assumption in practice.

The funding strategy

UBC decided that this programme must cover all costs, to be recovered from student fees, as the programme was aimed at a global lifelong learning market and would not receive any government subsidy. Furthermore, to ensure that this new programme would not be extra work for existing professors in the Faculty of Education, the programme had to generate enough revenues to cover the programme-related costs of all academic and administrative staff, including hiring additional tenured research professors to work on this programme (or to substitute for existing academics who wanted to work on this programme). The Distance Education and Technology unit (DE&T), which was a partner in the development and delivery of this programme, also had to cover all its costs of participation. In addition, supporting administrative units, such as the registry, library, and the Faculty of Graduate Studies, would also be paid for the extra costs of the programme.

Because of the need for start-up costs before fee revenues started flowing, the university provided a loan to the programme, which was then repaid with interest as revenues accrued. All initial start-up costs were charged against this loan until revenues started to flow. This allowed for instance two new tenured professors to be hired before the first courses were offered.

In order to get the loan, and in order to determine the level of student fee and the number of students required to cover all costs, it was necessary to develop a detailed business plan. The business plan included the costs of up-front planning, the development, delivery and maintenance of the course, all direct and identifiable indirect costs, student enrolment projections, and the generation and assignment of revenues. The assignment of revenues included cash flow back to the various departments participating in the programme. The business plan was jointly developed by staff from DE&T, the Faculty of Education, and the university treasury. Staff in DE&T drew heavily on their experience of costing the courses in the post-graduate certificate programme.

Components of the business plan

The business plan contained two separate but related components: the narrative, and a detailed budget spreadsheet. The narrative included the following elements:

- An introduction, briefly summarizing the reasons for the programme, and its main goals.
- Details of the programme, including target audience (working teachers in schools and post-secondary education), content (educational technology), type of accreditation (credit master, post-graduate), delivery

format (fully online), funding model (cost recovery from fees), recommended tuition fee, admission requirements, programme requirements and structure, language requirements, and recommended programme administration.

- Assumptions behind the business plan, such as the total number of courses to be offered, the projected annual enrolments, and the length of the programme.
- Calculation of annual student admissions and enrolments, based on demand, and taking into account attrition and rate of study (likely number of courses per year per student) and students opting to take single courses or a sub-set of courses towards a post-graduate certificate.
- Market research and marketing (including an analysis of similar programmes on the market, their enrolments and fee structures).
- Method and costs of student advising and admission.
- A detailed nine-year budget projection, including programme expenditures, student fees, and projected revenues.
- Three business options, based on different levels of risk related to different levels of student enrolments and fees.
- Conclusions and recommendations.

The business plan was an essential planning document for this new programme. It was the subject of intense discussion, and was eventually approved by the whole of the Faculty of Education, as well as by the university treasury (who were providing the loan), the Division of Continuing Studies (which took the risk on the loan), and the Vice-President Academic's office. The business plan went through over 30 iterations, and although it was signed off in the early days of the programme, it is still a living, dynamic document, as it is continually adjusted to take account of actual enrolments, revenues and expenditures each year.

The budget

The budget eventually projected over a nine-year period (it took four years to put the whole programme in place, and the remaining five years were projections for the programme in a steady state). The financial part of the business plan was in three parts: expenditures and revenues; disbursements; and assumptions. Using a spreadsheet, the assumptions could be changed, and the spreadsheet would automatically adjust the resulting revenues, expenditures and disbursements. This allowed for 'what-if' scenarios, such as, 'What if we get only 70 per cent of projected enrolments – what impact will that have on the fee if we are to break even?'

Revenues

The top part of the spreadsheet provided an annual summary of projected revenue. It provided details of projected enrolments, student fees (in total cash), admission fees, income from the loan, and total revenue. Total student fee and admission fee income was simply calculated by multiplying the level of the fees by the projected number of students each year.

For this programme, tuition fees were set at $1,250 per course. Students needed to take ten courses to qualify for the masters, making the total tuition fee C$12,500. A total of 12 courses developed by UBC would be available in any one year when fully operational, giving students a small amount of choice of courses. New enrolments were projected at 60 per year, and total enrolments when all courses would be available were projected at 280 students a year (this took account of projected attrition/drop-out and assumed a certain speed in which students would work through the programme). When the programme reached a steady state (Year 5), total revenues were projected to be approximately C$700,000 per year (and the loan would have been repaid).

Expenditures

Expenditures were more complicated. These can be divided into planning and management of the programme, course development, course maintenance, course delivery and operations and administration and overhead costs.

Planning and management

There were substantial costs in setting up and managing a large programme such as this, especially since it had many innovative features. This programme required major changes in university policy, required a whole Faculty to support the idea of a graduate programme being delivered entirely online to students from all over the world, it required agreement to work with another institution in another country, and it needed to get agreement on the business model, which had never been approved before by a Faculty. Altogether, the programme proposal went through 27 committee meetings for approval.

In the end, a total of almost $300,000 was included in the business plan to cover the cost of planning activities. However, to avoid the need for debt charges up front to cover these costs (most of which were incurred before the programme started), these costs were spread over nine years. There would still be considerable sunk planning costs on top (e.g. time spent by academics and managers at meetings such as Senate) that cannot be properly calculated.

In order to provide academic leadership and management of the programme, the Faculty of Education appointed a half-time programme co-ordinator, a senior academic who worked across the academic departments (this is an inter-disciplinary programme), finding professors to teach on the course, and managing the programme on behalf of the Faculty of Education.

Course development

Course development costs (that is, costs for developing the final first version of each of the 12 courses in the programme developed by UBC) were made up of costs for each academic subject expert (estimated at 12.5 days work), an academic reviewer (flat rate of $1,000), project management and instructional design (12 days per course), Web programming and graphic design (14 days per course), library resources (a librarian participated in course development to assist in identifying academic resources for the course and to prepare for student library services), copyright fees, and cash for multimedia production. The courses were produced using a tight project management model, with academic work being focused on content and teaching approach, and academic time spent on media production being kept to a minimum through the use of technology specialists. Course production costs were projected at around C$24,000 (US$18,000) per course on average, including costs of academic and course development time charged at a daily rate based on average salaries (including benefits).

Course maintenance

Web courses need considerable maintenance. Student feedback, analysis of exam or assignment results, changes to urls, new research and publications, and changes by the original author all need to be built into the cost of a programme. Thus costs were included for the time of academic(s), project manager, Web programmer, and graphic designer each year to maintain each course. This came to roughly C$3,700 per course per year. The advantage of this strategy is that it should prevent courses getting out of date, and thus would avoid the need for a major revision or replacement after five or so years.

Delivery and operations

These costs can be divided into a number of subheadings. The major cost was for 'tutoring' the courses. This programme required the main academic(s) to teach one section (20 students) of the course they developed, and contract instructors were hired for every additional section of 20 students. A fixed amount ($7,500) was allocated for the cost of the main professor teaching each course, who took the first 20 students. Contract instructors took the remaining students, and were paid $220 per student, or $4,400 for a full section (these costs reflect differences in the collective agreements for tenured academics and contract instructors at UBC). Thus costs would vary slightly according to the number of student enrolments in each offering of the course, but when fully operational with 280 students a year enrolled, the teaching costs were projected to be just over C$170,000 (US$127,500) a year.

The second group of costs for delivery could be called administrative. These were costs of programme admission, including selection of students, course registration costs, Faculty of Education administration, and technical support (help desk). This was projected to be just under C$60,000 (US$45,000) a year when fully operational.

Then there were costs for delivery of printed materials ($8,500 a year), the library tutor ($12,000 a year), marketing (about $5,000 a year when fully operational, but $22,000 in the first year), and travel to Mexico for liaison with Tec de Monterrey ($6,000 a year). Marketing costs may seem low, but most marketing is done online, using mail-lists often acquired from professional groups to which potential students belong. The total delivery costs when fully operational were estimated to be about C$260,000 (US$195,000) a year.

Overheads

Assigning overheads is one of the greatest challenges in costing Web-based learning. In a conventional campus-based research university such as UBC, almost half the costs of academic operation are assigned as overheads (building maintenance, library, President's office, and so forth). The aim in this programme was to reduce a general charge for overheads to a minimum, by estimating as accurately as possible the costs generated by the programme for each of the supporting departments. For instance, the cost of admitting and registering students was calculated and money was transferred to the administrative departments (registry, graduate studies) for this extra cost. Therefore there are line items in this budget that do not normally appear in face-to-face teaching budgets, except for the very few institutions operating on an activity-based costing model. The costing strategy was therefore a cross between activity-based costing where costs could be accurately calculated for a supporting department, and a remaining but smaller general overhead for other costs that could not be accurately calculated.

There are several sub-headings under overheads. *Operating* overheads were calculated as a percentage (20 per cent) of different direct expenditure items that were deemed to have indirect costs as well (e.g. the programme co-ordinator generated overhead costs in the dean's office). These operating overheads totalled approximately $57,000 a year. The university charged all credit programmes a small percentage of student fees (8.13 per cent) for a central fund that was used for *teaching improvements* (OHTS). This totalled $28,480. A small amount was set aside for *bad debts* ($5,600 a year). Overheads in total came to approximately $90,000 (US$67,500) a year, or $125,000 (US$93,750) a year if *planning costs* are included as overheads. Probably these overhead costs are underestimated, as many central university costs may not be measurable but nevertheless are real, if shared (for instance there are no costs charged for central IT services, which maintain the network).

Financing costs

A total of $225,000 was made available for loan purposes, although the maximum borrowed was $150,000 in Year 1. Interest charges were estimated to total $46,500.

Profit and loss

These figures can be summarized for the nine years of the programme (Table 8.1).

It can be seen that the financial plan was set up so that the programme never makes a significant operating loss in any year. This is the role of the loan, which counts as income in the first two years, and then as expenditure, in terms of repayment, over three years, as student numbers and hence revenues increase. By Year 5 (2006), all debts should have been cleared and a small surplus left. By Year 7 (2008) the programme should reach a steady state and generate an annual surplus of approximately $200,000 on revenues of $700,000 (a return of almost 30 per cent).

The surplus (or profit) may seem high, but then so are the risks. There is no guarantee that enrolments will reach and continue at 280 a year. Enrolments of 200 a year are required just to break even, yet tenured professors will have been hired on the guarantee of revenues to pay for them from this programme. (This is not as risky financially as it sounds – UBC will be replacing 40 per cent of its faculty in any case over the next five years due to retirements).

Risk management indeed was a critical part of the business plan. A number of decision points were identified that would enable the programme to be cancelled if demand proved inadequate, without sustaining substantive loss. For instance, the first course was due to open in September 2002 with a second opening in January 2003. A minimum figure of applications had to be received by June 2002 to begin the programme. Although a start would have been made on production of the first two courses, this could be stopped without major financial loss. No money was in fact borrowed until March, 2003, the end of the financial year, by which time the pattern of applications had become clear. The programme still has to ensure a steady stream of enrolments, but the longer the programme lasts, the less risk there is to both students and the university's finances.

The setting of the fee was probably the most difficult decision to make in the business plan. In Canada, students pay only a small proportion of the

Table 8.1 Projected profit and loss for the MET programme (C$)

	1	2	3	4	5	6	7	8	9
Revenue	305k*	407k*	482k	607k	707k	707k	707k	707k	707k
Expense	301k	410k	483k	607k	663k	506k	493k	493k	493k
Profit	4k	–3k	–1k	–	44k	201k	214k	214k	214k
No. of students	60	130	190	240	280	280	280	280	280

* includes loan as income; k = C$1,000; loan repayment included in expenses

cost of a university education. At the time the decision was made (early 2001) to charge $1,250 a course, or $12,500 for a full degree, students were paying less than $3,000 a year for an on-campus master's in education. Since then, all student fees in British Columbia have increased substantially, as a result of the government removing a freeze in tuition rates. The $12,500 for a master's degree is no longer out of line with many similar degrees being offered to lifelong learners.

The costs of Web-based learning

This case illustrates why it is difficult to say what an online programme costs. At $12,500 a student for a master's degree, one could say it costs $1,250 a course. However, if one takes away the profit, the figure is closer to $8,750, or $875 a course. But the profit may be necessary, to provide the motivation for academic departments to move into lifelong learning and to provide a safeguard against risk. Also, this case provides a more realistic assessment of the real costs of Web-based learning under operational conditions than studies on a course-by-course basis. This case does attempt to deal with the issue of administrative costs, overheads and financing, even though all overhead costs may not have been included. It also needs to be realized that the costs of this programme are very much dependent on the method of course production, using a tight project management model. Courses and programmes developed on the 'Lone Ranger' model (discussed later in this chapter) may have a very different cost structure, as will mixed mode courses.

Some may be concerned, as were some of the Faculty of Education, about the apparent privatization of graduate degree programmes. It is important though not to underestimate the value of this costing exercise, merely because it is based on a cost-recovery or revenue-generating model. This model can be used just as well for calculating the costs of programmes wholly or partly funded by government. Instead of the main revenues coming from student fees, the main revenue would come from the university's or college's main operating budget. Thus if student fees are estimated to cover approximately 20 per cent of income, and government funding the rest, then in this case students would pay a fee of $2,500 for the whole programme, and the university would allocate $10,000 per student (or $1,000 per student per course) from the general operating budget.

Lastly, it should be remembered that the costs for this programme are still projections. It will not be until 2007 that the actual costs of this programme will be clearly known. However, at the time of writing (June 2004), the programme was meeting its enrolment targets, producing courses on schedule, repaying its loan, keeping to budget and had produced its first batch of graduates.

Comparing costs

Comparing the costs of Web-based learning with the costs of other technologies through the analysis of the MET programme raises another set of problems. Administrative, overhead and financing costs are not always factored in when doing costing studies. Second, the MET programme costs include all activities carried out by the students, including assignments and reading print (most of the MET courses have accompanying textbooks and custom course material in print format, which the students buy). Thus to make comparable comparisons, we need to do some further calculations and make some assumptions.

As well as the tuition fee of C$1,250, there are also the costs of textbooks and supplementary readings, which average about C$100 per course per student. We could add a further C$100 for Internet provider fees per course (C$30 a month), and a further C$100 per course for depreciation for a student's computer. This would give a *total cost per student* of C$1,550 per student per course, or C$15,500 for the whole programme (US$11,625). This is probably the full total cost of the programme, but it assumes that students would not otherwise own a home computer and have Internet access, which in this particular case is an unlikely assumption.

The *break-even point* for this programme, if enrolment targets are met, is C$875 (US$656.25) per course, and this would be a better comparable figure with the other calculations in this book, which do not have a surplus built into their costing.

In addition, there are significant costs for administration and *overheads* in the MET programme. I list these in Table 8.2, based on the annual programme costs when the programme is in a steady state.

It can be seen then that administrative and overhead costs constitute 36.5 per cent of the total annual cost of the programme when in a steady state (the costs of financing turned out to be very small – a total of $46,570 in interest over the whole programme, or barely 1 per cent of all costs). In order to make comparisons, I will deduct 36.5 per cent from the $875 per course, giving a direct teaching cost of $555.63 per course. The average course size is projected to be between 23 and 24 students, for total enrolments of 280 per year over 12 courses in a steady state. Assuming that students spend approximately 100 hours studying per course, we then arrive at a total direct teaching cost of C$5.56 (US$4.17) per hour per student, including tutoring, assignments and print reading, or C$6.56 per student hour if the cost of textbooks and supplementary readings are added. This compares with approximately C$5.01 per student hour (including tutoring and textbooks) for a print-related course of 30 students from the same university (see Table 4.4, Chapter 4).

The figures for the MET programme are calculated somewhat differently from the costs of other technologies in this book. If we use the same data, but recalculate for comparative purposes in the same way as for other technologies, we arrive at the figures in Table 8.3.

Table 8.2 Administrative and overhead costs for the MET programme

Cost heading	Annual cost (C$)
Programme admissions (FoE)	15,000
Faculty of Graduate Studies (admissions)	4,043
Faculty of Education, Dean's Office	3,308
Student systems and support (FoE)	16,800
Student administration (Registry)	4,200
Operating overheads (FoE + DE&T)	56,850
Liaison with Tec de Monterrey	6,000
Planning (FoE + DE&T)	34,908
OHST	28,480
Bad debts	5,600
Total of overheads	180,189
Total annual programme cost	493,819

Table 8.3 Cost per course of a Web-based course at a dual-mode institution

Over 8 years	240 students (30 per year) C$	1,000 students (125 per year) C$	5,000 students (625 per year) C$	10,000 students (1,250 per year) C$	24,000 students (3,000 per year) C$
Development	18,000	18,000	18,000	18,000	18,000
Maintenance	19,425	19,425	19,425	19,425	19,425
Library	1,000	1,000	1,000	1,000	1,000
Print materials	2,700	11,250	56,250	112,500	270,000
Technical support	9,720	40,500	202,500	405,000	972,000
Total for Web development and delivery	50,845	90,175	297,175	555,925	1,280,425
Average cost per student	211.85	90.17	59.43	55.59	53.35
Tutor costs	41,925	167,325	827,325	1,652,325	3,962,325
Total institutional costs	92,410	257,500	1,125,500	2,208,250	5,242,750
Total per student	385.04	257.50	224.90	220.82	218.45
Per study hour (100 hours) – without textbooks	3.85	2.58	2.25	2.21	2.18

It can be seen we come to a similar figure for a class of 30 students (C\$3.85 for a cost per course of 30, compared with C\$5.56 for the costs for a course of 24 based on a whole programme, excluding textbooks). Given the many possible variations in costs, we are in the right ball-park, and thus can make comparisons calculated in the same way in this book from Table 8.3 with the costs of other technologies and thus for other sizes of course enrolments. Comparison of costs with other technologies will be discussed in the final chapter.

ORGANIZATIONAL ISSUES

At the time of writing, the greatest challenge for institutions moving to Web-based learning is to find appropriate organizational models that ensure quality while controlling cost.

Models of course development

There are many different ways in which a course can be developed and delivered (this is discussed in more detail in Bates, 2000, pp.59–75, and Bates and Poole, 2003, pp.139–45).

Lone Rangers

By far the most common model of course development is what I call the Lone Ranger approach (after an old Hollywood cowboy film and subsequent television series). Teachers work individually creating their own Web-based materials, usually using a course development platform such as WebCT or Blackboard, and sometimes helped by a graduate student. Lone Rangers are essential in most institutions for getting Web-based learning started. They are usually very enthusiastic, and put in a great deal of their own time on developing the materials. They demonstrate some of the potential of Web-based learning, not just to their colleagues, but also to the institutional administration. This model of Web-based development fits well with the autonomy of the individual teacher.

However, there are many problems with the Lone Ranger model. The main issues are quality, workload and scalability. Lone Rangers are usually self-taught, not just in the use of technology but also in course design. Often the materials are overloaded with content, fail to exploit the technical features of the Web, such as interactivity, and look poor in terms of graphical design. Put bluntly, they are amateurs, not professionals.

Because Lone Rangers have to deal with technical issues (such as access to and maintenance of the Web site), design issues (the sequencing of pages, the graphics, and the interactive elements), and content (keeping urls up to date, adding and removing content), the development and maintenance of the Web-based material takes more and more time. It is not surprising then that the Lone Ranger model is associated with very high costs. Particularly for professors with research responsibilities, it is very difficult for them to become experts or even experienced in all these areas without their research suffering. This results in many academics shying away from online learning, and hence the difficulty of scaling up.

There will always be the exceptional highly skilled individual who is able without assistance to develop sustainable and high-quality Web-based learning, especially when the online component is a minor support to face-to-face teaching. However, for most teachers, a different model is usually needed if Web-based learning is to be an integral part of the teaching, of high quality, and sustainable over the long haul.

Boutique course development

Hartman and Truman-Davis (2001) identified the boutique approach. This is basically one-on-one individual help for a teacher. Preferably close to where the teacher is located, there is a small learning support unit which operates on an 'on-demand' basis, meeting the specific needs of each teacher in developing online materials. Thus a teacher will drop in with a request for instance to move their PowerPoint slides from a lecture to the class Web site.

This is the model often most preferred by academics. However, often the help sought is technical rather than educational. Furthermore, the model starts to become unsustainable as demand increases, because of the resources needed. It causes particular difficulties for the learning support unit, as there is no obvious way to determine priorities between multiple requests for help, and there is no limit to the commitment for support. Nevertheless, the boutique model can be useful in helping individual professors get started in using technology in a systematic and professional way.

Collegial materials development

Collegial materials development is used particularly for developing learning objects. Several academics (often but not always from different institutions) work collaboratively to develop online or multimedia educational materials. By working collaboratively they can share ideas, jointly develop or share materials, and provide critical feedback to each other. In collegial materials development, each participant in the project is free to decide what materials to include in their own courses, and what materials to share with other colleagues. Rarely is a whole course produced. However, at some stage, even collegial development approaches are likely to get to a point where there is a need for more formal management of the process, some form of evaluation or peer review of the materials, and the need for professional design and graphics.

Project management

There are many models and approaches to project management. What they all have in common is that project development and delivery involves a team of individuals each contributing different skills. What defines project management is the process. It has a defined set of resources, usually determined at the outset of the project, a series of deadlines for different steps in a defined process, and a clear 'deliverable', in that it is clear what the project has to achieve and it is obvious when it is completed.

One great advantage of project management is that it enables costs to be controlled. Approximate standards can be established for the amount of time required of the academics and course development support staff to develop and to deliver a good quality online course. Thus the DE&T unit at UBC, partly based on research conducted within the unit but also driven by available resources, was able to establish an informal standard or guidelines for the development, delivery and maintenance of online courses. Table 8.4 provides an indication of the standards based on a typical one-semester course of 13 weeks. The standards assume an existing curriculum already taught face-to-face, and the use mainly of text and still graphics.

The model can be adapted to courses with different requirements, such as courses requiring more multimedia production, or courses where the curriculum or content is being designed from scratch, in which case more time would need to be allocated.

Project management was an essential tool for enabling the DE&T unit to double in size over the period 1995–2003 while at the same time increasing the quality of courses. The DE&T model enabled the university to hire as regular employees instructional designers (who doubled as project managers) and specialist Web designers, resulting in the development and sharing of professional expertise. The outcome was high quality, cost-effective online programming produced at the same or lower cost per student as face-to-face teaching.

Good project management should ensure that the academic has final control over all decisions regarding content and teaching methods. Furthermore, many academics found that working with a team of professionals from

Table 8.4 Standard times allocated to online courses at DE&T

	Initial development	*Course delivery (each year)*	*Maintenance (each year)*
Academic time	12 days	10 days	4 days
Project management/ instructional design	12 days	1.5 days	4 days
Web programming (including graphics)	12 days	1.5 days	4 days

DE&T was a very empowering experience, in that the quality of teaching and learning was dramatically improved by the contribution of all the team members.

However, many academics are strongly hostile to project management. Most would prefer the university to give them cash to develop online programming and to hire their own part-time graduate students to help. ('Leave the money at my door, and go away', one said). Some academics see project management as a threat to their academic freedom. The requirement for academics to sign a letter of agreement that spelled out responsibilities of the team members and intellectual property rights (essential in a project management model) eventually led to a grievance to the B.C. Labour Relations Board by the Faculty Association (the union for academics at UBC) in 2003. The Faculty Association won, on the grounds that the letter of agreement constituted conditions of employment, which had to be agreed by the Faculty Association as it had exclusive bargaining rights for academics at UBC. The university is appealing this decision.

Which approach?

The decision whether to adopt a Lone Ranger, boutique, collegial materials development or project management approach depends on a number of factors. The most critical are the size, complexity and originality of a project, and the resources available. In general, though, the more important the role of technology in a course, the more important a full project management approach becomes.

Thus a teacher thinking of adding PowerPoint presentations to her classroom teaching will not need project management for this (the boutique model would work best). It is more difficult to determine whether mixed mode courses, which combine a reduced face-to-face teaching load with substantive web-based learning, require a project management approach, but Twigg (2003) showed that major advantages could be gained by working with instructional designers to redesign mixed mode teaching. However, if a whole course is to be delivered online and at a distance, or if a multimedia expert system is to be developed, or if a large lecture class is to be completely redesigned, then instructional design and project management become essential.

Administrative requirements

Virtual universities and single mode distance education institutions are specifically designed to deal with the support and administration of distance learners. However, conventional campuses moving into Web-based learning will face increasing pressure to change their administrative arrangements as well. Campus-based students moving to online learning will expect many of their administrative services also to be delivered online. The administration of online students can be challenging even for institutions experienced in managing print-based distance education.

Admission and programme requirements

One reason for moving online may be to reach new markets. However, to reach these markets, admission policies may need to be revised. For instance, some institutions have a 'residency' requirement in that a certain proportion of courses need to be taken on campus. This requirement may not be appropriate for the new market – for example, lifelong learners who already have a degree, or students studying overseas.

Second, once a course is available fully online, should it be made available to other students who have not been admitted to the institution, and if so, how does the registry handle such students? Many governments are now pressing institutions to make their online courses available to anyone who wants to take them. Should such students be integrated with the regular students of an institution, treated separately, or ignored? UBC, which is a highly selective university, allowed students from the Open Learning Agency to take distance courses within the same class as the regular students, but the 'visiting' students obtained their qualification from OLA, not UBC. With the closure of the OLA, a new category of student had to be created, allowing individual courses to be taken by students who were not otherwise 'admitted' to UBC.

Online student services

Does it make sense for students to be taught online but have to come to campus for all administrative services? Can students find programme information, apply, be admitted, pay their fees, be registered for courses, be taught, and receive their grades, totally online? Even if academic policies can be changed, administrative computing systems may not be able to accommodate the changes without a great deal of work and changes in administrative procedures.

Once students are online, what services can they access from the institution? Many institutions are now developing student portals, which allow student information to be tailored for the individual student. Thus when a student logs on, the home page is customized so that the student's courses are listed, and through the use of a password, the student can access all the information needed to be a student, such as programme requirements, grades, and status within a course. Students can change courses, contact their teacher, and conduct administrative business through the portal. This is not only convenient for the student, but can also in the long run lead to major savings in administrative areas. For instance, students completing high school or travelling abroad can now apply online and admit themselves to UBC, if they think they will achieve the minimum grades needed for entry. Once they know their high school exam grades, they then submit their formal transcripts. All the university needs to do is to check the transcripts against the grade estimates provided by the student, thus reducing a huge amount of paperwork.

The more teaching moves away from the classroom-based model the more one must pay attention to administrative and marketing issues. Administrative inertia can be a major barrier to the development of Web-based teaching. For this reason, it is wise to develop an institution-wide strategy for the use of the Web, encompassing fund-raising, marketing, admission, registration, financial services, student services, purchasing, and e-commerce, as well as teaching and learning. UBC is attempting to do this through a university-wide e-strategy (http://www.e-strategy.ubc.ca).

Integrated or separate units for online learning?

It is clear that there is a continuum of online learning, from supporting classroom teaching right through to fully Web-based or distance courses. This is leading some administrators in dual-mode institutions to question the need for separate institutions or departments of distance education. If an academic department is responsible for developing Web-supplemented and mixed mode teaching, why should it not also take full responsibility for fully online courses? This was certainly the thinking at the University of British Columbia as it moved more and more towards online learning.

It could be claimed that Distance Education and Technology unit at UBC had been very successful. The number of distance courses available increased from 70 in 1995 to 130 by 2003, of which 70 were fully online, all of the Web-based courses being developed since 1996. Students facing increasing costs due to rising tuition fees and the need to work part-time welcomed the flexible options to face-to-face teaching that the distance education programme provided. The number of undergraduate students taking distance courses went from 3,520 in 1996 to 6,170 in 2003, an increase of 75 per cent, or 10 per cent per year (UBC's total enrolments increased by between 1.5 to 2 per cent per year over the same period). The distance education unit provided leadership in the development of graduate credit programmes in professional continuing education, such as the Master in Educational Technology, which were established on a sustainable cost-recovery basis.

The existence of a professional central unit resulted in a quality assurance approach to the development of distance education programmes, resulting in high completion rates and comparable exam performance to those taking face-to-face classes. The academic departments benefited in that distance education took pressure off face-to-face classes to some extent, particularly in the Faculty of Arts. The unit also provided economies of scale in the area of student support services, such as counselling, marketing and a help desk. The unit also attracted research funding, enabling the university to keep current with new developments in Web-based learning and distance education, and the unit also developed a consultancy service that generated revenues for the university.

Nevertheless, none of this was sufficient to protect the DE&T unit. Following a departmental review and the retirement of the director in 2003, the Vice-President Academic's Office decided that most of the resources and functions of the DE&T unit should be 'restructured'. In particular, course production and delivery were to be devolved to the faculties, and student services for distance education students to central administrative units such as the Registry. The DE&T unit would cease to exist by April 2005.

The weakness in the model developed by the Distance Education and Technology unit was that deans had little direct influence over distance education activities, and the growth of distance education enrolments did not result in increased revenues for the faculties (with the exception of the masters' programmes). With the central distance education unit managing most of the funding for undergraduate distance education courses, there was no significant financial incentive for either individual faculty members or for academic departments. As tuition fees and student enrolments increased, more and more revenue was going to DE&T. The senior administration believed a devolved model would be more consistent with the philosophy of decentralized control of teaching and the integration of learning technologies. In particular, the senior administration believed that by transferring the highly valued professionals from DE&T to the faculties, the use of Web-based learning in the classroom as well as for distance education would be strengthened.

It remains to be seen how this decision will benefit the students (who were not consulted about the changes) and how the decision will impact on the cost-effective use of resources. Faculties historically had shown little interest in the needs of distance learners, as most professors were already overwhelmed with increases in the size of face-to-face classes. Staff in DE&T were particularly concerned about the lack of understanding in the faculties of the special learner support needs of students studying fully at a distance, and the loss of a professional centre for distance education course design. As a result, some of the most experienced DE&T staff left to work in other organizations instead of transferring to other faculties or administrative departments at UBC.

In theory, it is right that the academic departments should give just as much attention to distance education as to other forms of delivery. However, in reality, this is unlikely to happen in a large research university. The focus is on recruiting the best students from high schools, and identifying those that will make the best research students. Lifelong learners and distance students are a distraction from the core business of building strong research departments. Also, there is a shortage of good instructional designers and project managers, and scattered across a large number of departments, their influence will be diminished. In any case, academic departments are unlikely to support project management models for reasons already discussed.

The challenge then for the senior administration at UBC will be to address the academics' current lack of interest in and commitment to distance education, and issues of quality control and cost-effectiveness in a highly decentralized system. It will be interesting to see whether the faculties do successfully integrate distance education into their core operations, while maintaining the quality and growth of the previous central unit.

The cycle of development in Web-based learning

In summary, most post-secondary institutions appear to go through the same cycle of development with respect to Web-based learning.

Stage 1: Lone Rangers

Individuals within an organization become interested in and excited by the technology. With little or no support from the institutional administration, they start developing their own Web-based teaching. This gradually gets the attention of other colleagues and the central administration.

Stage 2: Institutionally-funded project grants

Partly as a result of pressure from the Lone Rangers, but also sometimes as a result of financial encouragement from government, the senior administration becomes aware of the importance of Web-based learning, and offers a large number of relatively small grants or reduced teaching loads to encourage more Lone Rangers.

Stage 3: Rapid and unco-ordinated expansion

As a result of these incentives, many more teachers start developing Web-based materials. However, problems start arising because many of the new online teachers are less keen on doing the extra work required, and start demanding more support. There is a strong demand from teachers for more professional development for online learning, but mainly focused on technology training, not pedagogy. At the same time, the senior administration starts to be worried about the poor quality of many of the Web-based projects, the amount of duplication, and the high costs.

Stage 4: Focus, policies and regular funding

The senior administration then starts to organize learning technology committees to discuss and recommend policies and priorities. The administration encourages the establishment of one or more learning technology support units, and allocates regular funding to support Web-based learning activities. The institution starts to deal with issues of quality assurance, faculty development (including instructional design), teamwork, intellectual property, marketing, new programming, and rewards for innovative teaching through tenure and promotion committees.

Stage 5: Quality, sustainability and integration of Web services

The institution has now clearly identified the roles and priorities for Web-based learning, the amount and type of support needed and put in place a sustainable financial strategy to support Web-based learning. It has also recognized that Web-based learning needs to be supported by and integrated with other Web-based services, such as on-line student administration. As a result, where Web-based learning is used, it is consistently of a high quality and operates in a highly cost-effective manner. Few institutions have yet reached this point, but a significant number are moving in this direction.

Barriers to change

Lastly, it should be recognized that there are many institutional and cultural barriers that prevent greater development of online learning. Probably the biggest is the lack of interest of many teachers in using technology for teaching. In most cases, this is based on a very considered, rational decision. Without increased technical and instructional support from the institution, technology-based teaching and in particular the Lone Ranger model requires more skill and more effort than classroom teaching. When the rewards for appointment, tenure and promotion are driven primarily by research accomplishments, there is no incentive for professors to put more effort into their teaching.

Secondly, many university professors have no other model of teaching than the classroom method. University teaching is basically an apprenticeship system, watching the 'master' or more senior teachers and copying them. As a result, many university teachers are unaware of the knowledge acquired in the last forty years about the conditions needed to support effective learning, the need for flexible approaches to teaching to accommodate student differences within a class, the importance of instructional design, or team approaches to teaching with technology. The question then is: do teachers have the right, in the name of academic freedom, to inflict poor teaching on students when we know there are better ways to teach? Or should training in Web-based learning and teaching be a requirement now for at least all new teachers? Certainly at the moment there is no requirement in post-secondary education for teachers to receive such training. Until that requirement is in place, there will continue to be a need for instructional designers, Web programmers, project management and above all teamwork, if teachers are to develop and deliver high quality, cost-effective Web-based learning.

Probably though the biggest challenge is the lack of vision and the failure to use Web-based learning strategically. The focus of most campus-based institutions is still on the face-to-face student, and on enriching the classroom experience through technology. Web-based learning, however, allows institutions to deliver education globally, to reach out to the continuing professional education market, and to use technology to change in fundamental ways the organization and delivery of teaching. This will not happen though without major reorganization and cultural change within educational institutions.

CONCLUSIONS

We shall see in Chapter 11 that Web-based learning can be cost-competitive with print-based forms of distance education, and much more cost-effective than broadcasting technologies, for moderate numbers of students per course (30–100). Web-based learning increases quality through stronger interaction between teachers and learners without losing the flexibility of distance delivery. However, Web-based learning does not have the same economies of scale found with either print or broadcasting. In essence, with mass media delivery one is trading off quality of learning against cost, if one accepts that interaction between students is essential for higher quality learning outcomes.

More importantly, rather than *economies of scale*, Web-based learning offers the potential of *economies of scope*. It is possible to offer individual courses more cost effectively to smaller numbers of distance learners, because the fixed costs of development are not as high as for broadcast technologies. Online courses can be tailored more easily to the needs of individual students. It is only when the demand for an individual course is very high (over 3,000 students a year) that the costs of Web-based learning cease to be competitive with broadcast technologies.

If the mantra for selling real estate is 'location, location, location', the mantra for controlling the costs of Web-based learning is 'design, design, design'. Design drives both costs and effectiveness. Methods of working based on project management and/or teamwork are essential where Web-based learning constitutes a significant and essential component of the teaching. Although Web-based learning is still quite young, a great deal is known about how to design cost-effective courses and programmes. However, such design requires fundamental changes in the organization of teaching, and in particular in the way that teachers work.

If teachers can learn all the skills needed to design, develop, deliver and maintain Web-based materials in such a way that the technology is fully exploited, within reasonable constraints of time, then there is no need for the support of other professionals such as instructional designers, project managers and Web developers. However, in reality the effective use of Web-based learning requires such a range of different skills that few people are likely to meet this standard, at least not without damaging their personal life or their research.

Although in theory there may be a case for treating fully distant Web-based learning as just another method of delivering courses, and therefore merely an extension of an academic department's on-going responsibilities, in practice the requirements for cost-effective, high quality Web-based distance learning are very different from that of using Web-based learning to support classroom teaching. When academic departments can give equal priority to the needs of off-campus students, and can provide effective student support and course design for fully distant learners, then distance education can be integrated within the normal teaching duties of an academic department. However, until Nirvana arrives, to be assured of high quality, cost-effective courses delivered fully online we will probably still need specialist distance education units or organizations.

9   Audio-, video- and Web-conferencing: access and teaching issues

Co-authored with Janice Picard

Distance education has operated in several somewhat separate technological worlds. These can be summarized as: primarily broadcast (or one-to-many) technologies such as television and print; asynchronous online teaching through the Internet and the World Wide Web; and synchronous, two-way technologies, such as audio- and video-conferencing, and Web-conferencing. This chapter will focus on the potential and limitations of these synchronous or 'real-time' two-way telecommunications technologies for teaching and learning.

In this chapter four related two-way synchronous technologies are discussed:

- Audio-conferencing using standard telephone services.
- Narrow-band video-conferencing using standard or ISDN telephone services.
- Broad-band video-conferencing using high-speed networks (fibre-optic and/or satellite).
- synchronous conferencing over the Internet (Web-conferencing or IP-conferencing).

As well as describing the development and applications of these four technologies, the chapter discusses the role or place of synchronous technologies in modern distance education. Are synchronous tools really necessary in distance learning and in particular online education? Do synchronous methods compromise the individualized or flexible study models favoured by many distance educators? In what new ways do Web-based synchronous technologies, such as Web-conferencing, improve earlier forms of telecommunications-based instruction?

THE TECHNOLOGY

The obvious example of a synchronous two-way communications technology is the telephone, an invention of Alexander Graham Bell. An educator as well as an inventor, Alexander Graham Bell dreamed of bringing the wisdom and knowledge of great thinkers into ordinary people's lives through the use of technology.

Audio-conferencing

Audio-conferencing is a development of telephone technology, and is still found in some distance education programmes. Audio-conferencing can be used either with individuals in their homes or offices, or with groups in local centres, such as satellite campuses. For individual learners, the instructor calls a phone number to connect through a conference bridge, a special telephone switch that allows several lines to be shared at the same time, so all users can hear and speak to each other in real time. The student needs no special equipment other than a standard telephone. Audio-conference services can be booked through private companies offering conferencing services for a fee, or offered as an internal service if an institution owns its own bridge.

The second kind of audio-conferencing, group conferencing based on one or more remote sites with several students at each site, requires more sophisticated equipment. This may include loudspeakers, microphones that are button-operated by the student when they want to speak, or an omni-directional microphone that can pick up speakers in different parts of the room.

Early teaching through audio-conferencing was cumbersome, since participation was restricted to one speaker at a time, and line quality was often poor. These were strong disincentives for free-flowing and spontaneous discussions. More recently full duplex systems (i.e. several speakers can talk at the same time) and digital telephony have eliminated noisy lines, fading and disconnections to the extent that an audio-conference call should now be free of technical difficulties.

A limitation of audio-only conferencing is the lack of visual contact between students and instructor. Careful planning, design and presentation are needed to overcome these constraints (Wolcott, 1994). Computer-based audio-graphics were developed and combined with two-way audio to alleviate this problem. The instructor and students were able to transmit and view whiteboard or computer graphics, including annotations, in real time.

Audio-conferencing has diminished as a distance delivery tool, partly due to alternative forms of distance delivery such as video-conferencing (Hardy and Olcott, 1995) and the World Wide Web. However, some useful lessons have been learned from the experience of using audio-conferencing and audio-graphics for teaching that will also apply to the newer technologies of video- and Web-based conferencing.

Telephone-based video-conferencing

Early development of video-conferencing technology was carried out in the 1920s by Bell Telephone Laboratories, the research arm of AT&T, and aptly the same company founded by Alexander Graham Bell in 1877. Bell Labs initiated the first live video-conference in 1929 between Washington and New York City (Newton, 2002). The New York Daily Mirror reported that the audio was clear and the video 'inoffensive' (Rosen, 1996).

Despite the success of the trial, it would still be many years before two-way video and audio communication would be commonly available. Although 'one-way' satellite, cable and broadcast technologies were used extensively by educators in the 1970s and 1980s, two-way video-conferencing did not start making significant headway until the early 1990s (Boaz *et al.*, 1999), because of the high costs of equipment and facilities, the lack of common standards between different vendors, and user resistance: people still preferred to meet and conduct business in person (Trowt-Bayard, 1994).

The big break-through for telephone-based video-conferencing was compression technology. Video and audio signals can be originated in either analogue or digital format. Analogue signals can be converted to digital signals, and vice-versa, by using encoding and decoding equipment (known as codecs). Both analogue and digital signals can be carried by any medium, such as satellite, fibre optics, or even telephone cable, provided that the transmission and reception equipment uses the same format, or that there are codecs for conversion. Thus, for a digital video signal to be received on a standard analogue domestic television set, somewhere between origin and reception the signal must be transported and converted.

One way to reduce the bandwidth required for transmission, and hence costs, is to 'compress' the video image, that is, to digitize the signal and then to remove as much extraneous or redundant data as possible. Although a full-motion analogue television picture changes 30 times per second in North America (25 times per second in Europe), only a small part of the picture changes in each frame. For instance, with a 'talking head' against a still background, probably less than 10 per cent of the picture changes from frame to frame. Once the basic picture is captured, all that needs to be transmitted per frame are the changes. It follows that the more movement, and the faster the changes, the more difficult it becomes to compress without losing quality. Similarly, pictures transmitted at narrow band rates tend to be jerky and have problems with lip synchronization.

Compression technology has developed rapidly. Engineers have designed more and more powerful algorithms for converting from analogue to digital, allowing increasingly more data to be compressed without noticeable differences in the quality of the picture. Nevertheless, despite the improvement in compression technology, there can still be some loss of picture quality (jerkiness, blurring of movement), although for standard lectures using slides and a talking head, this is not a major problem, especially if six phone lines (384 kbs) are used. It becomes more of a problem if equipment or movement is being demonstrated or high quality video or graphics need to be shown.

A telephone-based video-conferencing system is likely to include a camera and two video monitors, one showing the 'active' connected remote site and the other the 'home' site. An omni-directional microphone will be placed on a table in the middle of the room, or there will be button-push individual microphones. A document camera will be available to display documents and printed graphics. A computer can be connected to display and transmit slides, Internet sites, or any other computer-generated materials. A self-managed operating console will be used to control camera and other inputs. Possibly some form of soundproofing and special lighting within the room will also be needed.

The system also requires a codec that converts and compresses video and audio signals for transmission over the standard telephone system, a connection to standard or ISDN telephone lines, and to a multipoint conferencing unit (MCU) if three or more locations are to be included. Telephone-based video-conferencing requires a minimum of two telephone lines operating in tandem (58–64 kbs $\times$ 2), although many systems now use six lines (58–64 $\times$ $6 = 348$–384 kbs). A common international standard (H.320) enables users to call video-conferencing sites almost anywhere in the world over dial-up, telephone networks. Thus the most popular form of video-conferencing at the time of writing is dial-up telephone-based compressed video-conferencing (although all video-conference systems sold today support both telephone dial-up and Web-supported connectivity).

Web-conferencing

Currently this is best described as very narrow-band or variable bandwidth conferencing. This allows users to communicate through their desktop computers in real time. Because of bandwidth restrictions to the desktop, Web-conferencing currently focuses more on audio, graphical and text communication in real time. Individuals can speak with one another and collaborate on text-based projects using data conferencing tools such as document sharing, white-boarding and typed 'chat'.

Web-conferencing is more and more integrating synchronous with asynchronous functions. The synchronous communications can be archived and accessed later by those unable to attend in real time (audio- or video-streaming), or by those who attended in real time but want to review or study the material more closely. Network connectivity is provided by ISDN, corporate intranets, or the Internet, and is beginning also to be provided through mobile telephony. Audio quality during a Web conference can be surprisingly good. However, in most cases audio is half duplex, supporting one speaker at a time, a situation that has much in common with early audio-conferencing applications.

Real-time, synchronous video applications are limited in Web-conferencing. Because of current bandwidth restrictions to most desktop computers, the video is dramatically compressed and usually appears in a small window on the computer screen. Even with a small compressed window, picture quality is currently quite poor. It is not possible at the moment to communicate video from more than two sites simultaneously, although some software allows the instructor to switch between several different sites in sequence. Current software for managing desk-top video-conferencing and integrating it with asynchronous functions is still crude and expensive, and tends to give all control of communication to the instructor. Consequently, applications of desk-top video-conferencing for teaching purposes will be quite limited until there are further improvements in bandwidth to and from the desktop, computer processing speeds and compression technology. For these reasons, the current growth in Web-conferencing places less emphasis on synchronous video communication.

Despite the restrictions on real-time video, there is growing interest in synchronous Web-based conferencing (Barron, 2001). An alternative to expensive and site-restricted technologies, Web-conferencing has been seen as the 'next generation' distance learning technology (Gillan and McBride, 2000). Eduventures, an eLearning market research company, forecast that live synchronous distance learning is not only gaining momentum in the online environment, it will soon overtake asynchronous online learning in corporate, government and post-secondary settings (e-Learning News, 2001).

Broadband video-conferencing

Broadband networks tend to be fully digital and multi-purpose, carrying telephone, fax, data, television and video-conferencing over fibre-optic cabling and/or microwave transmission. Where sites are connected through high-speed broadband networks then high quality, broadcast standard video-conferencing is possible. For connecting multiple sites at the same time, advanced digital switches are required. Higher quality cameras and equipment can be used. As a result, picture and sound quality tends to be much higher than with telephone-based video-conferencing.

The provincial government of Ontario, Canada, is investing C$78 million (US$54 million) in 3,700 kilometers of broadband optical network (the ORION network) to connect their 43 post-secondary institutions and over 50 publicly funded research institutions. ORION will also connect to Internet2 and other national and international high-speed networks, such as Canada's CANARIE cross-country high-speed network. ORION will have wavelength capacities of 10 gigahertz per second scalable to 320 gps capacity. The Indiana Telecommunications Network (ITN) is another public–private partnership. It provides a high-speed network between public institutions across the state of Indiana, allowing users access to high quality video-conferencing within the state. ITN bypasses public Internet and telephone networks to ensure high speed communications within the state.

Broadband networks require decision making at government or inter-institutional levels. Governments often make these decisions to ensure that their state or province is not left behind in the information technology race. The cost implications of this are discussed in the next chapter.

ACCESS AND FLEXIBILITY

During the 1980s, home access to the telephone system increased dramatically in most economically advanced countries. For instance, the number of homes in Britain with a telephone increased from 54% in 1974 to 86% in 1991. Consequently, audio-conferencing was extensively used for educational purposes in the 1980s. The British Open University was logging between 700 and 1,000 hours of small group audio-conferences in 1982. Robinson (1984) listed over 60 systems and 170 organizations in the USA at that time using educational audio-conferencing.

Home- or office-based audio-conferencing provides greater flexibility for learners than campus-based audio-conferencing. However, as telephones started to become ubiquitous in most homes in developed countries, video-conferencing and the Internet were already becoming established. Also, we shall see that the cost of home-based audio-conferencing is high. As a result, most educational uses of audio-conferencing, and almost all applications of video-conferencing, have been through campus-based sites, where groups of students could be served.

The advent of video-conferencing led to substantial growth in the number of traditional institutions offering 'distributed' courses. This method became particularly popular with campus-based US state universities, as these had a mandate for equal access to citizens wherever they were located in the state. Telecommunication technologies enabled institutions with such a mandate to make better use of limited teaching resources, as courses could be taught to larger numbers of learners across the state without instructors having to travel (Duning *et al.*, 1993). As Trowt-Bayard (1994) surmised, '... it's easier to move bits than bodies' (p.12).

However, although campus-based group conferencing enables students to access locally programmes coming from a distant provider, students still have to be present at a set time and a set place. This reduces flexibility compared with home-based technologies such as mail-delivered printed materials or home-based computing. Web-conferencing to the desktop or mobile telephone promises more flexibility and convenience. The ability to archive and access synchronous Web communication later provides added flexibility for those who cannot participate in real time. Software licensing costs though for Web-conferencing are currently high, and this restricts access, as does the need for higher speed Internet access and a high-end personal computer.

With respect to full desk-top video-conferencing, at the time of writing the necessary bandwidth to the desktop is just not there for most potential students, nor are the sophisticated software/interfaces that are needed to make this a user-friendly learning environment.

TEACHING AND LEARNING IMPLICATIONS OF SYNCHRONOUS CONFERENCING

Early distance learning, based on print-based correspondence and/or broadcasting technologies such as radio or television, was characterized by its distinctive lack of real time interaction between learners and an instructor. Interaction among learners was even more lacking. The development of two-way synchronous technologies enabled a transition from an individual print-based model of instruction where the learner studied in isolation, to an approach based more on distributed groups.

Audio-conferencing was the first conferencing technology to provide two-way capability as a supplementary or a main technology for teaching. As a supplement, it provided interactive support for print- or video-based systems such as satellite television. As a main technology, it supported a wide range of instructional applications, such as tutorials, lectures (Kirby and Boak, 1989), and learner support (Lalande, 1995). Students could still study from home but in a real-time group context. Similarly with video-conferencing, learning could take place synchronously at local study centers or at university or college satellite campuses (Collis, 1991).

With Web-conferencing, teacher and students can interact visually, graphically, and verbally. Students can step out of a synchronous session without disrupting the lesson, but still notifying participants that they have left the session. Students can hold conversations on the side, using text chat, or attract the attention of the presenter without having to interrupt. A student can have a private conversation with the presenter/instructor without disrupting the rest of the class.

Also with Web-conferencing, students and teacher can share word-processed documents, spreadsheets, and other computer applications. They can access Web sites, either as a group, or individually. Students can access multimedia, animated graphics, PowerPoint presentations and recorded events for playback. Students can be assessed through multiple-choice questions and receive immediate feedback of results. Students can also get online instructor evaluation either synchronously or asynchronously. Students can submit questions to an instructor (or the class) live verbally or through asynchronous messages. Instructors can get live polling of issues and see the results immediately. Thus desktop Web-conferencing allows both synchronous and asynchronous learning activities to be combined and integrated.

Modes of synchronous conferencing

There are several common modes of teaching by telephone or video-conferencing. In summary, these are:

Mode 1: Individual to individual

Mode 1 represents an instructor communicating on a one-to-one basis with a single student. Many distance teaching institutions still use the telephone in Mode 1 for individual tutoring and counselling, with print and other media providing the direct teaching. Although today the telephone is rarely used as the main source of teaching, and e-mail provides a less time-dependent mode of communication, the telephone can still provide critically important learning support or counselling to students studying at a distance.

Mode 2: Instructor to a single, remote group

Mode 2 represents a teacher or tutor in contact with a group of students at a remote site. This is sometimes used when the teacher is in one institution (and may incidentally have 'live' students before her in a classroom), and the remote group is at another campus, or in another institution. In this mode, it is generally used for direct instruction. It is particularly useful where there is a secondary or 'downtown' campus. No bridge is required in this situation, as only one remote site is connected. This mode can be supported either by audio- or video-conferencing. It is generally used as the main delivery medium.

Mode 3: Instructor to remote individuals

Mode 3 links a tutor or teacher with a number of individual students at individual sites – usually students at home. Through the use of a bridge, every person can speak to and hear every other person. A number of institutions have used Mode 3 extensively instead of (optional) face-to-face tutorials, especially where students are scattered over a wide area (Robinson, 1984). The telephone tutorials provide students with an opportunity to analyse and discuss the teaching materials provided through other media (print, television, audio-cassettes, or the Web). Currently, this mode is still limited mainly to audio-conferencing by telephone, although some software (e.g. Centra, http://www.centra.com) supports the transmission to the desktop of a small video picture as well as audio, provided the sender has a desktop video camera.

Because signals can be sent from only one site at any one time, such conferences require skill to manage, as the instructor has to pass the desktop 'baton' or microphone to the site that is to transmit. As a result, control over the design and conduct of this mode of conferencing usually remains firmly with the instructor, with most comments from the students directed to the instructor rather than to the other students.

Although technically it is possible to link a large number of sites together through audio- or Web-conferencing, the risk of technical difficulties rapidly increases with more than seven sites. An equally serious constraint is the number of students that can be effectively taught or tutored in this way at any single time. Generally, between 7 and 12 individual students are optimal for audio-conferencing and Web-conferencing in this mode, if a high level of interaction between teacher and student is to be maintained.

Mode 4: Instructor to multiple groups

Mode 4 links a teacher or tutor in one site to groups of students at multiple sites. Many universities and colleges in North America and Australia have used Mode 4 for direct instruction, with lectures delivered to campuses distributed around a state or province. Students respond with questions to be answered by the lecturer. Either audio-conferencing or video-conferencing may be used. In this situation, conferencing is likely to be the main form of direct instruction, accompanied by printed notes or a Web site. Several US state university systems, such as Wisconsin, Nebraska, and organizations such as the National Universities Telecommunications Consortium have used either audio- or video-conferencing or both for this form of delivery.

Mode 5: Self-help groups

One other mode of operation is really a variation on Modes 1 and 3. Students may be encouraged to set up self-help or task-oriented groups. Synchronous Web-conferencing is particularly useful for students working collaboratively online on an assignment or task. The activity is often helped if students can set up the task synchronously, then work on it asynchronously, coming back to a synchronous discussion to finalize the task.

Teaching roles for synchronous conferencing

Robinson (1984, p.129) found in a study she conducted that telephone tutorials with either individuals or small groups (Modes 3 or 4) were effective for the following tasks:

- To clarify student difficulties in course materials.
- To promote student discussion of specific issues and topics.
- To debate a topic.
- To discuss problems of recent written assignments, or strategies for tackling forthcoming ones.
- To discuss, analyse or work through previously-circulated printed materials (maths problems, graphs, diagrams, illustrations, raw data, etc.).
- To analyse a written text or musical score.
- To present short case-studies.
- To role-play an exercise.
- To practise and evaluate sight singing on a musical course.
- To negotiate the design of a project.

She also found the following were *not* considered effective:

- Lecturing.
- Constructing a complex diagram from scratch.
- Impromptu tutorials or unprepared topics.
- Tasks involving a large number of texts or sources.
- Groups with constantly changing membership.
- Some science, technology and maths topics where dynamic visuals were required.
- Conveying lengthy and detailed instructions.

Although this list was developed for audio-conferencing, nearly all of the positive and negative items would apply to the later forms of video- and Web-conferencing, although video-conferencing will also support subjects where there is a need for dynamic visuals.

Telephone conferencing can also be very useful for administration, disseminating information to regional staff, for meetings to avoid staff travelling to headquarters, and even for training staff. It is useful for planning and designing courses developed collaboratively by staff at different institutions or campuses. Because of its simplicity and reliability, and multi-point facility, telephone conferencing is often preferable to video-conferencing for this purpose.

Video-conferencing has been used in a wide range of applications. Duran and Sauer (1997) claim that distance learning has become '... *the* primary application of videoconferencing ...' (p.82). Many U.S. states have deployed large-scale video-conferencing systems. One example is the Georgia Statewide Academic and Medical System, a multi-site video-conference network consisting of 400 locations, with multi-point bridging connecting up to 16 locations at a time (Mode 4). Applications have included student debates, virtual field trips, tele-medicine, tele-rounds, tele-psychiatry, tele-education conferences, and distance learning. Since inception in 1992, GSAMS has successfully conducted over 100,000 video-conferences (Rhodes, 2001).

Video-conferencing can serve a variety of administrative and communication needs in addition to distance learning, such as meetings, job interviews, and candidacy exams. The ability to see whom they are talking to counters instructor resistance to earlier forms of synchronous technologies such as audio- and audio-graphics conferencing.

While video-conferencing to groups tends to focus on the transmission of information, Web-conferencing systems have placed greater emphasis on collaboration between individuals. Some of the other advantages claimed for Web-conferencing are:

- It can replace or enhance courses currently offered by video-conferencing, audio-conferencing or audio-graphic conferencing.
- It can enhance existing asynchronous courses, providing a blended learning approach.

- It provides off-campus learners with tools they can use to collaborate in real time with peers.
- It has potential to provide enhanced support to tele-health related applications as well as grand rounds for medical faculty.

Desktop video-conferencing has been used in distance learning as a replacement for larger, more expensive room systems, either for direct instruction or to provide learner support. Alberta North, a consortium of post-secondary institutions in Northern Alberta and the Rural Area Training, installed a network of desktop systems into local sites for distance learning meeting applications. Nichol and Watson (2000) found that desktop video-conferencing can be an effective medium for tutoring student teachers at a distance.

The importance of video in conferencing

To what degree is video needed in a networked working environment and what value if any does a 'talking head' contribute? Rosen (1996) reported on three studies undertaken by Sun Microsystems, Anderson Worldwide and the University of Michigan that examined the role of video in real-time collaborative communications. A summary of the studies is provided below:

- 84 per cent of participants indicated that video improved the quality of communication between colleagues; without video, the quality of the discussion was felt to be inferior.
- Video was particularly valuable in interpreting pauses in conversation; without video there was some anxiety and confusion.
- The University of Michigan study found that video had a strong effect on the satisfaction of group members and appeared to motivate individuals to work together.
- Sun Microsystems found that without video, collaboration declined among users.
- Collaborating with high quality video was perceived to be as good as face to face.
- When video was added to support remote collaboration, the number of e-mail messages dropped; when video was removed, although the collaborative tools were still available, the number of e-mail messages per day doubled.

These studies suggest that verbal communication may be less effective without video. These outcomes are in contrast to studies that suggest that remote learners can experience anxiety when they appear on camera, resulting in lower learner involvement and participation rates (Armstrong-Stassen *et al.*, 1998). One possible explanation is that Web-conferencing uses a desktop computer. This is a more personal and familiar medium of communication compared to the telephone-based video-conference classroom with its accompanying video cameras and large monitors.

Advantages and disadvantages of synchronous conferencing for teaching

There are many educators who believe that the closer technology comes to simulating face-to-face teaching, the better (University of Illinois, 1999). For those who believe this, technologies that come closest to supporting or replicating the type of interactions and communications processes that occur in a face-to-face classroom would have an advantage over other forms of delivery. Garrison, writing in 1989 about audio-conferencing, claimed that:

> Teleconferencing represents a paradigm shift in facilitating and supporting learning at a distance ... Of all the means used to support distance education, teleconferencing most closely simulates the transaction between teacher and students in a contiguous or conventional form of education. The exchange is conversational in nature, it may be spontaneous, and it is immediate. In these respects teleconferencing differs from all other technologies used to bridge the distance in distance education.
>
> (Garrison, 1989, p.66)

He identified three 'defining characteristics' of teleconferencing:

- A group method of learning.
- Regularity and immediacy of two-way communication.
- Suited to small and widely-dispersed target groups.

For these reasons, Garrison claimed that 'few if any traditional classroom techniques are not adaptable to teleconferencing'. This shift from individualized to group-based learning enhances opportunities for interaction and collaboration for those who are able to access such technology. Furthermore, video-conferencing technology in particular enables classroom teaching to be extended beyond the instructor's classroom with relatively little adaptation of teaching method.

The main issue that surrounds the value of synchronous technologies is whether, as Garrison stated, distance education should mirror as closely as possible face-to-face classroom teaching, or whether distance education should be based on an educational model fundamentally different from face-to-face classroom teaching. A second issue is the extent to which the various forms of synchronous communication can overcome some of the limitations of asynchronous technologies, and in particular text- and graphics-based Web courses. A third issue is the extent to which the design and use of synchronous technologies influences the effectiveness of the medium. Some of the arguments for and against the use of synchronous technologies are discussed below.

Real time interaction

We do know that interaction between learners and instructors, and interaction between a student and other students, are critical to successful distance learning (Moore and Kearsley, 1996). Guzley *et al.* (2001) have claimed that the combination of synchronous two-way audio and two-way video has the most promise for maximizing interaction in distance learning. The ability of video-conferencing to support 'side talk', namely spontaneous discussions at remote sites that occur during presentations, was also noted as being important. Oliver and Reeves (1996) reported on the strong attitudinal and motivational gains attributed to this form of social interaction.

In discussing asynchronous, Web-based online learning, Feenberg (1999) wrote that the online environment is essentially a space for written interaction. Donath *et al.* (1999, p.2) argue that this is both the strength and the limitation of asynchronous Web-based communication:

> Most on-line conversation is text. This is partly due to the history of the technology. Textual interfaces were the norm when e-mail, newsgroups and chat-rooms were developed. As a medium for exchanging ideas, text has a number of excellent qualities. It is highly adaptable. With the basic alphanumeric keyboard, people can assemble discourses on any topic. With skill, it can be quite expressive. Yet as a conversational medium, the austerity of text can be detrimental. In particular, it is difficult to convey many kinds of social information, such as conversational tone, patterns of activity – even the size of the conversational group is opaque in most text-based forums. Asynchronous discussions such as newsgroups or mailing lists are inherently persistent, and recorded logs bring persistence to the [otherwise] ephemeral synchronous text-based chats. Yet the drawbacks of the text-only interface [are evident] when perusing the archives of a discussion. The rhythms of the conversation's exchanges are obliterated and the reader is likely to approach the mass of accumulated archival material by searching or non-linear approaches, often losing in the process much of the conversation's context.

Research into desktop video-conferencing suggests that it could be successfully used to improve the quality of interaction between students and teachers. Harmon and MacNeil (1998) found that desktop video-conferencing provided a motivational as well as an informational/reflective role in distance learning for remote learners. Thus synchronous technologies that facilitate real-time, conversational interactive communication may have strong advantages over text-based asynchronous technologies with respect to inter-personal communication.

Immediacy

Some (for example, Hardy and Olcott, 1995) have argued that learners prefer having their instructor in close proximity, whether this is accomplished virtually or in person. Others (for example, Soo and Bonk, 1998) have argued that in synchronous learning there is a condensation of information and ideas that cannot easily be duplicated any other way, particularly in online learning environments. They argue that synchronous communication allows for immediate and timely feedback and creates a strong social presence more easily than asynchronous online environments.

Collaborative learning

According to Jonassen (1999), learning is more effective when it is undertaken with other learners rather than as a singular, solitary activity. Jonassen (1999) and Oliver and Reeves (1996) have argued that such forms of learning lead to higher quality learning outcomes. Sorensen and Baylen (2000) have argued that the two-way video and audio capability of video-conferencing can support increased student interactivity and collaborative work, and can help create social presence among distance learners.

Anytime, anywhere flexibility

The flexibility of distance learning has been seen as one of its advantages over traditional forms of education. Synchronous technologies, by their very nature, impose more constraints on learners. It is quite common for designers of existing online programmes that are largely asynchronously delivered to be resistant to providing live sessions for learners. As Anderson and Garrison (1995, p.40) have pointed out:

> Many distance educators have refused to incorporate, or have relegated to 'optional status', any interactions that restrict student access in terms of time or place. This ideological commitment to independent study denies interactive educational opportunities and choices to students and teachers.

In a study on learner perceptions of audio-conferencing, Anderson and Garrison (1995) examined the issue of flexibility. They found that for the majority of the learners surveyed, independence of time and place was not an issue (possibly because these learners had already made a commitment to attend classes at a learning centre).

Nevertheless, an asynchronous Web-based course is ideal for adults who travel frequently, or have erratic schedules. These learners require more flexibility in their learning than an adult learner who can attend a local face-to-face or synchronous conference class. On the other hand, a course based on synchronous conferencing may not have as much flexibility as an asynchronous online course, but it may provide a great deal more flexibility for learners than traditional instruction, if the traditional instruction requires lengthy travel time. Learners may rank real-time interaction via conferencing from a local site as being a particularly useful feature compared with the limitations of asynchronous online communication. For example, lawyers who attended a continuing professional development workshop that consisted of pre-recorded lectures and live group discussions by Web-conferencing reported that the key advantage of this way of learning was its flexibility over traditional face-to-face instruction, which required more time away from the office (Picard and Wood, 2002).

Thus we can see that adult learners have varying opinions of what constitutes flexibility within a course. A more fundamental issue is: should absolute flexibility be the overriding consideration in the design and delivery of all distance courses? The research thus far would suggest that distance learners not only benefit from a combination of synchronous and asynchronous technology, but they also prefer this approach.

Improve the quality of teaching

Can we achieve higher learning outcomes with new synchronous technologies? Results are inconclusive. Professors at Michigan State University taught a microeconomics course using live Web-casting technology (Brown and Liedholm, 2002). The study involved three cohorts of learners: face to face; hybrid (reduced face to face access but including access to Web-based tutorials); and off campus (Web-casting and Web-based tutorials). Evaluation results comparing the three groups showed no significant differences on knowledge and comprehension questions.

As we have seen, this is typical of most if not all carefully controlled media comparison studies. However, the results differed significantly with respect to the higher level skills of applying knowledge, particularly regarding complex applications, because the fully online learners significantly underperformed in comparison to the face-to-face and the hybrid learners.

Problem-solving and critical thinking vs. rote memory and comprehension

The limited research that has been done on learner–instructor interactions in the synchronous classroom indicates that the use of memory and content-level questioning is common (Kirby and Boak, 1989; Hardy and Olcott, 1995; Oliver and McLoughlin, 1997). According to Oliver and Reeves (1996), the majority of interactions found in synchronous settings are social and didactic in nature; cognitive interactions, which go beyond memory and comprehension to higher levels of thinking, are far less prevalent.

Oliver and Reeves' systematic analysis of the types of interactions that occur in virtual, synchronous classrooms (using the social, didactic and cognitive scale which they developed) suggests that most teaching tends to be content-focused, rather than focused on problem solving and critical thinking. More significantly, though, they also found that for a variety of reasons, teachers teach the same in virtual classrooms as they do in their regular classrooms. They question whether the live, interactive capabilities of the media are being used effectively.

Educators have often bolted existing methodologies and practices onto new forms of communication. The lecture method is the most common teaching application and as Oliver and Reeves have shown, such methods are easily transported to synchronous technologies. Thus although the question has been framed as to how well synchronous technologies support critical thinking, we might want to ask instead why is traditional classroom instruction so poor? Why do instructors tend to focus on lower level learning outcomes in their teaching, and why are these methods of classroom teaching carried over to technology-based teaching?

In the asynchronous computer-conferencing environment, instructors may be more selective in the types of questions they pose. Time on task may also partly explain higher levels of interaction in asynchronous computer conferencing. Ideally, learners read, reflect, formulate and respond to postings. In a synchronous environment, whether face-to-face or technology-mediated, learners' responses are usually immediate. Thus responses are given without benefit of lengthy reflection, unless questions have been assigned ahead of time as a way to encourage critical thinking in synchronous settings (an idea endorsed by Hardy and Olcott, 1995).

Synchronous technology suffers to some extent in its proximity to face-to-face teaching, in that sometimes forms of teaching that place emphasis on comprehension and understanding at the expense of critical thinking are more easily transferred to synchronous technology-based teaching. Certainly, asynchronous computer conferencing is quite different from the temporal, non-linear, spontaneous nature of synchronous environments, and communicating in print is quite different from communicating aurally.

Probably more significant though than the functional differences between asynchronous and synchronous technologies is the way that they are used. Teaching that is redesigned to exploit the advantages of either method is more likely to be successful than merely replicating classroom teaching. Ultimately, the issue is not which is the better technology, but how can they best be combined in ways that exploit their teaching potential.

CONCLUSIONS

Synchronous conferencing technologies continue to develop and improve. Through a combination of increased bandwidth, faster computer processing,

and improved compression technology, synchronous communications technology is becoming more and more accessible for distance learning. Desktop
Web-conferencing is clearly the next step in the evolution of synchronous
technologies, offering the promise of full two-way video and audio communication between instructors and students, when broadband technology to the
desktop is available.

One argument for the use of synchronous conferencing is that this most
closely resembles conventional face-to-face teaching. Although students are
not physically present, the students and instructor can communicate with
each other in almost exactly the same way they would if they were physically
present in a classroom.

The trouble with the argument that synchronous technologies best replicate
classroom teaching is that it assumes that conventional classroom teaching is
the best way to teach and cannot be improved. The argument denies the
possibility that technology may allow for different and possibly better ways
to teach. Certainly, there appear to be strong benefits in addition to increased
convenience and flexibility for learners (and instructors) from an asynchronous approach to learning, such as more time for reflection, more time on
task, and more opportunity for knowledge construction.

The second argument is that although there are benefits from asynchronous
approaches to learning, there are also disadvantages, and synchronous technologies can help overcome these. This is a more convincing argument. Synchronous communication offers immediacy and the opportunity for both instructor
and students to interpret body language, tone of voice and other more subtle
non-textual features of communication. Synchronous communication allows
for the more affective side of learning, such as creating vibrant and dynamic
discussions and increasing social presence.

However, these advantages tend to be lost if synchronous communication
is largely used for information transmission or for lecturing, and yet this is
the danger if instructors are not trained to understand the strengths and
limitations of the medium. In many of the quoted research studies, poor
results were obtained because of inappropriate use of the technology, rather
than any inherent weakness in the technology itself. Many distance learners
will often prefer the advantages of synchronous communication, even if it
means a trip to a local centre. Nevertheless, having said that, for many distance
learners, synchronous video-conferencing is either inconvenient or not a very
effective medium of communication. Web-conferencing may overcome some
of the inconvenience, but at the time of writing, we are just beginning to get
experience in this form of teaching, which is still restricted to audio, graphic
and textual communication.

In summary, technology has evolved to the point where individuals can
engage in academic discourse, both synchronously and asynchronously, at a
distance, using a wide range of tools. The discussion of research into the
benefits and limitations of various types of synchronous communication
indicates that there are no overwhelming educational arguments for one

particular type of conferencing over another. However, it is likely that in most circumstances a combination of synchronous and asynchronous communication will offer the best learning environment.

More importantly, there are no clear instructional guidelines as to what is best done synchronously and what asynchronously. Until we understand better these differences, the benefits of a particular synchronous technology are likely to be driven by other considerations, such as access, cost and organizational context. Thus it is important to look at the costs and organizational issues around the use of synchronous technologies, which is the subject of the next chapter.

10 Audio-, video- and Web-conferencing: costs and organizational issues

Co-authored with Janice Picard

In this chapter we look at the costs for synchronous technologies, and also the organizational issues involved. Because the technology is still evolving, it is difficult to find a stable basis for estimating costs or discussing organizational issues. However, although new technology developments may drive down absolute costs, the cost structures for synchronous technologies are surprisingly stable, and the organizational issues around synchronous technologies are becoming clear.

COSTS

Costs will vary depending on the particular technology, as well as on the actual circumstances of use. It is necessary then to look separately at the costs of each of the four technologies (audio-conferencing, telephone-based video-conferencing, Web-conferencing and broadband video-conferencing).

Audio-conferencing

Costs of teaching by telephone will be influenced by several factors:

- The mode and purpose of the teaching.
- The distance between participants.
- The pricing structure (tariffs) of the telephone company.
- The availability of special services, such as leased lines, ISDN and fibre-optic networks.
- The extent of regulation governing competition and monopoly of services.
- The policy of the teaching institution regarding payment of line-charges by students and tutors.

Pricing policies

There is great variation in practice between institutions, and even more so within an institution, between what is charged to a student and what is not.

Distance-teaching institutions in particular have difficulties in drawing the boundary between what the student pays and what the institution pays. Nowhere is this more apparent than in policies regarding telephone call charges.

Some institutions offer 'call-free' services, where the call is automatically charged to the institution, even if initiated by the student, to encourage greater student–tutor contact. In other institutions, costs of telephone calls are borne directly by the students. Where telephone tutoring is used in support of other media such as print, telephone teaching tends to be seen as a replacement for 'optional' face-to-face lectures, where these are uneconomic. The logic in such institutions of making students pay the line charges is that the institution does not pay for student travel to face-to-face sessions; why then should it pay for telephone costs?

Robinson (1990) reported that at the British Open University:

> Audio-conferencing is almost always cheaper than the cost of a face-to-face tutorial *when the travel costs of all participants are taken into account*. The more usual calculation done compares only the tutor's travel costs (paid for by the university) with the cost of a conference call. On this basis the cost of the conference call may not always be less.

It could be argued that telephone teaching has not been used as much as it might have been in distance education because students were charged for using the service; on the other hand, it is very difficult for institutions to control costs if students are allowed to charge back all their calls.

One general approach is for all 'development' costs to be paid by the institution and all delivery costs to be recovered from the students, either in the form of a general student tuition fee or through a set of direct costs for each service provided. This means that students are responsible for the variable costs, and in this way an institution can accommodate everyone who wishes to enrol for a course (provided they can afford the fees), since fees cover marginal costs.

However, if students pay the direct cost of their telephone calls, the more remote a student, or the further a student is away from the tutor, the more it will cost the student to use the telephone for study purposes. Thus although students may have equal *access* to telephones, they do not necessarily have equal *costs* to bear in using them. One argument for allowing students to charge their calls to the institution is that this avoids cost disadvantages due to distance. One approach is to allow students a set number of 'charged' calls (irrespective of distance); over that limit, the student pays.

Private networks

Another factor influencing costs is whether institutions have to go entirely through the public telephone system, and are charged per line and the amount of use, or whether they have access to a private network. If telephone teaching goes through the public network, line costs are variable, being dependent on the number of students, the distance of the call, and the amount of use. However, in some countries, an educational institution can lease or rent private lines from a telephone company or a telephone 're-seller'. The lease is a flat annual fee. Once the lease is paid, there are no further charges for calls between sites covered by the lease.

Thus an institution in one part of an educational system can offer courses not only to its own on-site students, but also to students at its own 'satellite' campuses or at other institutions elsewhere in the state or province, with no direct cost to the institution for the telephone lines, once the lease has been paid. This is particularly useful for small multi-campus institutions, where there are insufficient students or specialist staff at one site to teach a particular subject, but by 'pooling' students across several campuses, a viable number can be reached for a 'class'. Leased lines also provide a means for equalizing telephone costs for more remote campuses.

The Open Learning Agency leased lines that connected with most government offices, colleges and universities within the province of British Columbia. OLA not only used the audio-conferencing system for its own courses, but also managed it on behalf of the other post-secondary institutions in the province. OLA provided a conference bridge service for the colleges and universities. It paid an annual fixed charge of C$150,000 (US$112,500), plus C$780 (US$585) per line, for this service. This was a *fixed* cost, since the figure was independent of the amount of use. In addition, there were charges for calls that went outside the system. Calls from outside this particular leased system were charged at the rate to the nearest system 'point'. Thus if someone called into their local college, they paid at the rate to their local college, even though the college switchboard may then be networking them into an audio-conference across the whole province.

Bridge costs

For institutions that use audio-conferencing extensively, it is usually cheaper to buy and operate their own bridge, provided the institution has an adequate number of telephone lines. Alternatively, one could use a professional tele-conferencing company such as Darome, whose costs (in Canada) are 30 cents per minute per line within a local calling area and 50 cents per minute per line for calls outside the local calling area.

In 1990, a 40-port (line) bridge cost US$75,000. It is relatively easy to calculate whether or not to buy a bridge, if traffic can be estimated. Dividing the cost of the bridge plus the cost of providing one's own bridge operator, by the administrative charges of a tele-conferencing company, enables one to calculate the number of conferences that need to be made to make purchase of a bridge more cost-effective than using a professional tele-conferencing company.

Cost examples

Given the wide variation in cost policies between institutions, any example chosen of the actual costs of telephone teaching is likely to have limited relevance. However, by using examples, we can explore the *structure* of telephone teaching costs. I will base my examples on costs and practices at the Open Learning Agency. (All costs unless indicated otherwise are in C$.)

Example 1: Direct teaching by audio-conferencing using leased lines

This example is based on direct teaching to individual students in their homes. Where telephone teaching was the primary medium used, the teacher was paid a set fee, which included curriculum development, choice of set books, advice on supplementary reading, setting and marking of assignments and examinations, and tutoring/counselling of his or her students.

At the Open Learning Agency, for a one semester course of 13 weeks (roughly 150 hours of study) an instructor was paid approximately C$3,000 in 1990. Such a course would include a three-hour telephone tutorial, consisting of a lecture (sometimes given by a guest specialist, who might be paid in addition to the teacher) followed by an interactive discussion between students and teachers. Students would also be able to call the teacher during set 'office hours' for individual consultation. The direct fixed cost of the Open Learning Agency's audio-conferencing unit was C$91,700 in 1990/1 (see Table 10.1).

The Open Learning Agency in 1990/1 provided 1,185 hours of audio-conferencing. This worked out at a direct fixed cost of C$77 (US$57.75) per hour. The average 'class' size for an Open Learning Agency course delivered by audio-conferencing was about 12. Handling more than 12 individuals at 12 different sites becomes difficult, and interactivity for all students starts to drop off rapidly.

The instructor's cost of C$3,000 for 13 weeks at 12 hours a week, divided by 12 students = C$1.60 (US$1.20) per student per hour. (This includes all the work of the teacher, not just time spent on audio-conferencing.) There are probably additional costs, such as guest lecturer fees, mailing and library costs for supplementary reading, etc.

Using a leased line service, the instructional costs per student will increase with the number of students in steps of 12, until all 40 ports are being used. There is an additional cost for calls going outside the leased network and beyond local calls to the nearest leased 'node', for example, to students' homes in more remote areas. In 1990/1, these averaged about C$2 (US$1.50) per student per hour, plus another C$2 per hour per tutor, across all participants.

Calculating costs for audio-conferencing is particularly complex. Up to three 'sessions', each with 12 students and a tutor, can be handled simultaneously on a 40 port bridge. With each session lasting three hours, up to nine

Table 10.1 Direct fixed cost of OLA audio-conferencing service, 1990/1

Fixed costs per annum	C$	US$
Operator costs	40,000	30,000
Bridge costs (amortized over 8 years)	12,500	9,375
Leased lines: C$780 × 40 =	31,200	23,400
Other costs	8,000	6,000
Total	91,700	68,775

sessions could technically be handled per day, or 45 per five-day week. Even though many sessions will be held in evenings or weekends, when students are at home, I have assumed a maximum of 45 sessions per week. (Although evenings would allow for more conferences, once the number of sessions exceeds 45, an additional operator would be needed). This means that for every 540 students, a new bridge, set of leased lines and an operator would be needed. Table 10.2 is based on these assumptions.

It can be seen that there are slight economies of scale due to the semi-fixed costs of a bridge, an operator, and leased lines, but overall costs are high per student study hour. It is important to note that the figures in Table 10.2 refer just to the costs of the audio-conferences themselves, and not to the actual time spent on the course as a whole. The audio-conference itself is only one-quarter of the weekly workload for students, the rest of the time being devoted to print materials and assignments.

Example 2: Tutorials using audio-conferencing via direct lines

For telephone tutorials used in support of other media, such as print, tutors tend to be paid on an hourly rate, which was approximately C$22 per hour in the OLA in 1991. For a class of 12 students, this works out at C$1.83 per student per hour. In most cases, tutors get some form of reimbursement for their outgoing telephone calls to students, sometimes with a set limit.

Line costs through a commercial conference operator will average between 40 cents per minute, or $24 per hour per student, plus $18 per hour (30 cents per minute) for the tutor's call, or $1.50 per student per hour. Thus a one-hour telephone tutorial for 12 students, each in their own home, paying direct line costs, would cost $1.83 + $24 + $1.50 = $27.33 per student study hour. This would be in addition to the costs of other media used in the course.

Summary of the costs of audio-conferencing

The structure of costs for teaching by telephone are very different from those of 'one-way' media, such as print, broadcasting and cassettes. Telephone

Table 10.2 Costs of audio-conferencing per student study hour (based on OLA costs, 1990/1)

	30 students per annum (3 tutors) C$	120 students per annum (10 tutors) C$	625 students per annum (52 tutors) C$	1,250 students per annum (104 tutors) C$	3,000 students per annum (250 tutors) C$
Operator costs	320,000	320,000	640,000	960,000	1,920,000
Bridge costs	100,000	100,000	200,000	300,000	600,000
Leased lines	249,600	249,600	499,200	748,800	1,497,600
Other costs	64,000	64,000	128,000	256,000	384,000
Tutor contracts	72,000	240,000	1,248,000	2,496,000	6,000,000
Total (8 years)	805,000	973,600	2,715,200	4,760,800	10,401,000
Total (1 year)	100,625	121,700	339,400	595,100	1,300,125
Cost per student study hour (39 hours)	86.00 US$64.50	26.00 US$19.50	13.92 US$10.44	12.21 US$9.16	11.11 US$8.33

costs are variable, i.e. they rise roughly in proportion to the number of students using the service, unlike the 'one-way' technologies of print and broadcasting, although slight economies of scale are possible through the use of a bridge and leased lines. Telephone teaching to groups of students at several remote campuses would reduce average costs, but the cost structures would be similar to telephone-based video-conferencing, which in recent years has largely replaced audio-conferencing to groups.

Audio-conferencing may appear to be cheaper than it is because teaching departments often are not charged the fixed costs of an already existing service, and students have to pay the line charges. However, when the fixed costs or student phone costs are included, audio-conferencing is not so attractive.

Video-conferencing

For many years video-conferencing was a luxury few could afford. In the late 1970s and early 1980s, telecommunication costs for video-conferencing could cost organizations up to US$30,000 a month (Trowt-Bayard, 1994). The cost of hardware was also high. Codecs averaged US$250,000. Since then the costs of video-conferencing have been dropping dramatically. Prices will drop even more once broadband Internet access enables video-conferencing to the desktop, laptop or mobile phone. In the early part of the 2000s, though, the main form of video-conferencing is still telephone or cable-based, and thus this is the form of video-conferencing that we are most accurately able to cost.

There are four main categories of costs for telephone-based video-conferencing: instructor costs, equipment costs, line charges, and operational costs.

Instructor costs

Video-conferencing is quite demanding in preparation time. Content must be presented so that it can be clearly seen at remote sites on a relatively small television monitor. Strategies to ensure interaction and responses from students at remote sites must be considered. Additional readings and handouts, or even a Web site, may have to be developed in advance. If video-conferencing is also the main form of instruction, time also needs to be found for assessing students.

I have therefore assumed one hour of preparation time for every hour of direct instruction, and no savings in preparation time in subsequent years. I have also assumed one hour for marking each assignment and a total of three assignments per semester. Thus the cost for each hour of instruction will be $100 ($50 for preparation and $50 for instruction), plus marking time (dependent on student numbers).

Equipment costs

For a standard, room-based system, video-conferencing equipment costs average between $25,000 and $30,000 per site, including monitors, codecs, speakers, a desktop computer, and control units. Thus for an institution wanting to link up five sites (main campus plus four satellite campuses), the equipment costs will total around $125,000 to $150,000. Because of continual improvement in technical standards, a reasonable life for this kind of video-conferencing equipment is around four years. Thus if equipment costs are spread over four years, the average annual (amortized) capital cost would be $6,000 to $8,000 per site.

In addition to the hardware, there are the costs of room conversion. Appropriate lighting, the arrangement of tables and chairs, and above all proper sound insulation are each essential for successful video-conferencing. This can add another $20,000 per site, and wiring can add another $5,000, but once converted, the room can be used for at least 20 years, even as equipment improves and changes. Thus averaging room conversion costs over 20 years gives an annual room cost of $1,250 per year.

Line charges

These costs can depend on where the line costs originate, and in what year the costs are calculated. Currently, using ISDN one can rent six lines (386 kbs) at $65 an hour for connection anywhere in North America, or $1,100 a month. Trans-oceanic calls originating in North America would be about one-third higher ($90 to $100 an hour).

However, these are the costs for point-to-point calls (two sites). If more than two sites are to be connected, a bridge is needed. Connecting more than two sites requires either the purchase of a bridge, which for most institutions would not be justified unless there is a great deal of video-conferencing, or renting bridge time from a telecommunications company. Costs are in the order of $75 per hour per site, plus $95 for the outgoing call (from the site originating the conference to the telecom bridge).

Operational costs

Although modern equipment is now reliable and largely self-operated, equipment needs maintenance, rooms need to be booked, and trouble-shooting needs to be done from time to time. Thus most institutions using video-conferencing for regular teaching will need some full-time technical and operational support. One well-trained and experienced video-conference manager/technician can handle up to about six hours a day of conferencing, five days a week, from the originating site, at a cost of $50,000 a year (with benefits). In addition, technical support at each satellite campus will be needed on a part-time basis (half-time, or $20,000 a year per remote site).

Calculating costs for telephone-based video-conferencing

For the purposes of calculating typical costs, let us assume a video-conferencing studio operating 25 hours a week (i.e. 25 × one hour conferences) across four additional remote sites.

The room and equipment costs will average $8,000 a year at each site for a total of $40,000. The equipment is mainly used during semester time, so let us assume 40 weeks a year or 200 days for five hours a day, totalling 1,000 hours at the central site, and 750 hours at each of the four satellite campuses (not all conferences are likely to go to all sites). Thus:

- Room and equipment costs at the centre are $8 per hour ($8,000/1,000) and at the remote sites $10.67 an hour ($8,000/750).
- Staff costs at the centre are $50 per hour ($50,000/1,000) and at local sites $26.67 per hour ($20,000/750).
- Line charges are $95 per hour for the link to the bridge from the 'control' studio, and $75 an hour from the bridge to each of the four remote sites ($300) for a total of $395 per hour.

If we take a standard, five site video-conference with an average of six students at each site, or 30 students overall, and three lectures (each of one hour) per week, we obtain the costs that are set out in Table 10.3.

It can be seen that video-conferencing costs are still relatively high for teaching purposes, at over $20 per student study hour. There are no economies of scale once class enrolments exceed 30 students, and there are no

Table 10.3 Costs of 39 video-conferences over five sites, 30 students in total

Room/equipment centre	C$8 × 39	312.00
Room/equipment remote	C$10.67 × 39	416.91
Line charges to bridge	C$95 × 39	3,705.00
Line charges to remote sites	C$75 × 4 × 39	11,700.00
Instruction	C$50 × 39	1,950.00
Preparation	C$50 × 39	1,950.00
Marking	C$50 × 3 × 30	4,500.00
Manager	C$50 × 39	1,950.00
Site support	C$26.37 × 39	1,040.13
Total		27,524
Average cost per student		C$917.47
Average cost per student study hour		C$23.52
		US$17.64

accumulated economics over a period of years, as the teaching is more or less reproduced each year.

Some may argue that this is not the way that video-conferencing is commonly used. For instance, a common use is to take an existing face-to-face lecture course and add extra students at remote sites. The argument here is that video-conferencing is a marginal cost – the cost of the face-to-face lecture is already covered, so the only costs that should be added are the extra costs directly associated with the video-conferences. Assuming that 30 extra students were added, the preparation and instruction costs would be excluded (but not the additional student assessment costs). This would bring the marginal cost of the video-conference students down as shown in Table 10.4.

Thus it can be seen that the marginal costs are still high, although it could be argued that students will also spend time outside the conferencing doing assignments and other readings, thus bringing down the cost per student study hour.

Because of these high costs, most organizations eventually run into trouble with multi-point video-conferencing. For example, the School of Business at the University of Alberta phased out their Corporate Financial Diploma Program after examining the high costs associated with renting video-conferencing facilities in other cities, the cost of bridging the different locations, and the higher support costs of dealing with a more dispersed group of individuals.

Despite these high costs, there will still be situations where telephone-based video-conferencing will be considered worthwhile. In the corporate training sector, for instance, there are considerable costs incurred when employees have to travel for training. The savings made in travel, hotels, and

Table 10.4 Comparative costs of adding remote students by video-conference to a face-to-face lecture class

	Marginal cost (C$)	Full cost (C$)
Room/equipment (centre)	312.00	312.00
Room/equipment (remote)	416.91	416.91
Line charges (to bridge)	3,705.00	3,705.00
Line charges (to remote sites)	11,700.00	11,700.00
Instruction	0	1,950.00
Preparation	0	1,950.00
Marking	4,500.00	4,500.00
Manager	1,950.00	1,950.00
Site support	1,040.13	1,040.13
Total	23,625	27,524
Average cost per student	787.49	917.47
Average cost per student study hour	C$20.19 US$15.14	C$23.52 US$17.64

employees' time may well outweigh the costs of video-conferencing (for examples see Whalen and Wright, 2000). Video-conferencing may also be used when the video-conferencing costs, although high, remain a small proportion of the total tuition costs. The best example of this is the Queen's University MBA programme in Canada. At a cost of $45,000 per student for the MBA, the video-conferencing costs at around $7,000 per student are relatively minor. (However, the question remains: could the same quality of programme be delivered by less expensive methods?)

It is clear that telephone-based video-conferencing is too expensive to be considered the main medium of delivery for most academic purposes. Therefore telephone-based video-conferencing needs to be used very selectively. More importantly, because of its high cost, it should focus on those aspects of teaching that require real-time communication with remote learners. This is most likely to cover functions such as demonstrating procedural techniques, skills development, and in particular observing and providing feedback on the performance of remote learners. Thus in the distributed delivery of medical education between campuses in Vancouver, Victoria and Prince George, the University of British Columbia, the University of Victoria and the University of Northern British Columbia plan to make heavy use of video-conferencing.

The use of telephone-based video-conferencing for lectures, on the other hand, can be justified only in special circumstances. For instance, it can be much cheaper to bring a lecturer by video-conferencing into a large conference venue than to fly the presenter long distances, involving not only air fares but also accommodation and the time away from work. Telephone-based video-conferencing can also be useful for the occasional motivational lecture. On balance, though, it is an expensive medium for regular teaching.

Web-conferencing

Because Web-conferencing as a teaching technology is new, and at the time of writing there is no standard or dominant form in which it is used, there are almost no studies of the costs of Web-conferencing. However, it is possible to begin to build a costing model.

The most difficult element to estimate is the cost of course development. This could include instructor time, instructional design, project management and materials production. All these will depend on the chosen design. The simplest model would be an individual professor working on her own, using a combination of (text-based) chat, PowerPoint slides, audio lectures, online readings, and either multiple-choice testing or essay-type assessment. A more complex model would be based on a design team, consisting of the instructor, an instructional designer, and professional materials development. Since the claim for Web-conferencing is that it is easier and quicker to do than asynchronous online teaching, I will use the simpler model of course production (even though I believe it will lead to a lower quality course).

The course design consists of a weekly one-hour synchronous lecture, primarily audio but supported with PowerPoint slides and illustrations from Web sites, a one-hour weekly synchronous chat session, private individual study time for students of three hours a week following up on readings (either online or in textbooks), and three essay assignments, over a 13 week period. I have assumed a class of 25 undergraduate students, because the data I was able to obtain (from a Western Canadian research university) were based on a Web-conferencing software licence for a class of this size. I have estimated the instructor time at $50 per hour.

I have assumed an experienced and trained instructor, both in content and technology applications. She will need 90 minutes preparation time for each one-hour audio session. This includes the development of PowerPoint slides and finding appropriate Web sites to include. She will need to spend another 90 minutes on the one-hour synchronous chat session, to include preparation and follow-up. She will also need to spend another 75 hours on assignment marking, assuming one hour for marking for each essay assignment (25 × 3). In addition, she will spend 45 minutes per week on individual interaction with students with specific problems. In subsequent course offerings, the figures will be the same, except preparation time for the audio sessions will be reduced to one hour per week. Table 10.5 gives the following cost of Web-conferencing for instructor time.

Total study time per student per semester would be 13 hours for the audio lectures, 13 hours for online chat, 39 hours on follow-up work and 10 hours

Table 10.5 The costs of Web-conferencing: instructional costs

	No. of events × hours × C$ per hour	Year 1	Years 2–5	Total C$
Preparation time	13 × 1.5 × 50	975.00		
	13 × 1 × 4 × 50		2,600.00	3,575.00
Lecturing	13 × 50	650.00	2,600.00	3,250.00
Online chat	13 × 1.5 × 50	975.00	3,900.00	4,875.00
Marking	25 × 3 × 50	3,750.00	15,000.00	18,750.00
Learner support	.75 × 13	487.50	1,950.00	2,437.50
Total		6,837.50	26,050.00	32,887.00
Average instructor cost per year (over 5 years)				C$6,577.40 US$4,933.05

on each assignment (30 hours in all). This gives a total study time of 95 hours per student.

The original cost for software is $50,000 for a 25-seat licence of a leading Web-conferencing product, to be written off over 5 years. The software also requires an extended warranty payment of $8,437 a year. This gives an annual software cost of $18,437. Central server, hardware and network costs are approximately $3,000 a year (including high-speed Internet access but assuming the server is shared with other users), and technical support (including a help-desk) requires a 25 per cent share of a full-time position costing $12,000 a year (costs have been averaged out over five years). Table 10.6 aggregates all these costs.

The costs here are again high for Web-conferencing (although lower than for video-conferencing). This is partly because of the current high costs of

Table 10.6 The total costs of Web-conferencing

	Per annum (C$)
Instructor costs	6,577
Software costs	18,437
Server and network costs	3,000
Technical support	12,000
Total	40,014
Average cost per student	1,600
Average cost per student study hour	C$16.85 US$12.64

Web-conferencing software and server costs. This is a 'chicken-and-egg' problem: the high cost keeps down demand, and without a large market, there is high risk for product developers. Nevertheless, there are cost elements of synchronous technology (e.g. bandwidth and complexity) that make it inherently more expensive than asynchronous technology.

Once again, it is clear that if Web-conferencing technology is to be used, it needs to be used very selectively, and in particular we shall see that it needs to be used in conjunction with and not instead of asynchronous technology.

Broadband conferencing

As we saw in the previous chapter, a number of state and provincial governments have established broadband networks that link together educational and sometimes government and health centres. Such networks have multiple functions, such as digital telephone service, data transmission, Internet routing, and video-conferencing. As well as enabling a wide range of communications functions, such semi-private networks enable governments to bypass and thus reduce the direct telecommunications costs of commercial network providers, although in practice many of the government-financed broadband networks include private sector partners.

The business case for such investments needs detailed scrutiny on a case by-case basis. Initial investment costs are very high and the capital costs are often paid for at least in part by government, but once the network is established backbone infrastructure operational costs tend to be transferred to the user institutions and can be substantial. However, since the institutions have to pay these costs, irrespective of demand, end users such as academic departments are often offered these services without direct charge, to ensure the technologies are used.

This can have a distorting effect on the cost analysis of such technologies, making them appear cheaper to certain groups of people within the value chain than they really are. It illustrates once again the importance of determining the level of decision making when doing a cost analysis. Thus for those using the technology for teaching, broadband networks may look like a good deal, if the costs are not passed on to the department. At an institutional level, there may be more concern at having to pay the infrastructure bills irrespective of the demand for the service. For taxpayers, the economic benefits may not be so clear, when other possible uses for the money – for instance the hiring of more teachers – are taken into account.

What is clear about government-funded broadband networks is that investment is driven more by faith in the eventual value of wider and faster network connections than by any business case based on immediate educational demand and benefits, which probably explains the lack of cost-benefit publications in this area.

Summary of the costs of synchronous technologies

There are few economies of scale for synchronous teaching technologies. As a result, although costs may look reasonable for an individual class with relatively low numbers, when aggregated across the system, costs are in fact relatively very high. This means that synchronous technologies need to be used selectively, and economically it is hard to justify use of synchronous technologies as a main delivery medium for distance education.

ORGANIZATIONAL ISSUES

Asynchronous learning technologies such as WebCT became remarkably quickly incorporated into the teaching of many institutions during the latter half of the 1990s, mainly because the network infrastructure was already in place or being established for administrative purposes. Most of the organizational and technological infrastructure required for the adoption of synchronous technologies such as Web-conferencing will already be in place then in those institutions that have already adopted asynchronous Web-based learning strategies.

The initial moves into asynchronous Web-based teaching though also needed to be accompanied by a massive effort in supporting faculty in not only the technology, but also in how to use it best for teaching. This involved a steep learning curve for many instructors. The high cost of investment, and the commitment made to a particular technology, makes it increasingly difficult to move to more effective methods of delivery as new technology develops.

Thus there is likely to be organizational resistance towards introducing yet another round of technological innovation based on synchronous technologies, even though these new technologies themselves build on the existing Internet and Web infrastructure, and provide potential enhancements to teaching and learning. An organization that is spending thousands of dollars a year on a WebCT or Blackboard licence, and probably as much again on training and professional development to ensure the software is used well, is not going to move very fast to invest also in separate Web-conferencing technology.

A significant barrier to the spread of Web-conferencing in higher education is the current cost of software. Because of the high cost, projects to 'test' Web-conferencing will be treated as innovation or research projects. Such projects though often miss the essential issues of incorporating such technology on an institution-wide basis as a 'core' teaching tool.

Furthermore, the current pricing structure militates against the selective use of Web-conferencing. The licence fee, being based on users, is the same whether Web-conferencing occupies 10 per cent or 100 per cent of the learning time. WebCT and Blackboard are beginning to integrate elements of synchronous technologies into their platforms, but this pushes up the costs of licensing platforms. What is needed in any case is a software approach that starts from scratch on the basis of integrating synchronous and asynchronous technologies in an easy-to-use, seamless interface, and preferably one that will support equally well classroom-based and distance learners.

Thus although the move to Web-conferencing is not such a large leap as the move to Web-based asynchronous teaching, there remain significant organizational barriers to the widespread adoption of Web-conferencing in higher education.

CONCLUSIONS

In these conclusions I will summarize the main findings about the costs of synchronous communications technologies, and then reflect on the wider implications of these findings in the context of the educational issues discussed in the previous chapter.

Costs

The main drivers of synchronous communications costs are:

- The choice of technology (audio-conferencing, telephone based video-conferencing, Web-conferencing or broadband).
- Instructor preparation time.
- Number of hours of direct instruction through synchronous technologies.
- Instructor salaries/rate of pay.
- Delivery to individuals or to groups of learners.
- Telephone line charges (including the balance between local and long-distance charges) and who pays for them (student, institution or government through government-funded networks).
- Whether synchronous communication is a supplementary or main delivery technology.
- Class size (number of students per instructor).
- Whether materials are reusable.
- Hardware and software costs.
- Administrative and technical support staff costs.
- Whether the service is in-house or outsourced.
- For telephone-based video-conferencing, the cost of room conversion/adaptation.
- Hours of studying done by students 'off-line'.

With all these variables (and nearly all of them apply to all forms of synchronous technology), it is very difficult to provide general conclusions about the absolute cost of synchronous technologies. Nevertheless, there are some important generalizations that can be drawn.

A factor that does *not* significantly impact on the average student cost of synchronous technologies is the number of times a course or programme is offered, or student numbers for a particular course (provided class size remains the same, and the same class of instructor is hired). In these dimensions there are no economies of scale for synchronous communication technologies.

As a result, the average cost per student, and even more so, the average cost per student study hour through synchronous communications technology, is very high, irrespective of the technology used, or the number of students served. The reason why synchronous costs are so high is that the time students spend studying is directly linked to the time instructors spend teaching. This is a logical, causal relationship, if the definition of synchronous technology is that students and teacher are together at the same time.

There are two reasons why asynchronous technologies tend to be cheaper. The first is that *asynchronous technologies can achieve economies of scale resulting from the same materials being reused* by new cohorts of students. The second, and more significant, is that *asynchronous technologies shift the work from the teacher to the student*. Thus the student is able to work independently of the teacher.

On reflection, this is not surprising, of course. The rationale of all technology applications is to reduce the costs of labour. The fear in education indeed is that technology will replace teachers. However, it is not as simple as that. Teachers are still needed, not only to create and produce materials, but also to assist with the delivery of technology-based teaching. However, *asynchronous technologies allow for more time on task by students independent of the teacher*, partly through working independently with materials, but also through working collaboratively with other students, without the need for the teacher to be present *all the time*. This is the way average cost per student study hour can be driven down by technology, and if well designed, the way the time of teachers can be freed up for other activities.

Of course, it cannot be assumed that time is always used as productively in each form of delivery. Students, for instance, may learn a great deal more from one hour of inspired lecturing than from four hours of meaningless peer-group online discussion. This is why there will be occasions where synchronous technology will still justify the high cost. However, where costs are significantly different, learning gains must clearly be demonstrated for the higher cost medium or technology. In general, *higher cost technologies should be used only when they can demonstrate clear learning gains or other educational benefits over lower cost technologies*.

Thus, despite the much higher cost per student study hour of synchronous technologies, there will be occasions where same-time and even same-place approaches to teaching will be needed. However, synchronous technologies need to be used very selectively, as we now know that these technologies come at a high cost.

Implications for teaching and learning

As well as the opportunity for economies of scale and shifting work from teachers to learners, asynchronous technologies provide clear advantages for all students in moving them away from an overly rigid time and place model. However, it is also wise to retain key attributes of real time communication and combine them with key attributes of asynchronous online learning. By embracing a single model of teaching or a single technology, whether print-based distance education, broadcast television or a strictly asynchronous approach, we lose opportunities to meet new learning needs, improve learning performance, and to reach out to new target groups.

According to Downes (2002), the main problem with current online learning is its '... monolithic appearance and format', which replicates earlier forms of distance learning. The overemphasis on text has more to do with publishing than instruction. Although the overemphasis on Web publishing is easily avoided by good design, asynchronous Web-based technology benefits only a segment of potential learners, namely those that can already learn effectively through textual communication. Those learners who are less text-literate suffer. Furthermore, not all learners have the experience or discipline to learn independently, and this is inherent in an asynchronous mode, when learners can log on whenever they choose. Synchronous communication can provide a structure and timetable that keeps students working on schedule.

Blended learning is increasingly prevalent in the classroom, combining face-to-face instruction with the use of the Web. However, many students, especially adults, depend increasingly on virtual learning, both synchronous and asynchronous. The need is for sophisticated, flexible approaches to teaching and learning, matched to the needs of particular learners. This requires instructors to mix and match technologies. Thus it is very likely that another use of blended learning, this time defined as the careful use of Web-based tools to provide both synchronous and asynchronous learning opportunities, will be the next evolution of the training and education industry and the next phase in the digital evolution. However, the tools and the bandwidth are not quite there yet.

11 Executive summary: what have we learned?

CRITERIA FOR CHOICE

This is a book primarily about a method of approaching decision making in educational technology. I suggest that decision making should be based on an analysis of questions that each institution needs to ask, grouped under the following critieria:

A   Access: how accessible is a particular technology for learners? How flexible is it for a particular target group?
C   Costs: what is the cost structure of each technology? What is the unit cost per learner?
T   Teaching and learning: what kinds of learning are needed? What instructional approaches will best meet these needs? What are the best technologies for supporting this teaching and learning?
I   Interactivity and user-friendliness: what kind of interaction does this technology enable? How easy is it to use?
O   Organizational issues: What are the organizational requirements, and the barriers to be removed, before this technology can be used successfully? What changes in organization need to be made?
N   Novelty: how new is this technology?
S   Speed: how quickly can courses be mounted with this technology? How quickly can materials be changed?

In this chapter, I will summarize the conclusions drawn from applying these criteria to distance-learning technologies, and will also draw some more general conclusions about the use of technology, e-learning and distance education. My conclusions will be based on working in three different kinds of distance-learning organizations, a large national autonomous open university, a large campus-based research university, and a specialist open learning agency. Note though that Chapter 3 argues that the appropriate choice and use of technologies will depend on the particular context in which they are used. Thus if you were to apply the methodology to your own context, you may well reach different conclusions from mine.

ACCESS

Access is the most important criterion for deciding on the appropriateness of a technology for open or distance learning. Delivery to the home is usually the best way to widen access. Most people can learn at home. In terms of home access, television, radio, print, CD players, video cassettes, and the Internet are the most appropriate technologies in most economically advanced countries. In less economically advanced countries, print (depending on the literacy level of the target group), radio and television are likely to be the most appropriate technologies.

However, access depends on the specific priority target groups to be reached. Increasingly in open and distance learning, the 'market' is fragmenting into different types of target group, for instance, independent distance learners studying primarily at home, those in the work-force needing training, those who are combining part-time study with work, those who are studying full time, but only partly on-campus, or those who are combining one or more of these situations. For an increasing number of people, learning at the workplace is becoming more and more important. For some target groups, learning at local education centres, Internet cafés, or 'satellite' campuses may also be viable.

Even in less economically developed countries, the Internet may be an appropriate technology for selected target groups, while the Internet may not be appropriate for other target groups in the richest countries. The appropriate technology mix then depends on the nature of the target group and their location.

Even within these different 'markets', learners are not a homogeneous mass, but vary considerably in terms of educational background, income, age and learning experience. This diversity of the student body is growing fast. It will become increasingly important for educational organizations to be able to deliver their teaching in a variety of technological formats, depending on the needs of the individual, the teaching context, and the target groups to be reached.

In distance teaching, adequate interpersonal student support, in terms of contact with both 'human' counsellors and tutors, and with other students, is critical. This often leads to great importance being placed on local study or learning centres. Also, the establishment of local learning centres enables more sophisticated two-way equipment to be used than could be used for purely home-based students.

However, a number of issues arise from the placing of equipment in local centres. Quite difficult policy decisions need to be made about the extent to which students should be obliged to attend local centres. Access depends on the willingness and ability of the target group to get to local centres regularly. Making attendance compulsory at a local centre can reduce substantially the openness and flexibility of distance education. Making attendance optional though adds cost without benefiting all the intended target group, and raises questions about equity.

Although a technology may be widely available in people's homes, it may still not be very accessible. Although broadcast television and radio appear to be highly accessible, in reality programmes are often broadcast at times that are inconvenient or impossible for many potential students. Therefore asynchronous technologies such as CDs, video-cassettes, DVDs, and the Internet may be more accessible than synchronous technologies that have an apparent advantage in terms of home access.

Institutions and course designers are often caught between ensuring access to all and using more powerful teaching technologies. Distance teaching institutions often want to make use of newer technologies, but are held back by the need to reach minority groups, the working poor, or otherwise disadvantaged learners who do not have access to a wide range of technologies. In particular, even in economically advanced countries, open universities have been reluctant to make Internet access a requirement. Although understandable, this is probably now unduly cautious. Once access to a target group exceeds 70 per cent, it is unreasonable to deny the majority the advantage of a superior technology. Special arrangements can be made for the minority lacking access.

COSTS

Cost is also a strong discriminator between technologies. It is necessary to distinguish between 'one-way' technologies, which do not include the very substantial additional costs of tutorial support systems, and two-way technologies, within which tutorial-style interaction is usually incorporated. Also, it is important to distinguish between the cost of technologies for courses with low student numbers, and those with large student numbers. Lastly, each institution needs to analyse its own cost structures, as local context and differing assumptions about costs will influence the outcome of such an analysis.

Great care needs to be taken in comparing the costs of different technologies. Many of the examples in this book are based on hypothetical assumptions. Even where data have been drawn from actual cases, major differences in the data would be achieved by changing some of the assumptions. In particular, differences need to be substantial before they can be considered as having possible value. Nevertheless, there are clear cost *structures* that appear to be relatively stable and independent of context, as can be seen from Table 11.1, which summarizes and compares costs for the different technologies.

Figure 11.1 (derived from Table 11.2) indicates that there are some clear cost differences between technologies in open and distance learning.

Print, asynchronous web-based learning, audio-cassettes (and probably CDs) and radio for courses with over 1,000 students appear to be the lowest cost technologies (print data include direct tutorial costs). Broadcast TV made

Table 11.1 Comparison of costs per student study hour of technologies for different sizes of course

No. of students per course (over 8 years)	30	125	625	1,250	3,000
One-way technologies	*US$*	*US$*	*US$*	*US$*	*US$*
Broadcast TV (Table 5.1)*	460.00	110.00	22.00	11.00	4.58
Radio (Table 6.2)*	60.00	14.88	2.97	1.49	0.60
Audio-cassettes (OU) (Table 6.3)*	12.25	3.50	1.30	1.00	0.86
Print (without textbooks) (Table 4.2)					
Dual-mode	3.01	1.75	1.43	1.39	1.37
Open university	10.64	3.00	1.04	0.79	0.65
Two-way technologies					
Web-based learning (without textbooks) (Table 8.3)	3.85	2.57	2.25	2.21	2.18
Audio-conferencing (individuals)					
Main technology(Table 10.2)	64.50	19.50	10.44	9.16	8.33
Tutorials	27.33	27.33	27.33	27.33	27.33
Video-conferencing (groups) (Table 10.3)	17.64	17.64	17.64	17.64	17.64
Web-conferencing (Table 10.5)	12.64	12.64	12.64	12.64	12.64

* without tutorial costs: add $0.45 per study hour for tutorial costs

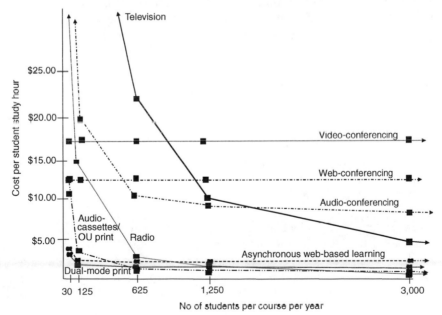

Figure 11.1 Comparison of costs of technologies for different sizes of course (US$)

by educational broadcasting organizations is clearly an expensive technology for courses with 3,000 students or fewer, but starts to become competitive in cost for very large numbers of students per course (6,000 students or more at $1.53 per hour – Table 5.1).

What stands out from Figure 11.1 is the high cost of synchronous conferencing. Web-conferencing costs will almost certainly come down as bandwidth and software costs are reduced, but synchronous conferencing cannot escape the high cost of labour, because these technologies provide no or very few economies of scale, and do not substitute the time of teachers with student activity.

The impression given by the graph in Figure 11.1 that there is little difference between the costs of print, audio-cassettes and Web-based learning is a little misleading. The cost of asynchronous Web-based learning is significantly higher than the costs of print or audio-cassettes for courses with over 600 students. Asynchronous Web-based learning has little economy of scale beyond this number. Thus for institutions aiming to reach very large numbers, there will be considerable cost advantages in combining print with audio cassettes or CDs, rather than in using the Internet.

A number of general points can be made about the balance of costs for different technologies:

- The major costs of using technologies for distance teaching are in production and delivery, and hence are recurrent, rather than capital. In general, the recurrent costs of producing and maintaining good quality technology-based materials tend to be underestimated.
- Audio cassettes, CDs and radio have low fixed *and* low variable costs.
- Face-to-face teaching and synchronous conferencing technologies have low fixed costs but high variable costs, that is, costs increase with student numbers.
- Good quality broadcast television has high fixed costs and zero variable costs.
- Asynchronous Web-based learning has moderate fixed costs and moderate variable costs.
- Delivery costs for technology-based materials are insignificant compared with production costs for most technologies, or with the costs of providing tutorial services for one-way technologies. It is important then to consider *all* costs when deciding on technologies.

It can be seen that student numbers are critical in comparing the costs of technology. Also, the long-term view needs to be taken: how will the costs work out over a number of years? Furthermore, what may look like a low cost for an individual department using synchronous conferencing may be a very high cost when added across the institution or even more so, the educational system.

Lastly, what these figures do not indicate are total costs. Unit costs per student may be very low for large numbers for some technologies such as broadcasting, but governments or institutions may not have the funds to reach the large numbers required to bring down unit costs. Even if funds are available, there may not be the demand for very large courses. What print, audio and asynchronous Web-based learning enable are economies of scope, thus allowing relatively small numbers of students to be served at moderate cost.

TEACHING AND LEARNING

Teaching and learning issues are less strong as discriminators compared with access or costs, partly because of the flexibility of different media and technologies and the ability of teachers and learners to make the best of any given situation. Nevertheless, from an analysis of the ways different media or technologies convey or transmit knowledge, several key features emerge.

Epistemological issues

There is an important relationship between beliefs about the nature of knowledge and knowing, the skills needed in a knowledge-based society, and the choice of technology. For instance, Postman (1993) argues that there is a strong link between technology and modes of thinking. Scientific thinking is heavily dependent on the 'objectivity' and linearity of printed material, allowing for descriptions of phenomena, analysis of argument and logic, and communication between scientists through printed journals. If we start to move from linear to lateral thinking, we may make some gains in creativity but we may lose some certainty and predictability. Thus there may be strong advantages in combining print with Web-based learning.

More importantly, there is a move to more constructivist approaches to develop the skills needed in a knowledge-based society. This places more emphasis on information management and analysis, knowledge construction, problem solving, and decision making, rather than on comprehension and memory. Technologies such as the Internet appear to facilitate this kind of learning more easily than print-based technology does. Once again, though, more research needs to be done on the relationship between technologies and the development of different kinds of knowledge.

Presentational features

Media differ in their presentational features. Some media are more restricted than others with respect to their presentational features. Thus print can handle large quantities of text, diagrams, and pictures. It can also handle colour, but at a high cost. Radio, audio cassettes, and audio-conferencing are restricted to sound only; asynchronous Web-based learning has been limited mainly to textual and graphical communication, but with medium-level bandwidth

(2 to 5 mgs) becoming widely available, audio and video components of asynchronous Web-based learning need to be exploited more. Television is the most complete medium in terms of its presentational qualities, although it is not a good medium for handling large quantities of text.

These presentational qualities have a direct relationship to teaching tasks. For instance, print can precisely represent facts, abstract ideas, rules and principles, and detailed, lengthy or complex arguments. It is a very dense medium, and consequently is still the great storehouse of knowledge. Radio can be used for lectures and studio discussions, but is not good for handling detail or dense amounts of information. Each medium also varies in the way it represents the world. Thus both television and radio can use drama or documentaries, while conferencing allows people to create or build their own interpretations of knowledge through discussion.

In particular, media differ in their ability to handle concrete or abstract knowledge. Abstract knowledge is handled primarily through language. While all media can handle language, either in written or spoken form, media vary in their ability to represent *concrete* knowledge. Video and audio are media that facilitate the link between concrete examples and abstract concepts. These representational possibilities of media are particularly important for non-academic learners, who often require concrete examples or demonstrations rather than abstract theory.

These are only some of the instructional differences between media. They do indicate though the importance of course designers identifying clearly not only the content of a course, but also how best to *present* knowledge in a particular subject area, and what *kinds* of learning are required (comprehension, analysis, application of principles to actual cases, problem-solving, interpersonal skills, mechanical skills, attitude change, and so forth). This means that a good understanding of what is required to teach a particular subject needs to be combined with good knowledge of the educational strengths and weaknesses of different media. Thus the selection of media is not just a technical issue, nor one that is purely academic.

Basically, every medium has its strengths and weaknesses in terms of its presentational qualities, but from an instructional point of view, some are clearly stronger than others. In particular, 'high-quality' television, for example, television that exploits its unique presentational qualities (as distinct from its use as a channel of communication) and multimedia are very strong, and radio, audio conferencing, and video-conferencing are all relatively weak, in presentational terms. Asynchronous Web-based learning and print lie somewhere in the middle of this range.

Structuring knowledge

Technologies also differ in the way they structure knowledge. The development of Web-based learning, the development of learning objects, and the move to more constructivist approaches to teaching offer many choices to teachers and course designers in ways to structure knowledge. This aspect of educational technology is probably the least well understood. However, there are some guidelines that can be followed.

First, knowledge needs to be structured in ways that best reflect the nature of the subject matter. Put another way, the epistemological roots of a subject may require a certain logical sequencing of information that needs to be followed, to avoid confusing the learner (see Bruner, 1966, for further discussion of this issue). The choice of technology should enable the representation of knowledge to be structured in ways that are appropriate for that subject matter.

The structuring of knowledge will also depend on the teacher's personal perspective on how students learn – or should learn. For instance, a teacher who believes that students need to take responsibility for their own learning is likely to offer a less structured approach to content than one who believes that their task is to present information clearly so that it is properly understood.

The extent and method by which content should be structured will depend on the learner's ability to navigate and organize information within the subject area. The less able they are to do this, the more the structure of the content will need to be determined by the teacher. Certain technologies (such as the Web) enable learners to navigate and organize knowledge better than others (such as a broadcast).

Teaching should progress from where learners need a tight knowledge structure to a context where learners are comfortable with loose content structures. This prepares learners better for dealing with conflicting evidence, the linking of seemingly disparate ideas, and hence creative thinking. The Web provides the potential for an environment where knowledge can be loosely structured yet managed by the teacher.

Developing skills

Another area where there appear to be differences between technologies (although this is an area where much more research is needed) is in their ability to develop different types of skills, as distinct from presenting knowledge or content. Thus asynchronous Web-based learning can develop skills of academic discourse, knowledge building and creative writing, while television, when used appropriately, can develop skills of analysis and evaluation.

Technologies that combine strong presentational qualities with strong student control over the technology are particularly good for developing skills. Thus well designed cassettes, CDs, and asynchronous Web-based learning are strong, and radio and video-conferencing are weak technologies for skills development.

Student assessment must reflect the objectives of the learning. If the objective is to enable learners to seek, find, analyse, and interpret information, this needs to be assessed as much as comprehension of the subject matter. The use of technology for instruction may also mean giving much more attention to the technology of assessment. Pencil and paper may not appropriately test the skills being developed through multi-media teaching. For instance, students may want to make Web-based portfolios of their work.

Therefore even in the more difficult area of pedagogical or instructional differences, there do appear to be profound instructional differences between technologies, from which it follows that they should be used carefully to exploit their strengths and avoid their weaknesses, rather than being used for just relaying a 'popular' mode of delivery, such as an entertainment-style broadcast or a televised lecture.

Unfortunately, though, it is common for educators and media specialists to carry over modes of design associated with an old technology to a newer technology, even though the new technology may have inherent design advantages (or disadvantages) over the old technology. Thus professors often use video-conferencing to relay lectures, rather than exploit the technology's presentational and interactive characteristics. It is therefore critical to reconsider the design of teaching and learning activities when technology is being used.

INTERACTIVITY AND USER-FRIENDLINESS

Some technologies allow for simultaneous or 'real-time' communication (synchronous), others for communication that can be stored and accessed when the teacher or learner is ready (asynchronous). Some technologies are one-way communication media; others are two-way. Some are permanent; others are transient. All these control features of technology impact on interactivity and user-friendliness.

Some 'one-way' technologies facilitate interaction with learning materials and provide feedback on student responses better than others. Interaction is at its most controlled in computer-based learning, where learners can be tested, corrected, or given remedial activities by the computer. However, computer-based learning has great difficulty in handling teaching contexts where individual interpretation or the development of argument is needed. The advantage of asynchronous Web-based learning is that it can combine computer-based testing with qualitative assessment from teachers.

Most two-way teaching technologies involve live or spontaneous contributions from the teacher. Where presentations are in real time ('live'), the time and opportunity for student communication is strictly controlled. Audio- and video-conferencing require the physical presence of a student at both a fixed time and often a fixed place other than the home. Furthermore, when the teaching is in 'real time', and ephemeral, the student is heavily dependent on understanding the presentation and discussions as they happen, and on taking good notes or on having a good memory.

Two-way communications media are valuable tools for distance educators; nevertheless, they are not always appropriate for all the jobs that need to be done. One-way communication technologies can, with careful design, provide a high level of interaction for students, and so still have an important role to play. In particular, they can provide economies of scale, and increase students' time on task. There is then a need for *both* high quality pre-prepared, permanent material, *and* for two-way communication between students and tutors.

One reason why the Internet has been more widely adopted in teaching and learning than many previous technologies is that it facilitates rather than inhibits interpersonal communication. Thus instead of replacing the teacher with a machine, the Internet facilitates interpersonal interaction both between teacher and learner, and among learners. The combination of computers and the Internet supports a wide range of theoretical approaches to teaching and learning. As a result, the design of learning experiences then becomes more critical than the choice of technology – which is as it should be.

Learner control

Two-way communication *under the students' control* allows students to interact easily not only with tutors, but also with other students. Until recently, the telephone has been the only means of doing this for students at a distance, and costs have been high. Asynchronous Web-based learning though now enables two-way communication at a distance, at asynchronous times, at relatively low cost, between students, and between students, tutors or even central academic staff. Computer-based communications have revolutionary implications for distance education, providing the means to free students from the centralized control of pre-prepared and constricted curricula.

The extent to which any particular medium encourages interaction or active learning depends to some extent on the way it is designed, but is also determined to some extent by the nature of the medium. What is clear is that *design* is a critical factor for the success or otherwise of e-learning and distance education. Multi-media materials that encourage active learning require considerable *pedagogical* as well as subject or production expertise.

ORGANIZATIONAL ISSUES

If technologies are to be exploited effectively in open and distance learning, it is clear that organizational structures and methods of working have to change. New technologies such as Web-based learning have a low threshold for entry. As a consequence, many individual teachers in dual-mode and previously conventional institutions are increasingly moving into distance learning with these technologies. One reason why these two-way technologies have become popular in conventional teaching institutions is because teachers can easily transfer their normal face-to-face teaching methods to the new technologies.

In contrast, one of the great contributions of distance teaching institutions has been to raise the quality of instructional design, resulting in extremely effective learning materials. This is a result of a great deal of preparation time and teamwork. High quality teaching materials are particularly important where students have a variety of educational backgrounds and experience of study, where entry to courses is open to all, and above all, when the technology allows or requires students to study independently.

However, in few cases have either campus-based or autonomous distance teaching institutions significantly restructured their internal organization or reallocated resources to exploit fully the possibilities of new technologies. In most cases, technology has been added onto traditional classroom activity or print-based correspondence courses. This results in additional costs, and additional work for students and teachers, with no clear, measurable benefits.

Few institutions, conventional or distance, have sought to restructure their teaching completely, to integrate the benefits of technology for both internal and external students. For instance, if teachers were organized in teams and given release time to create high quality learning materials supported by asynchronous Web-based tutoring, both 'on-campus' and distance students could equally benefit. Teaching staff would be freed from lecturing on a regular basis, and could give more time to individual face-to-face tutoring or group tutoring on-line.

Until teaching is thoroughly reorganized in these ways, though, there is still likely to be a requirement for a specialized distance education unit in dual-mode institutions, especially in research institutions, where there is less focus on off-campus students.

NOVELTY

While novelty should be the least important of all the criteria, in practice it is often easier to attract external funding for the use of new technologies. Also, suppliers of equipment and services will often offer attractive subsidies or 'free offers' for new products and services.

There are real dangers though in being driven by funding specifically linked to the use of new technologies. The first is the question of sustainability. If the technology is not cost-effective, an institution will find it difficult to continue with the technology when external funding or subsidies cease. Secondly, external funding for new technologies tends to be limited to capital investment in the technology, or subsidy of delivery costs, both of which are usually minor compared with the costs of course production and educational support during presentation of the course. Novelty then is very much a two-edged sword.

SPEED

In a society subject to such rapid change, it is essential to be able to change and revise content very quickly. One of the advantages of all the two-way technologies, plus radio, is their ability to bring students the latest information on research, social events, new developments in science and technology, and government policy changes.

In comparison, because of the long lead production times, or the high cost of changing material once made, broadcast television and print rate poorly on this criterion.

POLONIUS' ADVICE TO HAMLET

Lastly, I would like to propose twelve golden rules for using technology in education and training that apply whatever technologies are being used.

1. Good teaching matters

Clear objectives, good structuring of learning materials and relevance to learners' needs all apply to the use of any technology for teaching, and if these principles are ignored, then the teaching will fail, even if the unique characteristics of the medium are stylishly exploited. Good teaching may overcome a poor choice in the use of technology, but technology will never save bad teaching; usually it makes it worse.

2. Good design is essential

A lot is now known about how to design effective learning experiences, especially in distance education. Much of this will also apply to e-learning. Teaching needs to be redesigned to exploit the use of a particular technology. One size does not fit all, and in general the classroom lecture is the least effective design for technology-based teaching. To achieve good design usually means working with instructional designers.

3. Each medium has its own aesthetic

Professional production and design are important. Each medium and technology has a different range of production skills necessary to exploit its unique features; this means that 'quality' production counts – an asynchronous Web-based learning programme that does not fully utilize the special design features of the Web (for example, fails to use interaction, graphics, the structure of the Web, or the opportunities for discussion) will not work, even if in theory this was the most appropriate technology for the particular task. Effective teaching with technology usually means working with professional production staff, such as Web designers.

4. Educational technologies are flexible

Technologies are generally flexible and hence interchangeable in education and training, that is, what can be achieved educationally through one technology can usually be achieved through any other technology, given sufficient imagination, time and resources. Thus the absence or non-availability of a particular technology does not necessarily prevent learning goals from being achieved.

Each technology can be used in a wide variety of ways. Consequently, differences *within* a technology or medium (for instance, between two television programmes, one a televised lecture and the other a documentary) may be greater than differences *between* media (for instance, between a face-to-face lecture and a lecture given on the radio).

Nevertheless, intrinsic differences between technologies have been identified which have implications for teaching and learning. Although limitations of a particular technology can be overcome, this may require extra time, work or resources, and therefore technologies should be matched to learning needs as carefully as possible.

5. There is no 'super-technology'

All technologies have their strengths and weaknesses (yes, even the Web). They therefore need to be combined.

6. Make all five media available

In most open and distance learning, learners are not a homogeneous mass, but vary a great deal in terms of educational background, age, experience, and preferred learning style. Decision makers should therefore try to ensure that all five media (face-to-face, print, audio, video, digital multimedia) are available for teaching purposes, in one form or another. This will give variety to a course, not only providing an individual learner with different ways of approaching the same material, but accommodating different learning styles.

However, the greater the number of technologies used, the more complex the design process, and the greater the chance of redundancy and wasted expenditure; the aim therefore should be to use a limited range of technologies in any given context, but covering all the main media.

7. Interaction is essential

High quality interaction with learning materials, interaction between teachers and learners *and* interaction among learners, are all essential for effective learning. With good design, interpersonal interaction can be provided as effectively at a distance, through the use of appropriate technologies, as through face-to-face contact.

8. Student numbers are critical

The total number of learners to be served over the life of a course is a critical factor in technology selection. Some technologies are much more economical than others with large numbers; with other technologies, costs increase proportionately with student numbers. Take the long view; what may appear cheap in the first year may be more expensive over eight years – and vice versa.

9. New technologies are not necessarily better than old ones

There is no law that says new technologies will automatically be better for teaching than old ones. Judgement about new technologies should be made on educational and operational criteria, not by date stamp. Many of the lessons learned from the application of 'older' technologies will still apply to any newer technology. The needs of the target group may require the use of older technologies if new technologies won't get the job done.

10. Teamwork is essential

No one can know everything there is to know about the educational use and design of every technology now available, *and* be a subject expert, *and* be an effective researcher. Subject experts, media specialists and instructional designers are essential on every team.

11. Teachers need training to use technologies effectively

Teachers and instructors need training not just in the choice and use of appropriate technologies, but more fundamentally in how people learn, and how to teach with technology. Lack of appropriate training is the biggest barrier to the use of technology in higher education. Training will not replace the need for teamwork and other professionals, but will enable teachers to work more effectively in a team.

12. Technology is not the issue

The issue is: *how* and *what* do I want students to learn? And where? The effectiveness of technology-based open learning is now a non-issue (see Moore and Thompson, 1990); concentrate on designing the learning experience and not on testing the technology. There is more than enough technology around now to allow you to teach in whatever way you choose.

DOWN WITH LECTURES AND INCREMENTALISM!

A fundamental issue that is addressed in this book is whether to use technology to replicate 'traditional' instructional methods, or to use technology to change teaching methods to improve the quality of teaching and learning.

There is a predominant view, certainly amongst faculty in North American universities and colleges, that the traditional form of group face-to-face instruction is still the preferred and most effective form of education, and that the closer distance education can directly 'mimic' or imitate this, the more effective distance education will be. Also, where autonomous distance teaching institutions have introduced newer interactive technologies, they have merely added them to the high-cost, front-end development of print and television.

It is my view that neither of these approaches is adequate. It is increasingly difficult to defend the current system of teaching, as it applies to what is now mass post-secondary education. The 'old' methods of small classes and a direct and frequent person-to-person contact between scholar and young student worked well with an elite and restricted entry to higher education. Those days are long gone. Society is faced with a struggle for economic survival, where the future of developed countries depends on large numbers of people being educated to a high level, not just in late adolescence, but throughout their lives.

Also, the one-way transmission model of mass distance education practised by the autonomous distance teaching institutions needs to be modified. There is no longer a single mass market for adult continuing education, but an increasingly wider variety of needs, and increasingly smaller and unique target groups. This means more individualized approaches to open and distance learning.

Even more importantly, the model of transmission of information from teacher to student practised by both conventional institutions and the large, autonomous distance teaching universities is no longer sufficient in a society where knowledge is changing rapidly, and the skills needed both at work and in our social lives are becoming increasingly complex. People need to know how to communicate effectively, work in teams, search out and analyse new knowledge, participate actively in society, and generate as well as assimilate knowledge.

In particular, the predominance of the lecture-based classroom model in post-secondary education needs to be challenged. The ancient Greeks did not learn this way. Plato argued for dialogue rather than instruction. Indeed, the 'lecture', so prevalent in post-secondary education these days, is itself a technological artefact. The word 'lecture' comes from the Latin verb 'to read'. Because books in mediaeval times were painstakingly and beautifully written by hand by the monks, only one copy usually existed in each university. The one copy was so precious that the university professor literally read from the book to his students. Also, instruction was controlled by the church;

therefore control over access to knowledge was essential, to prevent unorth-odoxy. It is no accident that the invention of printing influenced not only the development of schools, but also the rise of Protestantism.

The industrial revolution, with its need to educate large numbers of people for commercial life, led to mass education, and the large group method of teaching was the most economical way to provide this. However, while in the twentieth-century technology has revolutionized communications, leading to the information society, our educational institutions are still pickled in the aspic of the industrial revolution.

Technology does provide an opportunity to teach differently, in a way that can meet the fundamental needs of a new and rapidly changing society. The evidence is now overwhelming that technology can both improve the quality of education and enable new target groups to be reached, at less cost than by using conventional methods.

This requires though new approaches to teaching and learning that exploit the unique features of different technologies in order to meet the widely different needs of many types of learners. These approaches must be based on the considerable amount of knowledge now available about how people learn and how to design effective learning environments, as well as on a good understanding of the educational strengths and limitations of different technologies.

What cannot be justified is continuing with a system of teaching that, while it may have served an élite well in the past, is very expensive and ineffective, in that it does not facilitate the vast majority of people to learn and think creatively and independently throughout their lives.

The need to redesign teaching and learning, and to reorganize institutions to support the use of technology in both teaching and administration, is the greatest challenge facing higher education today. In an era of mass higher education, institutions are failing to provide quality teaching to their students. In a survey of Canadian students in 2004, nearly half said that their first year campus experience was unsatisfactory. Large classes and lack of contact with tenured research staff were two of the main reasons.

Neither distance education nor e-learning are panaceas, but the technology is now at a stage where we can teach in a wide variety of ways. The challenge is to move beyond arguments about technology, distance and time, to focusing on the needs of learners, and the most cost-effective ways to meet those needs. I hope this book will help you with that challenge.

Appendix: unique characteristics of television and radio

This list was originally developed for the Broadcast and Audio-visual Sub-committee of the Open University, and referred specifically to television and radio and their advantages over printed text and home experiment kits. However, many of these functions apply equally well to non-broadcast use of video and audio. In particular, they can provide guidelines for use of video and audio in Web-based learning materials. The list was first published in Bates (1984).

TELEVISION

1 To demonstrate experiments or experimental situations, particularly:
   (a) where equipment or phenomena to be observed are large, micro-scopic, expensive, inaccessible or difficult to observe without special equipment;
   (b) where the experimental design is complex;
   (c) where the measurement of experimental behaviour is not easily reduced to a single scale or dimension (e.g. human behaviour);
   (d) where the experimental behaviour may be influenced by uncontrol-lable but observable variables.

2 To illustrate principles involving dynamic change or movement.
3 To illustrate abstract principles through the use of specially constructed physical models.
4 To illustrate principles involving three-dimensional space.
5 To use animated, slow-motion, or speeded-up video to demonstrate changes over time.
6 To teach certain advanced scientific or technological concepts (such as theories of relativity or quantum physics) without students having to master highly advanced mathematical techniques, through the use of models and/or animation.

7 To substitute for a field visit, to:

    (a) provide students with an accurate, comprehensive visual picture of the site, in order to place their study in context;

    (b) to demonstrate the relationship between different elements of the system being viewed (e.g. production processes, ecological balance);

    (c) to assist students to differentiate between different classes or categories of phenomena *in situ*;

    (d) to observe differences in scale and process between laboratory and mass-production techniques.

8 To bring students primary resource or case-study material, i.e. recording of naturally occurring events which, through editing and selection, demonstrate or illustrate principles covered elsewhere in the course. This may be used in several ways:

    (a) to enable students to recognize naturally occurring phenomena or classifications (e.g. teaching strategies, mental disorders, classroom behaviour) in context;

    (b) to enable students to analyse a situation, using principles covered elsewhere in the course; or to test students' ability to analyse phenomena in context;

    (c) to demonstrate ways in which abstract principles or concepts developed elsewhere in the course have been applied to real-world problems.

9 To demonstrate decision-making processes:

    (a) by recording the decision-making process as it occurs;

    (b) by dramatization;

    (c) by simulation or role-playing;

10 To change student attitudes:

    (a) by presenting material in a novel or unfamiliar perspective;

    (b) by presenting material in a dramatized form, enabling students to identify with someone with a different perspective;

11 To demonstrate methods or techniques of performance.

12 To interpret artistic performance (e.g. drama, spoken poetry, movies).

13 To analyse through a combination of sounds and graphics the structure of music.

14 To teach sketching, drawing or painting techniques.

15 To demonstrate the way in which instruments or tools can be used; to demonstrate the skills of craftsmen.

16 To record and archive events that are crucial to the course, but which may disappear or be destroyed in the near future.

17 To demonstrate practical activities to be carried out later by students.

18 To synthesize, summarize or condense contextually and media rich information relevant to the course.

AUDIO

Cassettes (or CDs)

1 To analyse or process detailed visual materials, such as mathematical equations, paintings, graphs, statistical tables, rock samples, maps, etc., by 'talking' students through the material.
2 To enable students through repetition and practice to master certain skills or techniques (e.g. language pronunciation, analysis of musical structure, mathematical computation).
3 To analyse or critique complex arguments or discussion between two or more people.

Cassettes or radio

1 To bring students primary audio resource material, either specially recorded or acquired from sound archives, for example:

   (a) recordings of naturally occurring events, e.g. political speeches, children talking, concerts or performances, eyewitness accounts;
   (b) a selection of sources of evidence for students to analyse.

2 To bring students the knowledge or wisdom of eminent people or leading researchers, through interviews.
3 To record the voices of key stakeholders or 'actors' to represent or illustrate concepts and ideas to be discussed within a course.
4 To change student attitudes:

   (a) by presenting material in a novel or unfamiliar perspective;
   (b) by presenting material in a dramatized form, enabling students to identify with someone with a different perspective.

5 To provide students with a condensed argument that may:

   (a) reinforce points made elsewhere in the course;
   (b) introduce new points not made elsewhere in the course;
   (c) provide an alternative viewpoint to the perspectives in the rest of the course;
   (d) analyse or critique materials elsewhere in the course;
   (e) summarize or condense the main ideas or major points covered in the course;
   (f) provide new evidence in support of or against the arguments or perspectives covered elsewhere in the course.

Radio

1 To provide corrections to the course, or deal with parts of the course where student feedback indicates difficulties.
2 To relate the course to current events (e.g. news stories) that emphasize the relevance or application of concepts within the course.
3 To update the course when the knowledge base changes, e.g. when new research is published.
4 To provide external criticism or alternative viewpoints to those in the course.

Bibliography

Agency for International Development (1990) *Interactive Radio Instruction*, Newton, MA: Education Development Centre.

Ahrens, S., Burt, G. and Gallagher, M. (1975) *M231: Analysis*, Milton Keynes: Open University Institute of Educational Technology.

Allen, I.E. and Seaman, J. (2003) *Sizing the Opportunity: The Quality and Extent of Online Education in the United States, 2002 and 2003*, Wellesley, MA: The Sloan Consortium.

Anderson, T. and Garrison, R. (1995) 'Transactional issues in distance education: the impact of design in audioteleconferencing', *The American Journal of Distance Education*, Vol. 9, No. 2, pp. 27–45.

Armstrong-Stassen, M., Landstrom, M. and Lumpkin, R. (1998) 'Students' reactions to the introduction of videoconferencing for classroom instruction', *The Information Society*, Vol. 14, pp. 153–64.

Barron, T. (2001) 'An e-learning industry update', *Learning Circuits*, Vol. 2, No. 7.

Bartolic-Zlomislic, S. and Bates, A. (1999) 'Investing in online learning: potential benefits and limitations', *Canadian Journal of Communication*, Vol. 24, pp. 349–66.

Bates, A.W. (1975) *Student Use of Open University Broadcasting*, Milton Keynes: Open University Institute of Educational Technology.

—— (1981) 'Some unique educational characteristics of television and some implications for teaching or learning', *Journal of Educational Television*, Vol. 7, No. 3.

—— (1984) *Broadcasting in Education*, London: Constable.

—— (1995a) *Technology, Open Learning and Distance Education*, London: Routledge.

—— (1995b) 'Research and development in distance education', in Lockwood, F. (ed.) *Open and Distance Learning Today*, London: Routledge.

—— (2000) *Managing Technological Change: Strategies for College and University Leaders*, San Francisco: Jossey-Bass.

Bates, A.W. and Gallagher, M. (1987) 'Improving the educational effectiveness of television case-studies and documentaries', in Boyd-Barrett, O. and Braham, P. (eds) *Media, Knowledge and Power*, London: Croom Helm.

Bates, A.W. and Poole, G. (2003) *Effective Teaching with Technology in Higher Education: Foundations for Success*, San Francisco: Jossey-Bass.

Bates, A.W. *et al.* (1981) *Radio: The Forgotten Medium?*, Milton Keynes: Open University Institute of Educational Technology.

Bloom, B., Englehart, M., Furst, E., Hill, W. and Krathwohl, D. (1956) *Taxonomy of Educational Objectives, Handbook I: The Cognitive Domain*, New York: Longmans Green.

Boaz, M., Elliott, B., Foshee, D., Hardy, D., Jarmon, C. and Olcott, D. (1999) *Teaching at a Distance: A Handbook for Instructors*, Mission Viejo, CA: League for Innovation in the Community College and Archipelago.

Boeke, M. (2001) *Technology Costing Methodology Casebook 2001*, Boulder, CO: Western Cooperative for Educational Telecommunications.

Bosch, A. (1997) 'Interactive radio instruction: 23 years of improving quality', *Education and Technology Technical Notes Series*, Vol.2, No.1, Washington, DC: World Bank.

Brookfield, S. (1987) *Developing Critical Thinkers: Challenging Adults to Explore Alternative Ways of Thinking and Acting*, San Francisco: Jossey-Bass.

Brown, B. and Liedholm, C. (2002) 'Can web courses replace the classroom in principles of microeconomics?', *American Economic Review* May (http://www.msu.edu/~brownb/vstudy.htm).

Brown, D. (1980) 'New students and radio at the Open University', *Educational Broadcasting International*, Vol. 13, No. 1.

Brown, S. (1983) *The 1982 Video-Cassette Loan Service: A Report on the First Year of Operation*, Milton Keynes: Open University Institute of Educational Technology.

Bruner, J. (1966) *Towards a Theory of Instruction*, Cambridge, MA: Harvard University Press.

Campion, M. and Renner, W. (1992) 'The supposed demise of Fordism – implications for distance education and open learning', *Distance Education*, Vol. 13, No. 1, pp. 7–28.

Clark, R. (1983) 'Reconsidering research on learning from media', *Review of Educational Research*, Vol. 53, pp. 445–59.

Collis, B.A. (1991) 'Telecommunications-based training in Europe: a state-of-the-art report', *American Journal of Distance Education*, Vol. 5, No. 2, pp. 31–40.

Cunningham, S., Ryan, Y., Stedman, L., Tapsall, S., Bagdon, K., Flew, T. and Coaldrake, P. (2000) *The Business of Borderless Education*, Canberra: Commonwealth of Australia, Department of Education, Training and Youth Affairs.

Daniel, J. (1996) *Mega-Universities and Knowledge Media: Technology Strategies for Higher Education*, London: Kogan Page.

Dirr, P. (2001) 'The development of new organizational arrangements in virtual learning', in Farrell, G. (ed.) *The Changing Faces of Virtual Education*, Vancouver, BC: Commonwealth of Learning.

Distance Education and Technology (2001) *Annual Report, 2000–2001*, Vancouver, BC: University of British Columbia.

Donath, J., Karahalios, K. and Viégas, F. (1999) 'Visualizing conversation', *Journal of Computer Mediated Communication*, Vol. 4, No. 4.

Downes, S. (2002) Problems and Issues in Online Learning, *The Learning Place*, October http://education.qld.gov.au/staff/learning/courses/sdownesoct.html.

Duning, B., Van Kekerix, J. and Zaborowski, L. (1993) *Reaching Learners Through Telecommunications*, San Francisco: Jossey-Bass.

Duran, J. and Sauer, C. (1997), *Mainstreaming Videoconferencing: A Developer's Guide to Distance Multimedia*, Reading, MA: Addison-Wesley.

Durbridge, N. (1981) 'The use of audio-cassettes', in Bates, A. *et al.* (eds) *Radio: The Forgotten Medium?*, Milton Keynes: Open University Institute of Educational Technology.

—— (1982) *EM235: Developing Mathematical Thinking*, Milton Keynes: Open University Institute of Educational Technology.

—— (1983) *Design Implications of Audio and Video Cassettes*, Milton Keynes: Open University Institute of Educational Technology.

Dziuban, C., Moskal, P., Juge, F., Truman-Davis, B., Sorg, S. and Hartman, J. (2001) 'Developing a web-based instructional program in a metropolitan university', in Geibert, B. and Harvey, S. (eds) *Web Wise Design: Lessons from the Field*, Englewood Cliffs, NJ: Educational Technology Publications.

E-learning News (2001) 'Eduventures forecasts $750 million market for "live" e-learning', *e-Learning News*, Vol. 111, No. 9, pp. 1–2.

Environics Research Group (1994) *National Survey of Post-Secondary Students' Preferences for Educational Material*, Toronto: Canadian Book Publishers' Council.

Farnes, N. (1993) 'Modes of Production: Fordism and Distance Education, *Open Learning*, Vol. 8, No. 1, pp. 10–20.

Feenberg, A. (1999) 'Distance learning: promise or threat', *National Crosstalk*, Vol. 7, No. 1.

Finkelstein, M., Frances, C., Jewett, F. and Scholz, M. (2000) *Dollars, Distance, and Online Education: The New Economics of College Teaching and Learning*, Westport, CT: American Council on Education/Oryx Press.

Fuenzalida, E. (1992) *Alfabetizacíon y Postalfabetización por Radio*, Madrid: Editorial Popular.

Gagné, R. (1977) *The Conditions of Learning*, New York: Holt, Rinehart & Winston.

—— (1985) *The Conditions of Learning* (4th edn), New York: Holt, Rinehart & Winston.

Gallagher, M. (1977) *Broadcasting and the Open University Student, 1976*, Milton Keynes: Open University Institute of Educational Technology.

Garrison, D. (1991) 'Critical thinking and adult education: a conceptual model for developing critical thinking in adult learners', *International Journal of Lifelong Education*, Vol. 10, No. 4, pp. 287–303.

Garrison, D.R. (1989) *Understanding Distance Education: A Framework for the Future*, London: Routledge.

Garrison, R. and Anderson, T. (1999) 'Avoiding the industrialization of research universities: big and little distance education', *American Journal of Distance Education*, Vol. 13, No. 2, pp. 48–63.

Gillan, R. and McBride, R. (2000) 'Linking video conferencing to the desktop', *Proceedings of SITE 2000*, Society for Information Technology & Teacher Education International Conference, San Diego, California.

Greenfield, P. (1984) *Mind and Media*, Cambridge, MA: Harvard University Press.

Grundin, H. (1978) *The Effect of Transmission Times on Students' Use of OU Broadcasts*, Milton Keynes: Open University Institute of Educational Technology.

—— (1980) *OU Broadcasting Times: A Study of Viewing and Listening Opportunities in 1978–79 and in the Future*, Milton Keynes: Open University Institute of Educational Technology.

—— (1981) *Open University Broadcasting Times and their Impact on Students' Viewing/Listening*, Milton Keynes: Open University Institute of Educational Technology.

—— (1983) *Audio-visual Media in the O.U.: Results of a Survey of 93 Courses*, Milton Keynes: Open University Institute of Educational Technology.

——(1985) *Report of the 1984 AV Media Survey*, Milton Keynes: Open University Institute of Educational Technology.

Guzley, R.M., Avanzino, S. and Bor, A. (2001) 'Simulated computer-mediated/video-interactive distance learning: a test of motivation, interaction satisfaction, delivery, learning and perceived effectiveness', *Journal of Computer-Mediated Communication*, Vol. 6, No. 3.

Harasim, L. (ed.) (1990) *Online Education: Perspectives on a New Environment*, New York: Praeger.

Harasim, L., Hiltz, S., Teles, L. and Turoff, M. (1995) *Learning Networks: A Field Guide to Teaching and Learning Online*, Cambridge, MA: MIT Press.

Hardy, D. and Olcott, D. (1995) 'Audio-teleconferencing and the adult learner: strategies for effective practice', *The American Journal of Distance Education*, Vol. 9, No. 1, pp. 44–59.

Harmon, S. and MacNeil, A. (1998) 'Facilitating interpersonal communication with technology in principal preparation programs', *Proceedings of SITE 98*, Society for Information Technology and Teacher Education International Conference, Washington, DC.

Harris, D. (1987) *Openness and Closure in Distance Education*, London: Falmer Press.

Hartman, J. and Truman-Davis, B. (2001) 'The Holy Grail: developing scalable and sustainable support solutions', in Barone, C. and Hagner, P. (eds) *Technology Enhanced Teaching and Learning*, San Francisco: Jossey-Bass.

Hawkridge, D. and Robinson, J. (1982) *Organizing Educational Broadcasting*, London: Croom Helm.

Hiltz, S. and Turoff, M. (1978) *The Network Nation*, Cambridge, MA: MIT Press.

Holmberg, B. (1983) 'Guided didactic conversation in distance education', in Sewart, D., Keegan, D. and Holmberg, B. (eds) *Distance Education: International Perspectives*, London: Croom Helm.

Hülsmann, T. (2000) *The Costs of Open Learning: A Handbook*, Oldenburg: Bibliotheks- und Informationssytem der Universität Oldenburg.

Idrus, R. (1993) 'Collaborative learning through teletutorials', *British Journal of Educational Technology*, Vol. 24, No. 3, pp. 179–84.

Iser, W. (1978) *The Act of Reading*, London: Routledge and Kegan Paul.

Jewett, F. (1999) *BRIDGE: A Campus Cost Simulation Model for Comparing the Costs of Mediated Instruction with Traditional Lecture/Lab Methods*, Seal Beach, CA: CSU/CO.

Jonassen, D. (1999) 'Designing constructivist learning environments', in Reigeluth, C. (ed.) *Instructional Design Theories and Models A New Paradigm of Instructional Theory*, Mahwah, NJ: Lawrence Erlbaum Associates.

Jonassen, D., Davidson, M., Collins, M., Campbell, J. and Haag, B. (1995) 'Constructivism and computer-mediated communication in distance education', *American Journal of Distance Education*, Vol. 9, No. 2, pp. 7–26.

Jones, D. (2001) *Technology Costing Methodology Handbook*, Boulder, CO: Western Cooperative for Educational Telecommunications.

Kaufman, D. (1989) 'Third generation course design in distance education', in Sweet, R. (ed.) *Post-Secondary Distance Education in Canada: Policies, Practices and Priorities*, Athabasca: Athabasca University/Canadian Society for Studies in Education.

Kirby, D. and Boak, C. (1989) 'Investigating instructional approaches in audio-teleconferencing classes' *Journal of Distance Education*, Vol. 4, No. 1, pp. 5–19.

Kirkwood, A. and Crooks, B. (1990) 'Video-cassettes by design', in Bates, A. (ed.) *Media and Technology in European Distance Education*, Heerlen: European Association of Distance Teaching Universities.

Lalande, V. (1995) 'Student support via audio teleconferencing: psycho-educational workshops for post-bachelor nursing students', *American Journal of Distance Education*, Vol. 9, No. 3, pp. 62–73.

Laurillard, D. (2001) *Rethinking University Teaching: A Framework for the Effective Use of Learning Technologies*, London: Routledge.

Li Chen, Liu Ying and Huang Ronghai (2003) *A Comprehensive Review of Modern Distance Education in the Mainland of China*, Beijing: Beijing Normal University.

McGreal, R. (ed.) (2004) *Online Education Using Learning Objects*, London and New York: Routledge.

MacKnight, C. (2001) 'Supporting critical thinking in interactive learning environments', in Maddux, C. and Lamont Johnson, D. (eds) *The Web in Higher Education*, Binghamton, NY: Haworth Press.

Manguel, A. (1996) *A History of Reading*, London: HarperCollins.

Marland, P., Patching, W., Putt, I. and Putt, R. (1990) 'Distance learners' interaction with texts while studying', *Distance Education*, Vol. 11, No. 1, pp. 71–91.

Marton, F. and Säljö, R. (1976) 'On qualitative differences in learning I. Outcome and process', *British Journal of Educational Psychology*, Vol. 46, pp. 4–11.

Meed, J. (1974) *Classification of Radio Broadcasts; Format and Technique*, Milton Keynes: Open University Institute of Educational Technology.

Meister, J. (1998) *Corporate Universities: Lessons in Building a World-class Workforce*, New York: McGraw-Hill.

Meyers, C. (1986) *Teaching Students to Think Critically*, San Francisco: Jossey-Bass.

Moore, M. and Kearsley, G. (1996) *Distance Education: A Systems View*, Belmont, CA: Wadsworth Publishing.

Moore, M. and Thompson, M. (1990) *The Effects of Distance Education: A Summary of the Literature*, University Park, PA: American Centre for the Study of Distance Education.

Naidoo, V. (2001) 'The changing venues for learning', in Farrell, G. (ed.) *The Changing Faces of Virtual Education*, Vancouver, BC: Commonwealth of Learning.

Newton, H. (2002) *Newton's Telecom Dictionary*, New York: CMP Books.

Nichol, J. and Watson, K. (2000) 'Videotutoring, non-verbal communication and initial teacher training', *British Journal of Educational Technology*, Vol. 31, No. 2, pp. 135–44.

Nipper, S. (1989) 'Third generation distance learning and computer conferencing', in Mason, R. and Kaye, A. (eds) *Mindweave: Communication, Computers and Distance Education*, Oxford: Pergamon.

Oliver, R. and McLoughlin, C. (1997) Interactions in audiographics teaching and learning environments, *American Journal of Distance Education*, Vol. 2, No. 1, pp. 34–54.

Oliver, R. and Reeves, T. (1996) 'Dimensions of effective interactive learning with telematics for distance education', *Educational Technology Research and Development*, Vol. 44, No. 4, pp. 45–56.

Olson, D. and Bruner, J. (1974) 'Learning through experience and learning through media', in *Media and Symbols: The Forms of Expression The 73rd NSSE Yearbook*, Chicago: University of Chicago Press.

Open University (1988) *Delivery Technologies*, Milton Keynes: Open University Visiting Committee VCO(88)20.

Open University (2003) Fact sheet: background information http://www3.open.ac.uk/media/factsheets/Information.

Ortner, G. and Nickolmann, F. (eds) (1999) *Socio-Economics of Virtual Universities*, Weinheim: Deutscher Studien Verlag.

Perry, W. (1976) *Open University*, Milton Keynes: Open University Press.

Peters, O. (1983) 'Distance teaching and industrial production: a comparative interpretation in outline', in Sewart, D., Keegan, D. and Holmberg, B. (eds) *Distance Education: International Perspectives*, London: Croom Helm.

—— (2002) *Distance Education in Transition*, Oldenburg: Biblioteks- und Informationssystem der Universität Oldenburg.

Peterson (2003) *Peterson's Guide to Distance Learning Programs*, Stamford, CT: Peterson/Thomson.

Piaget, J. and Inhelder, B. (1969) *The Psychology of the Child*, New York: Basic Books.

Picard, J.M. and Wood, P.F. (2002) 'An online blended learning approach to delivering business skills for professionals', North American Regional Conference of the International Council for Open and Distance Education, Calgary, Alberta. http://www.cade-aced.ca/icdepapers/wood-picard.htm.

Postman, N. (1993) *Technopoly: The Surrender of Culture to Technology*, New York: Vintage Books/Random House.

—— (1994) *The Disappearance of Childhood*, London: W.H. Allen.

Potashnik, M. and Adkins, D. (1996) 'Cost analysis of information technology projects in education: experiences from developing countries', *Education and Technology Series*, Vol. 1, No. 1, Washington, DC: World Bank.

Rhodes, J. (2001) *Videoconferencing for the Real World*, Boston, MA: Focal Press.

Robinson, B. (1984) 'Telephone teaching', in Bates, A.W. (ed.) *The Role of Technology in Distance Education*, London: Croom Helm.

Robinson, B. (1990) 'Telephone teaching and audio-conferencing at the British Open University', in Bates, A.W. (ed.) *Media and Technology in European Distance Education*, Heerlen: European Association of Distance Teaching Universities.

Robinson, J. (1982) *Learning Over the Air*, London: BBC.

Rogers, C. (1969) *Freedom to Learn*, Columbus, OH: Charles E. Merrill Publishing.

Rosen, E. (1996) *Personal Videoconferencing*, Ashland, OH: Manning Publications.

Rosenberg, M.J. (2001) *e-Learning*, New York: McGraw-Hill.

Ruhe, V. and Qayyum, A. (2000) *Learning through New Technologies, the Response of Adult Learners: Cross-case Report*, Vancouver: Distance Education and Technology, University of British Columbia.

Rumble, G. (1986) *The Planning and Management of Distance Education*, London: Croom Helm.

Russell, T.L. (1999) *The No Significant Difference Phenomenon*, Raleigh, NC: North Carolina State University, Office of Instructional Telecommunication.

Ryan, Y. and Steadman, L. (2002) *The Business of Borderless Education: 2001 Update*, Canberra: Commonwealth of Australia.

Salmon, G. (2000) *E-Moderating*, London: Kogan Page.

Salomon, G. (1983) *Using Television as a Unique Teaching Resource*, Milton Keynes: Open University Institute of Educational Technology.

Scardamalia, M. and Bereiter, C. (1999) 'Schools as knowledge-building organizations', in Keating, D. and Hertzman, C. (eds) *Today's Children, Tomorrow's Society: The Developmental Health and Wealth of Nations*, New York: Guilford.

Schramm, W. (1972) *Quality in Instructional Television*, Honolulu, HI: University Press of Hawaii.

—— (1977) *Big Media, Little Media*, San Francisco: Sage.

Senge, P. (1990) *The Fifth Discipline: The Art and Practice of the Learning Organization*, New York: Doubleday.

Skinner, B. (1969) *Contingencies of Reinforcement*, New York: Appleton-Century-Crofts.

Soo, K. and Bonk, C.J. (1998) 'Interaction: what does it mean in online distance education?', *Proceedings of ED-Media/Ed-Telecom 98*, World Conference on Educational Multimedia and Hypermedia and World Conference on Educational Telecommunications, Freiburg, Germany.

Sorensen, C. and Baylen, D. (2000) 'Interaction in interactive television instruction: perception versus reality', *Quarterly Review of Distance Education*, Vol. 1, No. 1, pp. 45–58.

Trenaman, J. (1967) *Communication and Comprehension*, London: Longmans.

Trowt-Bayard, T. (1994) *Videoconferencing: The Whole Picture*, Chelsea, MI: Flatiron.

Twigg, C. (2001) *Quality Assurance for Whom? Providers and Consumers in Today's Distributed Learning Environment*, Troy, NY: Pew Learning and Technology Program, Rensselaer Polytechnic Institute (http://www.center.rpi.edu/PewSym/mono3.html).

—— (2003) *Expanding Access to Learning: the Role of Virtual Universities*, Troy, NY: Center for Academic Transformation Rensselaer Polytechnic Institute (www.center.rpi.edu).

UNESCO (1986) *Statistical Yearbook, 1986*, Paris: UNESCO.

University of Illinois (1999) 'Teaching at an internet distance: the pedagogy of online teaching and learning', Report of a 1998–9 University of Illinois Faculty Seminar http://www.vpaa.uillinois.edu/tid/report/tid_report.html.

Whalen, T. and Wright, D. (2000) *The Business Case for Web-based Training*, Norwood, MA: Artech House.

Wolcott, L. (1994) 'Audio tools for distance education', in Willis, B. (ed.) *Distance Education: Strategies and Tools*, Englewood Cliffs, NJ: Educational Technology Publications.

Young, F. (1999) *Case Studies in Evaluating the Benefits and Cost of Mediated Instruction and Distributed Learning: Synopses/Summaries of Eight Cases*, Seal Beach, CA: Chancellor's Office, California State University.

Index